GLOBALIZATION
AND CITIZENSHIP

Globalization

Series Editors

Manfred B. Steger
*Royal Melbourne Institute of Technology
and University of Hawai'i–Mānoa*

Terrell Carver
University of Bristol

"Globalization" has become *the* buzzword of our time. But what does it mean? Rather than forcing a complicated social phenomenon into a single analytical framework, this series seeks to present globalization as a multidimensional process constituted by complex, often contradictory interactions of global, regional, and local aspects of social life. Since conventional disciplinary borders and lines of demarcation are losing their old rationales in a globalizing world, authors in this series apply an interdisciplinary framework to the study of globalization. In short, the main purpose and objective of this series is to support subject-specific inquiries into the dynamics and effects of contemporary globalization and its varying impacts across, between, and within societies.

Supported by the Globalization Research Center at the University of Hawai'i–Mānoa

GLOBALIZATION AND CITIZENSHIP

HANS SCHATTLE

ROWMAN & LITTLEFIELD PUBLISHERS, INC.
Lanham • Boulder • New York • Toronto • Plymouth, UK

Published by Rowman & Littlefield Publishers, Inc.
A wholly owned subsidiary of The Rowman & Littlefield Publishing Group, Inc.
4501 Forbes Boulevard, Suite 200, Lanham, Maryland 20706
www.rowman.com

Estover Road, Plymouth PL6 7PY, United Kingdom

British Library Cataloguing in Publication Information Available

Library of Congress Cataloging-in-Publication Data
Schattle, Hans.
  Globalization and citizenship / Hans Schattle.
  p.   cm. — (Globalization)
  Includes index.
  ISBN 978-0-7425-6845-7 (cloth : alk. paper) — ISBN 978-0-7425-6846-4 (pbk. : alk.
paper) — ISBN 978-0-7425-6847-1 (electronic)
  1. Globalization—Political aspects. 2. Citizenship—History—21st century. I. Title.
JZ1318.S335 2012
323.6—dc23
                                                                    2011044792

∞™ The paper used in this publication meets the minimum requirements of
American National Standard for Information Sciences—Permanence of Paper
for Printed Library Materials, ANSI/NISO Z39.48-1992.

Printed in the United States of America

For Louise and Benjamin

CONTENTS

Chapter 1

A Dual Dynamic between Globalization and Citizenship

As the twenty-first century moved into its second decade, several remarkable events around the world—some inspiring, some chilling—brought dramatic reminders of how so many key political, economic, and social issues today revolve around globalization and citizenship.

Across the Middle East and North Africa, citizens connected with each other through global social media platforms—such as Facebook and Twitter, as well as many local online social networking communities—and began holding protests to insist that longstanding dictatorships give way to democracies. Authoritarian governments in Tunisia and Egypt collapsed, while citizens in several other countries in the region, from Algeria to Bahrain, took to the streets in early 2011. Not all protests succeeded in securing peaceful political change, most notably in Syria, Yemen, and Libya, which erupted into civil war as revolutionaries clashed for months with forces loyal to Colonel

Muammar Gaddafi before taking control of Tripoli in August 2011. Still, the "Arab Spring" showed the world that freedom of association, freedom of assembly, and freedom of speech were gaining ground as universal values. More and more citizens around the world showed they were ready to make their voices heard—on the streets and on-line—even in the face of immediate obstacles, risks, and repression.

Just a few weeks before the revolutionary stirrings across North Africa and the Middle East captivated the world, two citizen activists and their respective organizations were suddenly catapulted into the global spotlight after years of toiling in relative obscurity. Liu Xiaobo, a Chinese literature scholar and political dissident, languished in prison in December 2010 as his quest to advance human rights and democracy received global validation in the form of the Nobel Peace Prize. Mean-while Julian Assange, the nomadic leader of the WikiLeaks website, which carved out its niche in the information age by publishing govern-ment documents originally intended to be kept secret, remained under house arrest in the United Kingdom as a result of rape charges filed against him in Sweden. This happened not long after his organization had collaborated with several leading newspapers to publish thousands of formerly confidential U.S. diplomatic cables leaked by an officer in the U.S. Army. The travails of both activists and their organizations, as they challenged two different global superpowers, underscored both the resilience of national legal authority and the growing impact of international civil society in the twenty-first century.

At the same time as campaigns by global citizen activists, their or-ganizations, and their network partners around the world continue to gain momentum, sharply growing resistance to immigration in several European countries and the United States highlighted yet another way that dynamics of globalization and citizenship interact—and often col-lide—in the present day. In September 2010 in France, the country's president, Nicolas Sarkozy—the son of an immigrant from Hungary—ordered the government to force about eight thousand undocumented Roma migrants to leave the country. National governments in Italy and Greece, two Mediterranean gateways for migrants heading into Europe, called for greater coordination from the European Union to tighten border controls and stop immigrants from entering the con-tinent. Even in the cosmopolitan haven of Switzerland, voters turned against the country's Muslim residents by approving a 2009 ban on the construction of minarets. Several national leaders in Europe—including German chancellor Angela Merkel and British prime minister David Cameron—gave speeches denouncing multiculturalism as anathema to their national cohesion, while far-right, anti-immigrant political parties across the continent continued to attract new supporters.

The tide also turned against immigration in the United States, the country historically regarded as the world's premier destination for immigrants. A new law in the state of Arizona that would give law enforcement authorities greater power to detain unauthorized immigrants awaited review by the U.S. Supreme Court. Scores of politicians tied to the populist Tea Party movement stepped up efforts to undo the equal citizenship provisions guaranteed by the Fourteenth Amendment to the U.S. Constitution. They initiated numerous proposals in state legislatures to abolish the tradition of "birthright citizenship" for children born in the United States to parents who do not have legal immigration status. Such frontal attacks on immigrants and attempts to narrow the scope of who counts as citizens in the world's most sought-after destination countries for immigrants remind us that nationalist backlashes are among the very processes of globalization. Indeed, many political movements against immigrants tap into public anxiety that their respective countries and local communities are perilously losing ground in the unremitting race of economic globalization. This anxiety, in turn, spurred yet another movement in the autumn of 2011: the Occupy Wall Street protests in lower Manhattan and their counterparts in nearly one hundred cities around the world, seeking to reverse the global political and economic currents of the past generation that have widened inequality between the very rich and everyone else.

Campaigns for civil rights and democracy by political activists who are influenced by international thinkers and actors are by no means a new phenomenon. Thousands of observers referred to the January 25 uprising in Egypt as the country's 1776 or 1789, and the American and French Revolutions themselves were influenced heavily by philosophers and activists well beyond the thirteen colonies. One of the key sources of inspiration for the Declaration of Independence had been written by political philosopher John Locke more than seventy-five years earlier, following the English Civil War. Locke's theory of legitimate government hinges on the consent of the people—with their natural rights to life, liberty, and property and the right to abolish any government falling short in this regard.[1] Moreover, one of history's most illustrious transnational activists, Thomas Paine, played a part in both revolutions; he arrived in Philadelphia from his native England in November 1774, and just over a year later, in January 1776, his pamphlet titled "Common Sense" became the best-selling booklet in history, with its lively, forceful argument against monarchy and for a republican constitution and total independence from Great Britain. More than 120,000 copies were sold in just three months—with about 500,000 copies sold overall—and the pamphlet fueled popular support for the revolution already under way. As an early supporter of equality for women, the abolition of slavery, and the elimination of all property requirements for citizenship, Paine traveled to France during the war for American independence to help secure aid for the revolution. After the dust settled in the United States, he returned to Europe to play a supporting role in the French Revolution, writing two volumes entitled *Rights of Man*—once again best sellers in their day—that defended the revolution and excoriated government by hereditary privilege. After migrating to France in 1792 to avoid arrest—the British government tried and convicted him in absentia on charges of sedition—Paine was elected to France's National Convention in late 1792 and served into 1793, voting for the formation of the French Republic and against the execution of the deposed king, Louis XVI, out of a moral objection to the death penalty.

What has changed in the present day are the background conditions of globalization and the digital media age as they accelerate and inten-sify today's citizen campaigns for civil rights and democracy. When I studied international relations as an undergraduate student almost twenty-five years ago—in the midst of the dismantling of the Berlin Wall, when the Velvet Revolution led to democratic transitions across Central and Eastern Europe and beyond, and ultimately the breakup of the Soviet Union—very few people were talking about either global-ization or citizenship. The dominant themes in international relations back then were the "East-West conflict," a phrase that seemed to re-duce world politics to a showdown between capitalist democracy and communist despotism, and the "North-South conflict" that emphasized sources of divergence and tension between the world's wealthier and poorer countries and regions. The two decades following the Cold War have taught us in spectacular ways that our world is far more complex than either set of fault lines suggested. Today the rapidly expanding transdisciplinary field of global studies stands alongside international relations and international studies and holds considerable influence within these more established fields as their outlooks continue to widen. Times have changed: globalization and citizenship now command tremendous interest in both the academic arena and public debate.

The cases above, and many more like them, highlight two fundamental, contrasting points about the interplay and tension between globalization and citizenship today: globalization is opening up new forms of political activity and civic engagement, often tied to networks rather than territory, thereby challenging, if not uncoupling, the ties of citizenship that bind individuals together with nation-states. However, even as public recognition of global interdependence continues to expand, the institution of national citizenship is now tightening and national identities are hardening in many countries. Many governments are cracking down on immigration and ethnic and cultural minority groups as a way of trying to reassure anxious and seemingly insecure publics that they retain some level of territorial control as globalization otherwise continues to proceed apace. Globalization continues to open up new opportunities for citizens to move across borders and get involved in political and social causes—for new voices to be heard in public debate, and for more established voices to resonate more widely. National citizenship, meanwhile, is becoming an increasingly powerful lever for governments seeking to control the destinies of their countries and assert authority and advance their perceived interests alongside globalization. These two key points—illustrating a dual dynamic, with more opportunities for citizens on the one hand, but more restrictions on the other—serve as the main propositions for inquiry and analysis in this book.

EXPLORING THE INTERPLAY AND TENSION BETWEEN GLOBALIZATION AND CITIZENSHIP

Just what is the meaning of citizenship? What exactly is globalization? And how has the recent period of globalization affected citizenship in the present day? Much debate surrounds these questions that are central to any study at the nexus of globalization and citizenship, and many competing interpretations of both concepts abound in the scholarly literature. Taking stock of the varying perspectives on citizenship, three main definitional frames come into focus: (1) rights and corresponding duties; (2) democratic empowerment and participation; and (3) sentiments of allegiance, belonging, loyalty, and identity.

RIGHTS AND DUTIES

The idea of democratic citizenship since modernity has been framed most commonly as a reciprocal relationship of rights and corresponding duties that exists between individuals and nation-states. Basic rights are typically cast as a series of valid claims made by individuals and groups upon their respective political communities; political philosopher Henry Shue, for example, defines "moral rights" as providing "(1) a rational basis for a justified demand (2) that the actual enjoyment of a substance be (3) socially guaranteed against standard threats."[2] Contemporary understandings of universal human rights cut across civil and political rights and social and economic rights. Civil and political rights include freedoms of speech, religion, and assembly and the rights to petition the government, vote, and receive proper treatment through "due process" within the legal system. Social and economic rights encompass rights to education, health care, basic living wages, fair and safe working conditions, unemployment insurance, and retirement pensions.

Much disagreement in political life revolves around how exactly national governments and societies should go about upholding and safeguarding these basic rights. Even within many constitutional democracies, plenty of debate carries forth over how extensively civil and political rights should be guaranteed. Consider the public rifts over issues such as capital punishment, same-sex marriages, and the extent that social and economic rights should be supported through public subsidies, regulation, and redistribution of wealth. In recent years, the principle of cultural rights has also figured heavily into citizenship debates, and scholars such as Will Kymlicka and the late Iris Marion Young have argued that ethnic, linguistic, and religious cultural minority groups within states should be granted differentiated citizenship rights depending on their circumstances. Other globally oriented political theorists base their arguments for international legal and political institutions on extending universal rights beyond the national realm. As Seyla Benhabib has noted, cosmopolitanism involves the recognition that all individuals are "entitled to legal protection in the virtue of the rights that accrue to them not as nationals, or members of an ethnic group, but as human beings."[3]

Despite enduring debates over which rights are truly fundamental and what kinds of measures are necessary to uphold them, rights have been cast in three centuries of Western political thought as inalienable—as held legitimately by all human persons from the moment of birth, regardless of one's national citizenship status, and as so essential to the human condition that no government can justify taking them away. In the United States the preamble to the Declaration of Independence clearly outlined this principle with the immortal words: "We hold these truths to be self-evident, that all men are created equal, that they are endowed by their Creator with certain unalienable Rights, that among these are Life, Liberty and the pursuit of Happiness. That to secure these rights, Governments are instituted among Men, deriving their just powers from the consent of the governed."[4]

The liberal model of citizenship is tied to the principles of universal equality and popular sovereignty as expressed in the declaration. This is the case despite the glaring gender exclusivity of the eighteenth-century wording and that, in practice, from the earliest years of U.S. history the full promises of both the declaration and the Bill of Rights, the first ten civil rights amendments to the U.S. Constitution, remained closed to women, slaves, aboriginal peoples, immigrants, and even many native-born white men not holding private property. The ongoing history of national citizenship in liberal democracies around the world has been filled with extended struggles for social standing and recognition among numerous groups of people—citizens as well as noncitizens—long excluded from the full privileges of membership and even basic entitlements and protections under the law.[5] Civil rights demonstrations and court battles have repeatedly functioned as the necessary vehicles pushing governments to deliver on their earlier founding promises of liberty and equality for all. The prolonged fight throughout the twentieth century to end segregation across the United States remains a sobering reminder of how long it has taken, at times, for the promises of citizenship to be fulfilled.

Note that rights-based understandings of citizenship emphasize formal membership status, namely, legal status, and also generally assume that citizenship carries corresponding duties. These range from compulsory obligations such as taxation, conscription into military service, and adherence to national laws, to voluntary responsibilities such as informed participation in politics, at least when voting. The broader political community, in turn, is assumed to fulfill basic duties to the citizens by creating conditions in which rights are upheld and all inhabitants—migrants as well as citizens and permanent residents—are respected equally and treated fairly. The common emphasis on citizenship as an exclusive category of people who share rights and duties implies the enforcement of legal distinctions between citizens and outsiders, or "aliens," as well as "in-betweens"[6] who are temporary or permanent residents of a state, with recognized legal status as migrants or guestworkers but not necessarily on track to becoming full members or citizens. Still, liberal democratic states generally hold themselves accountable to maintain basic human rights protections for citizens and noncitizens alike. They also confer upon citizens and permanent residents additional layers of rights and privileges—rights to work, to vote and hold public office, to travel abroad and receive diplomatic protection while away, and so forth. And struggles to overthrow dictatorships and establish democracies are precisely to set up the kinds of governments in which *both* citizens and noncitizens have various rights and corresponding duties upheld by the rule of law rather than the arbitrary whims of individual rulers or ruling cliques.

DEMOCRATIC EMPOWERMENT AND PARTICIPATION

Citizenship as a way of life dedicated to the art of self-government is a much older tradition, hearkening to the city-states of ancient Greece, in which citizenship was considered an office that included periods of deliberation in the public forum as well as periods of service in the military and on juries. For Aristotle, Cicero, Machiavelli, Rousseau, and many other classical thinkers—and also for their followers in contemporary social and political thought—the civic republican tradition hinges upon motivated and responsible citizens willing to invest the time, energy, and resources to seek out the public good through reasoned and inclusive discussion and debate. This ancient way of thinking about citizenship has affinities with the ways that many twenty-first-century global citizen activists involve themselves in transnational political and social causes around the world, irrespective of their national citizenship status and the territorial limitations this might otherwise seem to impose. Today growing numbers of global activists seek to hold international institutions as well as national governments accountable to principles of justice, equality, and transparency, while also challenging perceived inequities in the global marketplace. On the other hand, skeptics who believe that transnational advocacy does not necessarily lead to global citizenship also turn to Aristotle and his civic republican descendants to argue that good citizens need local proximity to each other in order to properly evaluate each other's character so to carry out their mutual responsibilities. While ancient Greece distinguished between citizens and slaves and restricted full citizenship status to male property owners in ways that would be distasteful to contemporary sensibilities, for Aristotle, the opposites of "citizens" were not slaves but idiots, as in those who saw themselves as unaffected by public affairs and selfishly refused any form of political engagement, withdrawing into isolation from the *polis* as they attended narrowly to their own concerns. This reflected Aristotle's view that to be fully human, and to lead the highest and best form of life, one needed to be politically active.[7]

While the civic republican tradition is often framed in contemporary political thought as a corrective to liberal individualism, the attainment of the liberal model of citizenship has depended for generations on channels of democratic empowerment and participation. What people across the world's democracies today take for granted as basic citizenship rights emerged only after extensive and persistent campaigns led by social movements. Women in the United States, for example, finally secured the right to vote in 1920, nearly a century after activists such as Lucretia Mott and Elizabeth Cady Stanton helped lead the international movement fighting for the franchise as well as the abolition of slavery, while African Americans continued to face formidable barriers that delayed their right to vote, in practice, until extensive civil rights protests led to the passage of national legislation and key court decisions in the 1960s. Switzerland's all-male electorate extended voting rights to women even later, in 1971, despite resistance even then from many who believed that the social roles of women should be kept to "kinder, küche, und kirche"—children, kitchen, and church. Social and economic rights began to gain recognition after the rise of industrialization and struggles in the labor movement for better working conditions; today, however, they are being rolled back in many countries as governments tighten their belts in the face of continuing global economic pressure. British university students in England and Wales, for example, no longer have free access to higher education and have been fighting sharp increases in tuition fees, and in early 2011 the state of Wisconsin revoked the right to collective bargaining for most of the state's workers.

ALLEGIANCE, BELONGING, IDENTITY, AND LOYALTY

The more psychological, even sentimental, aspects of citizenship relate to how individuals place themselves as both members and participants of the political communities that they—and their forebears—have chosen to construct and sustain together. Benedict Anderson famously defined the nation as an "imagined political community—and imagined as both inherently limited and sovereign,"[8] with historical developments such as the invention of the printing press and the increasing accessibility of vernaculars giving rise to nationalism, especially as the American and French Revolutions erupted in the late eighteenth century. T. H. Marshall notes that "modern national consciousness" accompanied the advent of modern civil rights, and that citizenship depends on "a direct sense of community membership based on loyalty to a civilisation which is a common possession."[9] Today's advances in technology and communication likewise inspire rising numbers of people, similar to philosophers and visionaries from ages past, to imagine their political communities and regard their corresponding loyalties as extending beyond the nation. Especially within the younger generations, notions of allegiance, belonging, and loyalty now work across legally established communities, namely, national and regional political jurisdictions, as well as advocacy networks revolving around shared causes and affinities. Many people now identify, for instance, primarily as women, environmentalists, or members of online communities rather than primarily as citizens of their native countries.

Conversely, some scholars who do privilege the more familiar historical notions of citizen identity within domestic political communities, initially city-states and later nation-states, insist that identity can force harsh distinctions between insiders and outsiders. As political theorist Adrian Oldfield once argued:

> Citizenship is not about altruism: it is about acknowledging the community's goals as one's own, choosing them, and committing oneself to them. Altruism is the response of one human being to another. Citizenship is exclusive: it is not a person's humanity that one is responding to, it is the fact that he or she is a fellow citizen, or a stranger. In choosing an identity for ourselves, we recognize both who our fellow citizens are, and those who are not members of our community, and thus who are potential enemies. . . . This does not entail an aggressive posture toward strangers. It simply means that to remain a citizen one cannot always treat everyone like a human being.[10]

Advocates of cosmopolitanism and the related notion of global citizenship disagree sharply with the limits to citizenship that Oldfield proposes as necessary and instead argue that today's global era challenges citizens to acknowledge and embrace the goals of transnational communities as their own. As cultural sociologist Joshua Yates has written: "There is something inherent in the global situation that asks us to extend our moral commitments and concerns to greater categories of people and across further social and geographic distances, and makes us believe in the efficacy of our efforts in this regard."[11] Then again, as we shall see in later chapters, Oldfield's point of view can help explain much of the anti-immigrant politics festering today in the United States and Europe. Whether identities, allegiances, and loyalties are deployed outward or turned inward, this definitional frame of citizenship is the realm of patriotic sentiment and also public opinion surveys such as Eurobarometer and the World Values Survey that measure the extent that some citizens—often young, educated, and affluent—mediate entrenched national identities with emerging supranational and cosmopolitan identities.

Many scholars insist that one of the three definitional frames above takes priority as *the* ultimate essence of citizenship. Some political scientists focus primarily on the first frame that emphasizes rights and duties and tend to privilege narrow definitions of citizenship that rest precisely upon formal membership and legal jurisdiction of nation-states. The fields of history, sociology, and cultural anthropology, in contrast, often allow more latitude for all three definitional frames to flow beyond the nation-state. Meanwhile, growing numbers of people with the resources and drive to pursue educational, professional, or voluntary service opportunities outside their native countries—or people who have jumped at opportunities to immerse themselves in international enclaves within their native countries—are finding it easier to relate themselves as citizens to different sets of political communities. For example, some of my students at Yonsei University in Seoul, South Korea, carry Korean passports and think of themselves as Korean citizens in terms of rights and duties—particularly young men facing military service—but identify more as Americans after having attended school for many years in the United States, while they also participate in global advocacy campaigns that point them toward cosmopolitanism. Also moving across the definitional frames for citizenship are so-called third-culture kids—dubbed by essayist Pico Iyer as the "privileged homeless"[12]—typically the children of professionals such as business executives, diplomats, and missionaries working abroad who have grown up as "global nomads" outside their native countries and often encounter difficulty adjusting whenever they return "home" once again. The current global era lends itself especially well to multifaceted understandings of citizenship.

THE RELATIONSHIP BETWEEN GLOBALIZATION AND CITIZENSHIP

Globalization extends back to the cross-continental wanderings of nomadic hunter gatherers twelve thousand years ago, the ancient Silk Road trading route that linked the Mediterranean region with India and China, and the European maritime explorers and imperial conquests that would shape and dominate political arrangements and economic exchanges across much of the planet until the two world wars of the twentieth century. Today's globalization scholars work across a multitude of themes—culture, economics, media, politics, social change, and technology—and definitions of globalization that prevail and operate across the concept's many themes, rather than concentrating mainly on economic globalization, tend to cast globalization as a series of processes in which the world becomes more intensely and extensively interdependent and interconnected and at faster and faster rates over time. David Held and his collaborators, for instance, emphasized "extensity, intensity, velocity and impact" when they framed globalization as a "transformation in the spatial organization of social relations and transactions" flowing across international borders but also affecting matters within nation-states.[13] Likewise, Ulrich Beck has defined globalization as "the processes through which sovereign national states are crisscrossed and undermined by transnational actors with varying prospects of power, orientations, identities and networks."[14] Anthony Giddens, meanwhile, focuses on interdependence across distance when he defines globalization as "the intensification of worldwide social relations which link distant localities in such a way that local happenings are shaped by events occurring many miles away and vice versa."[15]

As a fluid, ever-changing set of processes, globalization also involves dual forces of integration and fragmentation—criticism, resistance, and nationalist reactions against globalization in all its forms, in which citizens and their political leaders turn inward—that amount to reactionary dynamics that emerge as part of globalization itself. International relations theorist James Rosenau coined the term "fragmegration" to capture the continuous sense of interplay and contestation between globalization and localization, or more broadly, centralization and decentralization.[16] And while some wonder if globalization might be all too vaguely synonymous with many other kinds of "-izations"—since partial accounts of globalization all contain elements of Americanization, Europeanization, hybridization, industrialization, liberalization, urbanization, and Westernization—international relations theorist Jan Aart Scholte argues that ultimately globalization involves "respatialization," as in a "reconfiguration of social geography with increased planetary connections between people."[17] Note that in many of these definitions, "global" is framed not so much as a synonym for "planetary" or "worldwide" but as sets of processes or forces that bring the world closer together than before.

If citizenship is understood chiefly as a fixed or static concept, signifying passive legal relationships between individuals and their respective states, then globalization might appear to have little to say about citizenship other than influencing, if not transforming, this binary relationship as it evolves from generation to generation. However, if citizenship is also understood as a verb signaling activity in politics and society—as a series of habits, dispositions, and practices in which individuals situate themselves in all kinds of communities and immerse themselves into public initiatives, as well as public debate and often public controversy and struggle, then the idea of citizenship takes on some of the same dynamic qualities as globalization. Just as the consciousness of individuals and groups figures into some understandings of citizenship and nationalism, Roland Robertson and Habib Haque Khondker have noted that "in its most basic sense globalization involves the compression of the entire world, on the one hand, and a rapid increase in consciousness of the whole world, on the other."[18] Malcolm Waters also relies heavily on consciousness when he calls globalization "a social process in which the constraints of geography on social and cultural arrangements recede and in which people become increasingly aware that they are receding."[19] Such perspectives on globalization converge quite nicely with democratic theorist Benjamin Barber's take on citizenship as "a dynamic relationship among strangers who are transformed into neighbors, whose commonality derives from expanding consciousness rather than geographical proximity."[20] When globalization and citizenship are both viewed as interactive, then globalization can be viewed as an open invitation to citizenship and a way of thinking and living within new geographical, intellectual, and moral horizons.

Before globalization began to capture the public imagination, scholars were debating whether citizenship within the arena of domestic politics finds its ultimate expression in procedures and laws upholding the basic civil, political, and social rights of individuals or in the habits and practices of everyday people choosing to pour their energy into political life and engage in debate and deliberation—and at times, outright struggle—over what kinds of public policies would best serve the common good. "Communitarian" scholars such as Michael Walzer, Charles Taylor, and Mary Anne Glendon worried that Western constitutional democracies were veering too far in the direction of individualism and even extreme forms of "atomism," and that overly assertive manifestations of rights language could undermine civic virtue and social solidarity that a robustly democratic political community requires. "Liberal" scholars, meanwhile, framed individual rights and a sturdy bedrock of constitutional law as necessary trumps against abuses of public power, and political theorists such as William Galston and Stephen Macedo also emphasized that respect for diversity and difference amounted to liberal virtues that could be reconciled with the pursuit of common interests, if not an overarching common good. As noted by political theorist Judith Shklar: "There is no notion more central in politics than citizenship, and none more variable in history, or contested in theory."[21]

Contestation over the meaning of citizenship has only increased—and expanded in many new directions—since Shklar wrote that sentence back in 1991, in the midst of what became known as the liberal-communitarian debate. Since then, great strides in the spread of democracy around the globe, along with many other changes, have fueled interest in framing the notion of citizenship past the confines of the nation-state and, in many instances, beyond conventional politics altogether. Stunning advances in digital communications technology, heightening public recognition of the ways the world's economy has been coalescing into a single interdependent unit, and the growing social, political, and cross-cultural interaction beyond international borders—as well as across entrenched dividing lines within nation-states—all have played a part. Three debates about the relationship between citizenship and globalization have emerged in ways that overlap the three definitional frames of citizenship noted above.

First, an enduring *normative* debate has renewed itself as to whether cosmopolitanism—or global citizenship—is superior to patriotism or nationalism as an ethical basis for political identity and belonging. Much of this debate focuses on whether it is morally desirable for individual persons to think of themselves and live as citizens of the world as well as citizens of their respective countries and more immediate political communities. Moral philosopher Martha Nussbaum, echoing the Cynics and Stoics of ancient Greece, set this debate in motion in the United States with her widely cited essay, first published in 1994, claiming that world citizenship, with an emphasis on universal rights and reason—rather than national belonging—should be the basis for civic education. Nussbaum made her case with four main justifications: (1) that the study of humanity from a global perspective, in which people look at themselves "through the lens of the other," also has the effect of clarifying perspectives and enriching knowledge about one's native country and traditions; (2) cosmopolitan education will encourage recognition of a shared global future and help the next generation engage in more productive dialogue to solve the world's most pressing problems; (3) people who think of themselves as global citizens are more disposed to recognize moral obligations to the rest of the world; (4) encouraging young people to cross boundaries in their minds and imaginations will spare them from giving undue privilege to "morally arbitrary" national boundaries.[22] Nussbaum also turned to rights language to seal her argument: "In making choices in both political and economic matters we should most seriously consider the right of other human beings to life, liberty and the pursuit of happiness, and that we should work to acquire the knowledge that will enable us to deliberate well about those rights."[23]

Nussbaum has since modified her position to extend greater moral weight to a "globally sensitive patriotism,"[24] but her case for world citizenship remains one of the most eloquent and lucid arguments for giving moral priority to the notion of global citizenship. Her many critics, in turn, presented forceful responses that global citizenship should be dismissed as too abstract and remote from democratic political life and meaningful attachments to family, friends, and neighbors; that cosmopolitanism gives too little credit to the inspiring universal principles flowing from American patriotism, such as the idea of inalienable rights and assertions of universal equality; and that cosmopolitanism and patriotism need not exist in tension but rather can be seen as mutually reinforcing. This final point, made in response to Nussbaum by philosopher and cultural theorist Kwame Anthony Appiah, helped set the tone for a great deal of the debate that followed.

The more recent literature has moved away from cosmopolitanism as a universal ethic in favor of "rooted" approaches to cosmopolitanism that hold out the possibility that local loyalties and universal responsibilities can coexist harmoniously and facilitate dialogue and interaction across lines of difference—cultural, ethnic, and religious—at home and abroad.[25] As Appiah has written: "Cosmopolitanism shouldn't be seen as some exalted attainment: it begins with the simple idea that in the human community, as in national communities, we need to develop habits of co-existence: conversation in its older meaning of living together, association."[26] Other thinkers, such as Peter Singer, have taken a firmer stance in arguing that "in the present situation we have duties to foreigners that override duties to our fellow citizens. . . . Reducing the number of human beings living in absolute poverty is surely a more urgent priority than reducing the relative poverty caused by some people living in palaces while others live in houses that are merely adequate."[27]

Second, an *institutional* debate is focused on whether the limited advances in supranational governing institutions, most notably the European Union, and the growing impact of international organizations alongside national governments, have created the conditions for an expansion of citizenship beyond the jurisdictions of nation-states—or at least underscore the need for more cohesive and powerful global governing institutions to catch up with the realities of the global market. The institutional debate over the feasibility of an international model of citizenship revolves substantially around aspirations for democracy, both within nation-states and beyond them. David Held has captured the essence of the institutional debate by arguing that although nation-states retain legal supremacy and immense power, as well as "access to a formidable range of resources, bureaucratic infrastructural capacity and technologies of coordination and control,"[28] nearly all countries have become "enmeshed in and functionally part of a larger pattern of global flows and global transformations," with everything from investment capital, consumer goods, and fashion trends to weapons, pollutants, and diseases moving readily across international borders. In Held's view, a new and interconnected global order has emerged, "marked by dense patterns of exchange as well as by power, hierarchy and unevenness,"[29] that bears profound implications for the nature of citizenship, with networks gaining ground alongside territory. As Held puts it:

> The determination of political community and the nature of political identity within it become less a territorial matter and more a matter of transaction, exchange, and bargaining across a complex set of transnational networks. At the very least, national political communities by no means simply determine the structure, education and cultural flows in and through which their citizens are cultivated. Citizens' values and judgments are now formed in a complex web of national, international and global cultural exchange.[30]

In light of such developments, Held calls for a new multilayered system of "cosmopolitan governance" that would foster greater participatory democracy at the local level and also create new global governing institutions, such as an elected world parliament and a sweeping international court. In his view, these would serve as venues for global citizenship and render national governments more democratic and accountable to the public than the current international system predicated mainly on nation-states. Similar to Nussbaum's call for an ethic of world citizenship, Held's proposed institutional approach to global citizenship also generated skeptical responses. Political theorist Will Kymlicka, echoing an argument made years earlier by democratic theorist Robert Dahl,[31] responded to Held by claiming it is more realistic to hold international institutions *indirectly* accountable through national public debate. Kymlicka also maintained that despite the legal institution of European Union citizenship, in which all citizens of the twenty-seven member states also hold rights across the EU itself, most Europeans actually debate European issues within their own national public spaces. While he noted that he would welcome more direct public accountability from international institutions, for Kymlicka the essence of citizenship is "collective deliberation and decision-making" that he believes can hold individuals together only within domestic political communities. In his words:

> Transnational activism is a good thing, as is the exchange of information across borders, but the only forum in which genuine democracy occurs is within national boundaries. Transnational activism by individuals or NGOs is not the same as democratic citizenship. Moreover, attempts to create a genuinely democratic form of transnational citizenship could have negative consequences for democratic citizenship at the domestic level. . . . In short, globalization is undoubtedly producing a new civil society, but it has not yet produced anything we can recognize as transnational democratic citizenship. Nor is it clear to me that we should aspire to such a new form of citizenship.[32]

Another skeptic, international relations theorist Alexander Wendt, has argued that it would not likely be feasible for David Held's version of cosmopolitan democracy to function as a democracy of individual citizens, rather than groups. Wendt suspects that even those sympathetic in principle to the idea of cosmopolitan democracy—and the notion of a supranational government directly accountable to individuals—would oppose, in practice, the logical extensions of cosmopolitan democracy, such as freedom of movement and equal voting rights for all. While both freedom of movement and equal voting rights are widely accepted as basic rights within the world's democracies, Wendt says that "one can imagine our respondents demanding, as a condition for their entry into a cosmopolitan democracy, strong constitutional protection for the survival of their distinct cultural communities"[33] and especially the preservation of the social and economic advantages of the more affluent countries, thereby carrying over existing inequalities into any emergent system of cosmopolitan governance.

Third, a *sociological* debate has unfolded over whether certain groups of people are already, in effect, global citizens. Many pathways to possible global citizenship have been identified in this regard: international migration, managerial roles within international organizations and enterprises, and especially activism on behalf of causes that can be viewed as promoting "global public goods"—such as safeguarding the natural environment, overcoming world poverty, advancing human rights for all, and curbing shared threats such as climate change, diseases, terrorism, and the spread of nuclear weapons. International relations theorist Richard Falk and sociologist John Urry each set forth prospective categories of global citizens—global activists, global managers, global executives, and so forth—although many individuals within these categories do not necessarily perceive themselves to be global citizens or choose to act as engaged or responsible members of a formative global political and moral community. Those transnational activists who occasionally mobilize campaigns in an effort to hold international institutions more accountable to democratic norms, as political sociologist Sidney Tarrow has shown, remain "both constrained and supported by domestic politics" as they make temporary forays into the international arena and then retreat back into their local communities to maintain smaller-scale but sustained commitments to civic and political life. As Tarrow notes: "When the demonstrations die down, more significant, though more difficult to measure, is the learning they bring back to their own societies and the ties they have developed across borders."[34]

Those who stay away from political activism but share a global consciousness of sorts and consider themselves morally implicated as to how their actions and consumer choices interact with the fates of distant and often disadvantaged workers in the global economy—people who buy "fair trade" coffee or "Rugmark" carpets certified as immune from sweatshops—often are political, business, and intellectual elites far from representative of the general public even in the world's more affluent countries, much less the majority of the world's population who live on the equivalent of just a few U.S. dollars per day. Still, thanks to the satellite technology that has made continuous global news coverage something to be taken for granted, masses of people have many more opportunities now to identify with and reach out to people in distress. Natural disasters such as the earthquakes and tsunamis that in recent years have devastated communities in Haiti, Thailand, Indonesia, and Japan became global events in which people around the world reacted immediately with empathy and solidarity, although in many cases international aid campaigns continue to come up short in helping the afflicted communities rebuild.

Some specialists in migration, such as Yasemin Soysal, have argued over the years that universal human rights protections have extended to migrants a form of "postnational membership." Such assertions have been sharply contested by skeptics such as Christian Joppke and Randall Hansen who hold that the rights of migrants are ultimately dependent on nationality laws, immigration policies, and national judiciaries. In fact, great disparities remain among host countries over how immigrants are received and treated in domestic legal and political systems. The sociological literature on cosmopolitanism focuses heavily on "people out of place" such as refugees and asylum seekers; slaves and victims of human trafficking; migrant women who often toil as nannies, nurses, and sex workers; and children in sweatshops, orphanages, and brothels.[35] While the sociological debate on an international dimension of citizenship is inconclusive as to the desirability and feasibility of a model of global citizenship, it provides many compelling illustrations of how fates across humanity continue to become more clearly intertwined each passing day. It also highlights how the concept of citizenship has uncoupled itself from the nation-state and has morphed into many binary versions: cultural citizenship, digital citizenship, ecological citizenship, feminist citizenship, grassroots citizenship, green citizenship, queer citizenship, transnational citizenship, and so forth.

CITIZENSHIP IN A GLOBAL ERA: MIGRATION, POLITICAL ACTIVITY, AND PUBLIC SPACE

What's new, then, about globalization and citizenship? And where do we see the most interplay and tension between these two concepts?

International migration, political activity, and public space are three of the keys to understanding the current mixed and sometimes complicated relationship between globalization and citizenship.

More people than ever before, and more *kinds* of people, with widely varying fates and fortunes tied considerably to the passports they carry—or do not carry—now move across borders: representatives of governments and international organizations, corporate executives on international postings, students on academic exchange programs, expatriate professionals such as teachers and nurses often residing abroad on guestworker sojourns, labor migrants and soldiers, refugees and asylum seekers, people smuggled by human traffickers who are left particularly vulnerable to slavery and exploitation—all of these classes of migrants push up against national citizenship as an "international filing system" separating insiders and outsiders.[36] Worldwide, the estimated number of international migrants increased in the first decade of the twenty-first century, from 150 million people in 2000 to 214 million people in 2010—enough to make up the world's fifth largest country.

This recent increase in the number of migrants, however, is only in absolute terms; the proportion of migrants relative to the total worldwide population remained largely the same for the first decade of this century, a statistic that foreshadows how the overall climate in many destination countries is not becoming more hospitable toward migrants.[37] While growing numbers of migrants are now moving around within Asia, Africa, and Latin America, international migrant workers also remain a large and important presence across the world's wealthiest countries, even as they suffer from long hours, low pay, and ill treatment in jobs often shunned by natives. In Western Europe, people born outside the continent now make up about 10 percent of the workforce, and according to United Nations statistics, close to 40 percent of all workers in the small oil-rich states along the Persian Gulf hail from abroad, while international workers in the United Arab Emirates make up more than 80 percent of the population.[38] Nearly half the world's migrants are women, and all together, migrants send more than US$400 billion in remittances back home each year.[39]

The vast immigrant populations that have accompanied the current period of globalization have brought rich tapestries of ethnic diversity into many "global cities" around the world. Hundreds of languages are spoken in the public schools in London, Toronto, and New York, and cultural expectations are often upturned: some of the best pizza chefs in Boston are Brazilian, not Italian; one of New York's most popular bagel chefs is not Jewish but Egyptian; and travelers in Ireland now commonly find Russian or Polish immigrants looking after them at the country's bed and breakfasts. And yet, as we shall examine in chapters 4 and 5, public hostility against immigrants—and especially undocumented immigration—has been growing alongside public angst over the risk and uncertainty brought on by economic globalization and has become a driving force in national politics across Europe and in the United States. Deportations in the United States have more than tripled since 2001, with a record number of 387,790 persons removed from the country in 2009 as Barack Obama's administration cracked down more sternly on immigrants convicted of crimes.[40] Scholars have also identified a rising trend of "circular migration," with more immigrants juggling intermittent periods of time working abroad to raise money while continuing to anchor the most meaningful aspects of their lives—and their most fundamental loyalties and senses of duty and obligation—within their native local communities.[41]

  While legal citizenship status, for most human beings, remains largely an accident of birth, global citizen action is entirely a matter of choice. Globalization and emerging digital media platforms have opened up new venues for citizens around the world to raise their voices and get involved in causes that matter to them. First, interactive "netizens" transformed global civil society, with Jody Williams and the International Campaign to Ban Landmines receiving the Nobel Peace Prize in 1997 following the successful campaign that led more than one hundred countries to sign the treaty banning landmines as a weapon of war, and now the Twitter "microblogging" phenomenon has created "twitizens" who keep in contact, minute by minute, with many people they interact with only in cyberspace.[42] Transnational activism reaches back into history; for example, networks of activists expanded greatly in the years leading up to the twentieth century with campaigns to abolish slavery, secure voting rights for women, and end the abusive custom of foot binding, which had long prevailed for girls and young women in traditional China. When domestic grassroots organizations fail to secure political change at home, they can join forces with like-minded international organizations to mount both internal and external pressure on their national governments; political scientists Margaret Keck and Kathryn Sikkink call this dynamic a "boomerang effect."[43]

Looking at the big picture, the standard-bearers such as Amnesty International, Human Rights Watch, Oxfam, Greenpeace, Friends of the Earth, and Transparency International now coexist with corporate offshoots such as the Bill and Melinda Gates Foundation and the Open Society Institute bankrolled by financier George Soros as well as church-affiliated transnational organizations such as World Vision and Catholic Relief Services. And the recent proliferation of international nongovernmental organizations that describe themselves as "without borders"—Architects Without Borders, Doctors Without Borders, Engineers Without Borders, Pharmacists Without Borders, Teachers Without Borders, just to name a few—reminds us how pervasive the new transnational activism has become. At the very least, citizens too busy for the front lines of political activity can engage themselves in "checkbook participation" by supporting the work of organizations seeking to advance their interests and values, much in the same way that many citizens in the United States regularly send contributions to interest groups such as the American Association of Retired Persons, the National Organization for Women, and the National Rifle Association. The ideological cacophony that resounds across the landscape of domestic citizen participation also emerges in the international arena as well as in cyberspace. On the issue of immigration, for example, for every activist, interest group, or blog advocating for undocumented immigrants, refugee populations, or people who fall prey to human traffickers, there are others who call for greater restrictions on immigration and, in many cases, spew out hate speech.

Indeed, the expansive corridors of global public space have eased the way for small-time, narrow-minded local citizens to make their voices heard around the globe. Consider the case of Terry Jones, the pastor of the Dove World Outreach Center, a tiny congregation in Gainesville, Florida, with about fifty nondenominational Christian followers. It all began on Facebook in July 2010, when a "Burn the Koran" group on the social networking website asked followers to send photos of how they planned to set fire to the most sacred text for Muslims on the ninth anniversary of the September 11, 2001, terrorist attacks on New York and Washington, D.C. Religion News Service picked up the story and quoted Jones as saying that his church would hold an

"International Burn a Koran Day" on September 11.[44] Jones followed up by posting a video on YouTube (since removed) in which he held up a copy of the Koran and declared, "This book is responsible for 9/11." CNN brought Jones further into the spotlight with a television interview in late July. The mayor of Gainesville tried to defuse the story by dismissing the church as a "tiny fringe group and an embarrassment to our community," and pundits and netizens alike called Jones a "backwater redneck" and an "international hate figure"—antonyms of sorts for a "global citizen"—but Jones became a household name just the same. Fans and critics around the world descended upon Facebook to debate the issue and the conflict it highlighted between respect for pluralism and freedom of expression. Religious leaders urged Jones to cancel the publicity stunt; street demonstrations occurred from New York City to Kabul, where about five hundred protesters chanted "Long Live Islam" and "Death to America" as they burned the American flag and a cardboard effigy of Jones.

The U.S. military commander in Afghanistan, General David Petraeus, then warned in a written statement that Jones's plan "could cause significant problems" in Afghanistan and endanger U.S. troops worldwide. CNN gave Jones a chance to respond to Petraeus, and he told network anchor Anderson Cooper: "The general needs to point his finger to radical Islam and tell them to shut up, tell them to stop, tell them that we will not bow our knees to them."[45] Two days later, on the morning of September 9, President Obama called Jones's plan "a recruitment bonanza for Al Qaeda" and warned that it could lead to suicide bombings around the world. "If he's listening," Obama told George Stephanopoulos of *ABC News*, "I just hope he understands that what he's proposing to do is completely contrary to our values. . . . This country has been built on the notions of religious freedom and religious tolerance."[46] By the time Jones canceled his planned burning later that day, he had succeeded in sparking a worldwide brouhaha and gained attention for his previously obscure book, *Islam Is of the Devil*. Jones also tapped into growing anxiety about Islam in the United States as debate raged over a plan to build a mosque and Islamic cultural center near the site of Ground Zero in lower Manhattan; public opinion surveys taken at the time showed that about 53 percent of Americans viewed Islam unfavorably.[47] After several months out of the limelight, Jones went ahead and burned a single copy of the Koran on March 20,

2011, in what he called "International Judge the Koran Day." Thirty of his followers joined him for the event, which at first barely received any attention within the United States; however, an Internet video of the burning Koran was shown on television in Afghanistan and Pakistan, and thousands of people in both countries then held protests that claimed the lives of at least twenty people—including seven United Nations workers.

The Jones episode reminds us that global public space by no means privileges a cosmopolitan ethic in which, as Joshua Cohen once noted, "our highest allegiance must be to the community of humankind, and the first principles of our practical thought must respect the equal worth of all members of that community."[48] On the contrary, global public space often seems to have amplified voices of extremism and xenophobia, and dynamics of globalization have prompted many people to turn inward. Global public space is not necessarily globalist, cosmopolitan, or even liberal, as in the most basic model of liberalism that emphasizes universal freedom and the rights of all individuals. And yet, genuinely democratic citizenship depends on public space for mobilization, contestation, and deliberation. In this book, we treat public space as the myriad of venues in politics and society—from town meeting halls to online communities—conducive to ongoing, sustained public dialogue and deliberation. As we shall see in this book, the advent of cyberspace has transformed public space profoundly. Globalization has motivated some individuals and groups to broaden their social, political, and moral horizons beyond the nation-state and to work toward expanding public space in the international arena to help solve common problems. On the other hand, the institution of national citizenship remains highly resilient and is growing more restrictive, in many ways, while nationalism and tribalism are rising in much of the world partly in response to globalization.

In the chapters that follow, themes related to international migration, political activity, and public space converge in a variety of cases that illustrate the present-day interplay and tension between globalization and citizenship. Chapter 2 looks at the recent uprisings in North Africa and the Middle East, particularly the Jasmine Revolution in Tunisia, and the January 25 uprising in Egypt, emphasizing the role of social media in bringing together a new generation of globally aware and technologically astute activists—and also the tactics employed by national governments to disrupt these movements in cyberspace as well as on the streets. Chapter 3 focuses on how Chinese democracy activist Liu Xiaobo and WikiLeaks cofounder Julian Assange landed in the global spotlight in 2010 in very different ways and how their respective organizations and network partners have clashed with the world's two most powerful governments: the United States and China. Chapter 4 turns to Europe and examines the recent crackdowns on immigrants and backlashes against multiculturalism in countries such as France, Italy, Greece, and Switzerland that underscore how narrow and reactionary understandings of public space have been gaining momentum on the continent. Chapter 5 then shifts to the United States and explores how Arizona's controversial immigration law, the ongoing attempts to repeal birthright citizenship, and the perennial failure of legislation that would ease the way for children of undocumented immigrants to gain U.S. citizenship speak to rising public anxiety in the United States, reflecting concerns about economic globalization and the recent economic downturn. The concluding chapter ties together these cases and themes while raising some additional issues that cast light on the complex relationship between globalization and citizenship in the early twenty-first century.

CHAPTER 2

GLOBAL MEDIA, MOBILIZATION, AND REVOLUTION: THE ARAB SPRING

January 2011 ushered in a momentous new year—and perhaps a new era—across the Middle East and North Africa. First the people of Tunisia ousted dictator Zine al-Abidine Ben Ali, who fled the country after twenty-three years in power, in what became known as the "Jasmine Revolution," named after the country's national flower. Just eleven days later, on January 25, in the political and cultural heart of the Arab world, Egyptians flocked to the center of Cairo to insist that Hosni Mubarak step down. The demonstrations captivated the world for seventeen days until Mubarak left the presidential palace on February after nearly thirty years in power. Equipped with online social networking tools hardly envisioned during the fall of Soviet communism twenty years earlier, citizen activists inspired by their neighbors in Tunisia and Egypt, and also linked through wall-to-wall television news coverage by Al Jazeera, took to the streets and called for political change in

27

Yemen, Bahrain, Jordan, Syria, Algeria, and Libya. The protest movements, however, met severe government crackdowns and violence, and Libya erupted into civil war as its longtime military dictator, Colonel Muammar Gaddafi, insisted on staying in power and turned his forces against his own people in an effort to quash the revolutionaries; a larger war followed with airstrikes from the United States, Britain, and France targeting Gaddafi's forces. Gaddafi lost control of Tripoli in August and was captured, beaten, and killed by a group of rebels in October. Although the outcome remains uncertain, the "Arab Spring" has given the world fascinating lessons as to how an emerging, emboldened generation of citizen activists harnessed the new global media platforms, first to connect with each other, exchange ideas and organize campaigns and strategies, and then to communicate to the outside world their overwhelming frustration with failed national dictators as well as their alternative political and social visions for their countries.

The Arab Spring, then, provides many illustrations of how dynamics related to globalization set the stage for powerful struggles for democratic citizenship as an amalgam of rights and responsibilities, democratic empowerment and participation, and allegiance, belonging, identity, and loyalty. As citizens called for change, they insisted that freedoms of assembly and speech—online as well as in person—are fundamental rights in the twenty-first century. The round-the-clock vigils lasting for weeks in public squares in several national capitals demonstrated what it means for citizens to empower themselves, raise their voices, and join together—men and women; young and old; Muslims, Christians, and nonbelievers, all for the sake of creating new models of democracy. The activists also made it clear that they were engaging the global platforms of communication to display their loyalty and allegiances to renewed visions for their particular countries; the revolutions in Tunisia and Egypt, for instance, were widely recognized as the collective efforts of Tunisians and Egyptians themselves.

The interplay here between global citizen activism and national public space is striking. Many of the Arab Spring's leading citizen activists saw themselves as carrying out decisive roles within an emerging transnational movement for political and social change, truly inspired by universal human rights and democratic principles. But even as they communicated their ideas and aspirations for the future across a formative global online public space, with ideas and sources of inspiration migrating quickly from country to country, the citizens across North Africa and the Middle East resolutely carried out their campaigns and struggles within national public spaces—and they often had to find ways to enlist the backing of military leaders representing the coercive authority of their respective nation-states. The exceptional events of early 2011 have yet to be resolved, and it remains unclear just what kinds of democracies might emerge in Egypt and Tunisia, and elsewhere, or whether robust democracies will emerge at all. In February 2011, Václav Havel, the Czech playwright and democracy activist turned national leader after the Velvet Revolution, noted that the new generation of protesters in the Arab world has it much harder than his generation in Central and Eastern Europe because they lack historical experiences of democracy as well as established civil society institutions that can emerge quickly as alternative powers.[1] At the very least, many of the events and key players of the Arab Spring provide living and breathing narratives vitally related to the dual dynamic at the heart of this book: dynamics of globalization continue to open up new forms of bottom-up political activity and civic engagement—in these cases simultaneously tied to both networks and territory—at the same time that some autocrats across the Arab world and beyond still hold power even as the political sands shift beneath their feet.

LEADING UP TO THE ARAB SPRING: IRAN'S GREEN REVOLUTION

We can begin by tracing the recent origins of the Arab Spring to Iran, when in June 2009 vast numbers of citizens, linked by social media platforms, organized massive protests on the streets of Tehran following the country's disputed presidential election. While Iran's official leadership ultimately did not change and the incumbent president, Mahmoud Ahmadinejad, remained in power, the election became the moment in which the world learned how citizens could use social media platforms to organize political opposition and raise their voices on the global stage to challenge the legitimacy of their national governments. This marked the first time large numbers of supporters of a defeated national candidate communicated their frustration to the rest of the world by relying heavily on text messages and posts on Twitter and Facebook, as well as the bottom-up "webcasting" platform of

YouTube. In many ways, Iran's contested presidential election illustrated the rapidly accelerating globalization of social media as a tool in
political communication to empower everyday people, alongside established global news organizations, and in direct challenge to government
officials seeking to mute dissent.

The 2009 presidential election took place exactly thirty years after Iran's Islamic Revolution in 1979, and the official, disputed result
held that Ahmadinejad won with 63 percent of the vote. While Russia,
China, and India were quick to accept the official tally and congratulate
Ahmadinejad, several Western governments and international journalists raised doubts. The strongest of the three defeated challengers was
Mir-Hossein Mousavi, a former prime minister who gained much support among younger voters discontented with a weak economy and an
unemployment rate as high as 30 percent, and in search of widespread
political reforms. His campaign color happened to be green, leading this
period to be remembered as the "Green Revolution," though some also
took to calling it the "Twitter Revolution." Mousavi and his supporters
appealed without success for the results of the election to be canceled
and a new election to be held, noting that as many as fourteen million
unused ballots were missing and could have been cast fraudulently; the
number of missing unused ballots amounted to 37 percent of the thirty-
eight million ballots counted. Iran does not allow international election
monitors, and questions about the extent of possible fraud remain.

On the other hand, the impact of social media in energizing public debate in Iran was crystal clear: even before the balloting took
place on June 12, 2009, the number of text messages sent via mobile
phones in Iran rocketed from the usual 60 million messages per day
to more than 110 million messages per day. As more and more supporters of the challengers began communicating with each other via
Facebook—including an estimated 6,600 supporters of Mousavi's
Facebook page—the government blocked access to Facebook on May
23, three weeks before the election, only to restore access three days
later following public outrage at home and abroad. And then, on the
day of the election, mobile phone communications were suddenly interrupted and even the BBC reported that its television broadcasts were
disrupted by "heavy electronic jamming." A battle emerged between
Ahmadinejad's government and numerous media platforms, ranging
from Western news organizations such as BBC and CNN to the nascent

citizen media percolating from within, to become a powerful political movement unto itself. This rising force of citizen demonstrators in Iran was not always peaceful: even before the election authorities declared Ahmadinejad the winner, street demonstrators in Tehran set buses and cars on fire and threw rocks at police to protest what they viewed as an illegitimate victory in the making.

Once Ahmadinejad was declared the winner on June 14, supporters of Mousavi organized the strongest show of discontent since the 1979 revolution. Thousands of people marched in Tehran in search of a global audience with rallying cries (in Persian) such as "Where is my vote?" and "Death to the dictator!" Protests also took place outside Iranian embassies around the world. Iran's government wasted no time in fighting back, shutting off access to portions of the Internet for a half hour on the day after the election—and also shutting down Twitter, Facebook, and numerous text messaging services. Western journalists reported it was often difficult during this period to place calls on mobile phones, as Iranian authorities tried to stop activists from communicating with each other to organize additional protests.[2] Despite the growing obstacles and outbreaks of violence, Mousavi held a public rally in Tehran on June 15, with hundreds of thousands of his supporters—some estimated the crowd at more than one million—in what turned out to be the largest demonstration in Iran since the 1979 revolution. The very next day, Ahmadinejad followed up with a rally of his supporters, as Mousavi's supporters marched once again.

Iranian dissidents living in exile around the world were amazed, as they watched the election and its contentious aftermath, by the new wave of public protest back in their native country. Hamid Dabashi, a native of Iran and critic of Ahmadinejad who presents a weekly opposition webcast via YouTube that went "viral" during this period, told the BBC that the "absolutely extraordinary and unprecedented" postelection demonstrations happened only because of the mobilization that emerged online: "Nobody called for it except on the Internet. Cyberspace was buzzing with information that there was to be a demonstration from this square to that square."[3] Bottom-up networking, coupled with an element of coordination among some organizers at the top, seemed to carry the day. Experts in Internet censorship, meanwhile, found that Iranian government officials struggled to keep up with the activists using websites and social media platforms to communicate.

According to Austin Heap, executive director of the Censorship Research Center in San Francisco: "If you look at what was going on after the election, it was very clear that they [government officials] had no solid plan in place—the way they were filtering, what they were filtering. . . . Just basic things like the speed the Internet was operating at would change day by day, week by week."[4]

The filtering operations on the part of Iran's government seemed to grow more coordinated as time passed, along with growing cases of outright interference on press freedom. Several international news organizations reported that Iranian authorities confiscated cameras and other news gathering equipment, and Al Jazeera reported that some domestic newspapers were ordered to change their editorials and news headlines. BBC correspondent Jon Leyne—forced out of Iran by the government, along with several other international journalists—said he found that both sides struggled to gain the upper hand: the government's filtering attempts were "crude and ineffective," while computer programs designed to prevent filtering were eventually blocked by government censors. Leyne also noted that cyberspace in Iran throughout the campaign season was tempered by "mood swings" that peaked in the days immediately following the election. As Leyne wrote several months later: "One morning the whole BBC website would be inaccessible, and even usually secure connections were blocked. On other days the controls would be mysteriously lifted, enabling us to use the Internet to broadcast live from our office in Tehran."[5]

When the BBC Persian website was up and running, it served as a digital public square of sorts in the unfolding drama, registering 50 million page impressions for the month of June 2009 compared with 16 million one month earlier. Its online television streaming service was requested by Internet users 8 million times in June, and citizens on the streets provided much of the content, sending in thousands of e-mail messages, videos, and photos that often described and depicted incriminating images of police brutally beating protesters. Most notably, on June 15, as protests peaked three days after the election, citizen activists sent the BBC horrifying images of university students being beaten by plainclothes militia troops who dragged them from their dormitory beds. Online forwarding also turned global public opinion sharply against Iran's sitting government, especially after 40 seconds of video footage of a young woman bleeding to death from bullet wounds believed to have been inflicted by Iranian government militia troops went viral. The video was shown repeatedly on CNN after being e-mailed via mobile phone from a man in Tehran to the Voice of America, the *Guardian* newspaper in London, and five other people in Europe with the message "Please show the world." While Iran's government denied responsibility for shooting twenty-six-year-old Neda Agha Soltan on a quiet street in Tehran, the millions of people worldwide who watched the video thought otherwise.

Since the election, the Iranian government and Iranian dissidents have continued to compete for the upper hand in cyberspace and also more widely in the public space of the global media. Iran's Revolutionary Guards have reportedly drafted many of the country's most technologically adept young people, sometimes against their will, to help the government clamp down on its domestic critics by forming a new "cyber army" that has coordinated attacks on Twitter and websites associated with political opposition movements. Computer mavens in Iran and around the world, in turn, take these new methods of online censorship and suppression as a challenge. At least in Iran, however, the government of Mahmoud Ahmadinejad remained in power even as renewed protests against his rule picked up in February 2011 on the heels of the successful revolutions in Tunisia and Egypt. Authorities in Iran responded to the protests by placing Mir-Hossein Mousavi, as well as several other leaders of the citizen groups that still make up the country's Green Movement, under house arrest.

THE ONSET OF THE ARAB SPRING: TUNISIA'S JASMINE REVOLUTION

Before the end of 2010, the small North African country of Tunisia, with a population just above ten million, had a reputation as a stable but politically stifling outpost of the Arab world. Two events in December 2010 began to set in motion dynamics for change leading to the overthrow in January 2011 of Zine al-Abidine Ben Ali, the country's president since taking power in a bloodless coup in 1987. First, there were reports that Tunisia had blocked the public from accessing the website of a Lebanese newspaper, *al-Akhbar*, which had published a formerly confidential memo, written in July 2009 by the U.S. ambassador to Tunisia, calling the country a "police state" and sharply criticizing

Ben Ali and his family members. Released to news organizations by WikiLeaks, the memo by U.S. ambassador Robert Godec was titled, "Troubled Tunisia: What Should We Do?" and stated the following:

> The problem is clear. Tunisia has been ruled by the same president for 22 years. He has no successor. And, while President Ben Ali deserves credit for continuing many of the progressive policies of President [Habib] Bourguiba,[6] he and his regime have lost touch with the Tunisian people. They tolerate no advice or criticism, whether domestic or international. Increasingly, they rely on the police for control and focus on preserving power.
>
> Corruption in the inner circle is growing. Even average Tunisians are now keenly aware of it, and the chorus of complaints is rising. Tunisians intensely dislike, even hate, first lady Leila Trabelsi and her family. In private, regime opponents mock her; even those close to the government express dismay at her reported behavior. Meanwhile, anger is growing at Tunisia's high unemployment and regional inequities. As a consequence, the risks to the regime's long-term stability are increasing.[7]

While the government tried to suppress the information, citizens within Tunisia along with their friends and family members abroad easily worked around the official censorship, which banned WikiLeaks as well as other Internet communication critical of the government. Wherever they were at any given moment, critics of the government eagerly circulated via e-mail and postings on Facebook international accounts detailing extravagant lifestyles enjoyed by Ben Ali and his family in the face of the country's low incomes and stagnant economy.

A Local Incident Sets National and Global Sparks

The unflattering picture of Tunisia's political leadership confirmed the public's negative instincts about the government, further eroding its already low credibility just days before the death of Mohamed Bouazizi, twenty-six years old, who had been selling fruits and vegetables to support his family since he was ten years old. Bouazizi, according to media reports, had been bullied on a daily basis by police officers, who frequently confiscated his unlicensed vendor's stall and his merchandise. On December 17, Bouazizi used paint thinner to set himself on fire after the governor of his hometown, Sidi Bouzid, refused to meet with him to listen to his complaints about a female town official who allegedly slapped him in the face, spat at him, took away his scales, and tossed aside his vendor's cart. He died eighteen days later at a local hospital, and his family members said chronic humiliation, not poverty, threw him over the edge. Affectionately known as "Basboosa" on the streets of Sidi Bouzid and just twenty-six years old when he died, Bouazizi was a popular figure in the inland provincial city who would regularly give away fruits and vegetables to very poor families.[8] Protesters carrying "a rock in one hand, a cell phone in the other"[9] began marching on the streets of Sidi Bouzid just hours after Bouazizi set himself on fire, with political activists calling him a martyr. As word spread of the incident, several other unemployed young people in Tunisia and across the region also began trying to take their own lives, and some actually did. While the state-controlled domestic media in Tunisia avoided covering the story until December 29, the television network Al Jazeera showed a video clip of the protest that its producers found on Facebook. This linkage, once again, between social networking platforms and global news organizations proved crucial in boosting momentum and garnering worldwide attention for the protest movement. Journalists and commentators around the world came to rely on Twitter feeds of citizens tweeting instant updates and holding online conversations directly from the center of the action. One such tweet from the crowd of six thousand outside Tunisia's interior ministry declared just hours before Ben Ali fled: "Tunis now: the chants continue 'No to Ben Ali even if we die.'"[10]

The demonstrations attracted citizens from every age group and social and professional class who were fed up with high unemployment, political corruption, police brutality, and the absence of basic political rights, such as freedom of speech and freedom of assembly. The protests quickly spread from outposts such as Sidi Bouzid into the country's larger cities, especially once activists in the country's sole labor union, UGTT, began organizing rallies and marches; the protests reached the coastal capital of Tunis on December 27. The next two weeks of clashes between protesters and police turned bloody at times, with reports of police killing at least twenty-one civilians, and protesters injuring numerous police officers. Official figures later released by the government said that seventy-eight protesters died and another ninety-four were injured during the demonstrations leading up to January 14. While official state television showed little about the uprising on the streets, Tunisian citizen activists turned to the Internet to provide updates to the rest of the world. They used video cameras on their mobile phones to record harrowing clips of fires and lootings, and the digital recording files were routinely forwarded to contacts outside the country to post on websites such as YouTube.

As the pressure to step down intensified, President Ben Ali himself visited Bouazizi, who was covered in bandages, in his hospital room on December 28; Ben Ali also promised Bouazizi's mother, at a meeting in his presidential office, to send Bouazizi to France for more extensive treatment. But it was too late for both the protester and the president— Bouazizi died on January 4, and the protests drove Ben Ali out of the country ten days later.[11] Under protection from Libya, Ben Ali flew to Saudi Arabia, with French media sources reporting that their country's president, Nicolas Sarkozy, had refused him entry after earlier seeming to stand by him in public statements. On January 28 the new leaders back in Tunis asked Interpol, the cross-border police agency, for assistance in locating Ben Ali and securing his arrest; the government later asked Saudi Arabia to extradite Ben Ali back to Tunisia. Saudi Arabia refused, even after a court in Tunisia convicted Ben Ali and his wife, Leila Trabelsi, of embezzlement in June 2011 after a six-hour trial dismissed by many critics as a hasty charade on the part of the country's new authorities. The country's prime minister, Mohamed Ghannouchi, took over as the country's president, and he then quickly transferred power to the country's parliamentary speaker after being overruled by Tunisia's constitutional court.

Prospects for a successful democratic transition in Tunisia were questionable from the start, given that many of the people who actually ran Ben Ali's police state remained politically active in Tunis. Parliamentary elections took place in October 2011 to form a temporary government, charged with the task of drafting a constitution, and the new ruling coalition elected as interim president Moncef Marzouki, a human rights activist who had been imprisoned for opposing Ben Ali and then exiled in France for many years before returning to Tunisia once Ben Ali fled. As Marzouki noted at his inaugural ceremony in December: "Other nations are watching us as a laboratory of democracy."[12] While his election was billed as a power-sharing deal between the dominant, moderate Islamist party and its smaller, secular coalition partners, about forty opposition party members of the interim assembly protested the vote, casting blank ballots and emphasizing that the prime minister, Hamadi Jebali from the Ennahda party, would hold much more power for the time being. "This was a piece of theatre," said Najib Chebbi, head of Tunisia's Progressive Democratic Party. "He has accepted a presidency which is just democratic window-dressing without any real functions."[13] The current government and its prime minister will face another round of elections once a new constitution is written.

TUNISIA'S SOCIAL MEDIA SHOWDOWN

While the Ben Ali government tried to censor and obstruct the usage of social media among the citizens, the global high-tech companies themselves began to respond in ways that would give the people a shot at regaining their edge against the government authorities. As technology journalist and historian Alexis Madrigal uncovered in a fascinating account published by the *Atlantic*, staffers at Facebook's headquarters in Palo Alto, California, began to notice that something was amiss in Tunisia on Christmas Day 2010: the company began receiving reports that some political protest pages on the site were getting hacked. As recalled by Facebook's chief security officer, Joe Sullivan, it turned out to be an extraordinary cyberattack orchestrated by Tunisia's authorities: "We were getting anecdotal reports saying, 'It looks like someone logged into my account and deleted it.'"[14] As Sullivan's security team looked more closely at the data, they could not prove anything was wrong, but already citizens in Tunisia sensed interference from "Ammar 404," the nickname they had given to the country's Internet censors.

As the unrest in Tunisia increased in December and the government successfully blocked many video-sharing websites, Facebook's platform remained the one key web venue where activists managed to continue uploading videos as they shared information and made plans for their next moves. As Madrigal explained:

> The videos—shot shakily with camera phones—created a link between what was happening on the streets in the poor areas of the country and the broader Tunisian population. Many are graphic. In one video— since taken down, apparently—a young man is lying on a gurney with his skull cracked open. Brain oozes out. Cries are heard all around. The video focuses in on the man's face and as the camera pulls back,

we see that there are two other people with cameraphones recording the injury. Video after video of the revolutionary events captures other people videoing the same event. Those videos, and the actions they recorded, became the raw material for a much greater online apparatus that could amplify each injury, death, and protest.

But it wasn't just videos that people were sharing. All kinds of information passed between Tunisians. For activists as well as everyday people, Facebook became an indispensable resource for tracking the minute-by-minute development of the situation. By January 8, Facebook says that it had several hundred thousand more users than it had ever had before in Tunisia, a country with a few more people than Michigan. Scaled up to the size to the U.S., the burst of activity was like adding 10 million users in a week. And the average time spent on the site more than doubled what it had been before.[15]

Even activists who previously had avoided Facebook began to find the social networking tool indispensable. "It basically went from being a waste of time or procrastination tool, to my go-to source on up-to-date information," said Rim Abida, a development consultant born in Tunisia, educated at Harvard, and now living in Rio de Janeiro. "My mom is back in Tunisia on her own, and my Tunisian network on Facebook was posting the most up-to-date info on what was happening on the ground. It was stuff the major media channels weren't reporting, such as numbers to call to reach the military and what was happening when in what specific neighborhood."[16] It all amounted to a dramatic case of a global media platform leading the way in providing the most immediate local information in a moment of great turmoil.

By January 5, however, as protests in Tunisia swelled to a crescendo, Facebook's security team figured out that Internet service providers in Tunisia were running malicious software that recorded the login information of web users when they signed onto Facebook and similar social networking websites. As Madrigal explained: "The software was basically a country-level keystroke logger, with the passwords presumably being fed from the ISPs to the Ben Ali regime." At the same time as Tunisia was going through its biggest political uprising in more than twenty years, the government was stealing the passwords of the country's Facebook users so authorities could then change—or delete—Facebook accounts they considered offensive or damaging. In response, Sullivan's team at Facebook headquarters rerouted all Internet requests for Facebook coming from Tunisia to a more secure "https" server commonly used to encrypt information and keep it out of view of the Tunisian Internet service providers and their spying. More innovatively, Facebook also implemented what the company called a "roadblock" for all users in Tunisia as they logged in and out of Facebook, with users in Tunisia now required to identify their friends in photos before log-ins would be accepted; this additional layer especially sought to outmaneuver the censors and monitors. These changes to Facebook's interface in Tunisia took effect on Monday, January 10. Four days later, Ben Ali left the country.

The incident in Tunisia brought a sobering reminder that Facebook not only facilitates political activism but also creates new ways for government authorities to interfere with Internet access and entrap activists, learning their true identities and monitoring their every move in cyberspace. Facebook, in particular, has insisted that its users, activists included, use their real names rather than pseudonyms and has not put in place special measures for dissidents seeking to keep their identities hidden, even as it becomes all too obvious that online dissidents are vulnerable to being "outed" and, in extreme cases, killed by their respective governments. Madrigal wondered if Facebook would soon find it necessary to become more accommodating with activists, and his reasoning converged with the widening recognition that Facebook increasingly is filling a central role in the formation of global public space:

> If Facebook really is becoming the public sphere—and wants to remain central to people's real sociopolitically embedded lives—maybe they're going to have to think beyond the situational technical fix. Facebook needs to own [up to] its position as a part of The Way the World Works and provide protections for political speech and actors. Because the protests and overthrow of Ben Ali were just the beginning of this story. Hopes are high, but as we've seen so many times in the global south, the exit of one corrupt dictator usually means the entrance of another. To avoid that fate, politically active Tunisians will be using all of the tools at their disposal, including and maybe especially, Facebook.[17]

Clearly a battle over cyberspace continues to unfold in North Africa and the Middle East. It involves a great deal of push and pull between activists and dissidents on the one hand, authoritarian governments on the other, and global social networking sites and Internet service providers—with their offices well beyond the borders of the countries in question—monitoring the turns of events and making decisions that often amount to taking sides. The departure of Ben Ali signaled a moment for celebration in the activist ranks; online communities across North Africa and the Middle East were filled with jubilant congratulations for the activists and online conversations calling for political change in their respective countries. A YouTube user identified as Algeriansunited1, who had previously posted videos of demonstrations in Algeria, posted a message congratulating the Tunisian people. Many Facebook users within Tunisia and beyond changed their profile images to that of the red Tunisian flag—and a Facebook group with the name "Bye Bye 3ammar 404" (a poke at the "Ammar 404" moniker that protesters in Tunisia gave to the departed regime's Internet censors) posted a message (in Arabic) that stated: "A new day and the sun rises on a Tunis without the great traitor Ben Ali. Long live Tunis, free and independent."[18]

Especially in Egypt, which leads the Arab world in its number of Facebook users, many bloggers expressed their solidarity with the activists in Tunisia and hoped for a similar turn of events at home. Indeed, if the people of Tunisia could overturn their longstanding government and force Ben Ali and his family to flee, then possibly it could also be done in Egypt where far more people live in poverty, ruled by a dictator who had held onto power even longer. The very day Ben Ali fled the country, a well-known Egyptian blogger, Bint Masreya, posted a picture of the Tunisian flag and commented (in Arabic): "Tunisia: we are proud of your people; may the same happen to us."[19] A young Egyptian woman, Gigi Ibrahim, identified on Twitter as Gsquare86, tweeted these words as Ben Ali left the country: "Goosebumps all over. I can't believe I lived through an Arab revolution!! Thank you, Tunisia! The power of the masses is capable of toppling any dictatorship. Today was Tunisia. Tomorrow is Egypt, Jordan. LONG LIVE REVOLUTION!"[20]

EGYPT'S DEMOCRATIC UPRISING: THE JANUARY 25 REVOLUTION

Just as the death of Mohamed Bouazizi, at the young age of twenty-six, sparked the protest movement in Tunisia, the murder of a twenty-eight-year-old businessman, Khaled Said, galvanized activists in the months leading up to the January 25 uprising in Egypt. The timing of this incident, on June 6, 2010, in the coastal city of Alexandria, coincided with the rise of social media among political and social activists in the Arab world and also by younger generations of middle-class people poised to jump into political action once the window of opportunity opened. While police in Alexandria claimed that Said had choked to death after swallowing drugs he tried to hide from officers, photos of his body told a completely different and gruesome story: missing teeth, a broken jaw, and blood coming from his head. His family members told human rights activists that two police officers had dragged Said out of an Internet café and beaten him to death after he posted a video showing a group of officers sharing the spoils from a drug bust. More than a thousand people attended Said's funeral in Alexandria and held an impromptu protest; and many other protests around the country, filled with demands that Egypt's longtime and much despised interior minister be fired, continued throughout the summer of 2010. Activists also tried to hold a street demonstration in downtown Cairo, but according to a Reuters journalist, "the gathering was swiftly dispersed after state security men beat and detained demonstrators."[21] A group of Egyptian rappers made a music video, posted on YouTube, scoffing at the official account of Said's death with a phrase (in Arabic) that resonated among Egypt's protesters: "They think the people are stupid!"[22] Following tremendous public pressure, in July 2010 the two police officers in question were charged with "illegal arrest, using physical torture and brutality." After many delays, a court in Alexandria found the officers guilty, but the public furiously rejected the seven-year prison sentences they each received in October 2011 as far too lenient, and yet another wave of street protests followed.

FROM SOCIAL MEDIA TO STREET PROTESTS

Such allegations of torture were hardly new in Egypt; what has changed recently across the Arab world is the ability of citizen activists to chronicle human rights abuses, spur international awareness of the problems, and mobilize in response. Another crucial moment in raising consciousness in Egypt emerged in August 2010 when a woman went on television and accused police of raping her along a deserted rural road in the Nile Delta, north of Cairo.[23] Amid the outpouring of public criticism, a veteran Egyptian human rights activist who has focused especially on the rights of women and victims of torture in the country launched a website in 2010 with a hotline to report incidents of abuse or mistreatment by police, and the advocacy group El Nadim Centre for Rehabilitation of Victims of Violence began publishing an online diary to document allegations of abuse at the hands of Egypt's authorities.[24]

The murder of Said and the images of the severe torture he suffered at the hands of police, just moments before his death, outraged Egyptians and international observers alike and prompted strong demands for Egypt's government to make fundamental changes in its police system. Amnesty International called the "shocking pictures . . . [a] rare, firsthand glimpse of the routine use of brutal force by the Egyptian security forces, who expect to operate in a climate of impunity, with no questions asked."[25] A Facebook community started anonymously—with the title "We Are All Khaled Said"—along with its companion website quickly evolved into a clearinghouse of information about the broader iniquity of police brutality in Egypt, with numerous grotesque and detailed accounts of the Egyptian government's practices of torture that accompanied President Hosni Mubarak's thirty years in power under continual martial law. On the day after Tunisia's deposed president, Zine al-Abidine Ben Ali, fled the country, about seven thousand followers of this Facebook community held a special online event calling for action in Egypt, with this summary: "Enough of being silent. . . . We are not less than Tunisia. . . .Tens of thousands took to the streets in Tunisia and succeeded in their quest to achieve liberty. . . . We want our rights. . . . We do not want repression in Egypt. . . . We want to be free."[26] As noted in August 2010 by Mona Eltahawy, a journalist born in Egypt and now based in New York, the Said murder had the effect of taking Egypt's online activism to a higher level than before:

> If social media in the Arab world were merely outlets for venting or "stress relief"—as detractors claim—then Said's fate would have ended with some angry comments on Facebook and a tweet or two railing at the Egyptian regime. . . . Instead, thanks to social media's increasing popularity and ability to connect activists with ordinary people, Egyptians are protesting police brutality in unprecedented numbers. . . . There is a difference, of course, between the real world and the virtual world. Social media won't overthrow regimes. But such sites have given a voice and platform to young people long marginalized by those regimes.[27]

Several underlying problems in Egypt, bearing a resemblance to the sources of discontent that had long festered in Tunisia, triggered the uprising in Egypt just two weeks after Ben Ali lost power: frustration with high unemployment and low economic opportunity for all but the elites, political corruption and repression despite three decades of empty promises from Mubarak about prospects for democracy, as well as tiresome justifications for the country's harsh policing tactics. Indeed, Tuesday, January 25, the date that mass demonstrations centered on Cairo's Tahrir Square, or Liberation Square, coincided with Police Day, a national holiday observing the massacre of Egyptian police officers by British forces in 1952.

Also similar to Tunisia's Jasmine Revolution, Facebook groups based in Egypt were key to mobilizing protesters on January 25. One group that called itself "January 25: the revolution of liberty" had close to four hundred thousand fans as of January 25 and displayed the message: "Dear people of Tunisia, the sun of the revolution will not disappear!" Another group called "Day of Revolution" claimed it recruited more than eighty thousand of its online followers across Egypt to participate in street protests. While many activists in Egypt used social media to coordinate demonstrations and round up participants, others around the world posted messages of support and words of caution: one Egyptian Twitter user in California, identified as Lobna Darwish, tweeted this advice to the protesters: "To avoid electric shocks, put on several layers of clothing, particularly wool."[28] Others posted messages on Facebook advising activists about how to react if beaten by police and how to respond if taken away by officers. And some Facebook groups became forums expressing skepticism about whether the uprising would be effective; members of one such group, called "Révolution égyptienne blanche," or "Egyptian White Revolution," voiced concerns that the protests were being manipulated by the country's opposition parties. As one Facebook user posted on this group as the January 25 uprising began: "I'm a young Egyptian woman and I don't understand what you want with this revolution, who will benefit?"[29]

Several elder Egyptian opposition figures also began using Twitter, especially after the demise of Ben Ali in Tunisia, to communicate with their followers and direct their messages toward a global audience shortly before the mass demonstrations began in Cairo. Egypt's most prominent opposition figure, Mohamed ElBaradei, a leading Mubarak opponent in exile and the former head of the International Atomic Energy Agency run under the auspices of the United Nations, posted this statement on his Twitter feed on January 13: "Tunisia: repression + absence of social justice + denial of channels for peaceful change = a ticking bomb."[30] And the leader of Egypt's opposition Al-Ghad Party, Ayman Noor, sent several tweets from his Twitter account in advance of the protests; one tweet in January 2011 read: "From Ceausescu to Ben Ali, I say to those who are frustrated, you must learn your lesson: dictatorship continues to resist; it tries to tighten its grip; but suddenly it falls in the last minute."[31]

Religious organizations in Egypt also turned to social media in reaching out to their supporters. The Facebook page of a group called "No More Silence After This Day" included quotes from the Koran and a link to an Islamic organization calling upon its members to join the protests. Across the many different points of view, #Jan25 and #Cairo quickly became the Twitter hashtags most often used in Egypt and beyond to check out the latest developments. Cutting to the heart of the matter, a Facebook page run by protesters listed their demands of Mubarak: (1) declare that neither he nor his son, Gamal, will run for president in the 2011 elections; (2) dissolve the parliament immediately and hold new elections; (3) end the emergency laws giving police seemingly unlimited powers of arrest and detention; (4) release all prisoners including protesters and those who have been in jail for years without charge or trial; (5) fire the interior minister immediately—a final demand that hearkened back to the murder the previous summer of Khaled Said.

After initially responding to the protests with excessive force, Egypt's police lost their authority as the country's military sided decisively with the protesters by making it clear that soldiers would not fire against peaceful demonstrators. This move made a mockery of the government's attempts to impose daily curfews as early as 3 p.m. and keep people off the streets by closing roads and public transportation services. Christians and Muslims as well as the rich and the poor across the country called in unison for Mubarak and his government to resign immediately and flatly rejected his initial response to the protesters, communicated in a speech to the nation on February 1, that he would stay in office until regularly scheduled elections were held in September. Two journalists from the Associated Press captured the atmosphere at this moment among the remarkably diverse crowd of protesters:

The uprising united the economically struggling and the prosperous, the secular and the religious. The country's most popular opposition group, the Islamist Muslim Brotherhood, did not advertise its presence and it was not immediately clear how much of a role it played in bringing people to the streets. Many protesters chanted "God is great!" and stopped their demonstrations to pray. Young men in one downtown square clambered onto a statue of Talat Harb, a pioneering Egyptian economist, and unfurled a large green banner that proclaimed "The Middle Class" in white Arabic lettering. Women dressed in black veils and wide, flowing robes followed women with expensive hairdos, tight jeans and American sneakers. The crowd included Christian men with key rings of the cross swinging from their pockets and young men dressed in fast-food restaurant uniforms. When a man sporting a long beard and a white robe began chanting an Islamist slogan, he was grabbed and shaken by another protester telling him to keep the slogans patriotic and not religious. Women were largely unmolested in a city where sexual harassment on the streets is persistent.[32]

Older Egyptian activists watched their younger, web-savvy counterparts with much excitement and anticipation as the protests continued. Egyptian novelist Alaa Al Aswany—the founder of an earlier political movement in Egypt that also had opposed Mubarak's presidency and the prospect of a power transfer to his son—spoke to the younger activists on January 27, two days after the uprising began, and wrote his impressions later that day: "Most of them are university students who find themselves with no hope for the future. They are unable to find work, and hence unable to marry. And they are motivated by an untameable anger and a profound sense of injustice. I will always be in awe of these revolutionaries. Everything they have said shows a sharp political awareness and a death-defying desire for freedom."[33] Likewise, Egyptian novelist Ahdaf Soueif, the best-selling author of *The Map of Love* and many other books, noted how the old and the young, as well as the secular and the devout, were strongly joined together in "solidarity in action." As Soueif wrote in a column published January 27 in the *Guardian*:

In Tahrir Square, in the centre of Cairo, on Tuesday night Egypt refound and celebrated its diversity. The activists formed a minor part of the gathering, what was there was The People. Young people of every background and social class marched and sang together. Older, respected figures went round with food and blankets. Cigarette-smoking women in jeans sat next to their niqab-wearing sisters on the pavement. Old comrades from the student movement of the 1970s met for the first time in decades. Young people went round collecting litter. People who stayed at home phoned nearby restaurants with orders to deliver food to the protesters. Not one religious or sectarian slogan was heard. The solidarity was palpable. And if this sounds romantic, well, it was and is.[34]

THE JANUARY 25 UPRISING BUILDS MOMENTUM

The grassroots activists who mobilized the uprising quickly gained the backing of Egypt's largest and most influential opposition group, the Muslim Brotherhood, which otherwise kept a fairly low profile as it remained officially banned in Egypt. Mubarak's security officials responded by arresting several of its leaders as well as at least five members of parliament critical of the ruling party in the days immediately following January 25. The elder statesman within Egypt's political opposition, Mohamed ElBaradei, returned to Egypt on the evening of Thursday, January 27; the very next day, he was soaked by water cannons fired by police as he billed himself as a possible successor to Mubarak, saying that he hoped to lead a peaceful transition to democracy in Egypt if he could win the backing of the country's younger generations. On Sunday, January 30—the sixth day of protests—ElBaradei spoke before thousands in Tahrir Square and called for Mubarak to step down as fighter jets flew low over Cairo. It remained to be seen if ElBaradei could unify the country's fractious opposition forces and also overcome widespread perceptions of him in Egypt as an elitist and expatriate out of touch with the country's problems after years of living abroad, first as an Egyptian diplomat and later with the United Nations.

Even as Mubarak insisted in a speech on February 1 that he would stay in power for the short term, protesters intensified their calls for him to depart immediately and for the country to draft a new constitution, remove the ruling party from power, and bring Mubarak and his associates to trial—demands that were more ambitious than what the protesters had initially called for just one week earlier. An estimated two hundred and fifty thousand men, women, and children marched on Tahrir Square to reject Mubarak's speech, escalating the public pressure for him to resign. One protester carried a cardboard sign displaying song lyrics by an Egyptian pop icon, Abdel Halim Hafez, that captured the spirit of the marchers: "And we won when the army rose and revolted, when we ignited a revolution and fire, when we fought corruption, when we liberated the country, when we realized independence, and we won, we won, we won."[35] The visual images at the protests underscored the extent to which national uprisings now often take on the qualities of global events, in the ways that protesters rely on technology and also seek to reach a worldwide audience. One popular sign carried by hundreds, if not thousands, of protesters was directed at the English-speaking world and seen again and again in news photos: "Mubarak You're Down, Just Leave!" Another protester carried a sign in French with a local adaptation of a phrase that had made a great impact a few weeks earlier on the streets of Tunis: "Dégage, Mubarak!" Mubarak did just that on Friday, February 11, when he gave up his attempt to stay in office until the country's September elections and left the presidential palace for the Red Sea resort town of Sharm el-Sheikh. He and his two sons went on trial in August 2011 on charges of "intentional murder, attempted murder of demonstrators, abuse of power to intentionally waste public funds and unlawfully profiting from public funds for them and for others."[36]

As citizens around the world watched the uprising in Egypt gain strength, a gap emerged in many countries between restrained and muted responses from national leaders and assertive calls from citizens for Mubarak to resign. This gap emerged with particular clarity in the United States, where in early February 2011 President Barack Obama continued to call for a transition to democracy in Egypt without publicly calling for Mubarak to leave office immediately. As former U.S. vice president Dick Cheney went so far as to call Mubarak "a good man, a good friend and ally to the United States,"[37] many Americans sent a different message to Egypt as protests emerged in cities from Atlanta to New Orleans to Seattle, where about two hundred people gathered at Westlake Park carrying signs saying "Step down now" and "Free Egypt." Ghada Ellithy, an Egyptian immigrant, carried a handmade paper Egyptian flag—declaring "Go Egypt"—and said she wanted to support her mother and brother in Cairo who were among the protesters at that moment in Tahrir Square. Near Detroit, a group of demonstrators carried signs bearing messages to Mubarak such as "Get Out Grandpa," and one man carried a sign showing the Egyptian and U.S. flags and the slogan: "2011 is Egypt's 1776."

THE REGIME FIGHTS BACK: DETAINMENTS AND DARKNESS ONLINE

The dual dynamic between citizen activists using global media platforms to communicate with each other and raise their voices, on the one hand, and the imposition of power by national governments on the other, emerged with great clarity in Egypt when authorities managed to cut off the country's Internet access practically in one fell swoop. It was the first time a single country suddenly went dark, so to speak, in cyberspace, and it happened as journalists from Al Jazeera, facing the forced closure of its Cairo bureau, asked Egypt's citizens to post eyewitness accounts and videos online showing the protests in Tahrir Square so the television network could broadcast them, just as in Tunisia. In response, Egypt's authorities disrupted access to social media sites, first on Thursday, January 27, when users of Facebook and Twitter found the websites off-line; mobile phone communication and text messaging services also were patchy on this day. Then, Internet communication ceased nationwide beginning at 12:34 a.m. Cairo time on Friday, January 28, when a major Internet service provider for Egypt reported that no Internet traffic was going in or out of the country. Those who monitored the effects of the protests on the Internet in Egypt pointed out the similarities with Iran's Internet tampering in 2009 during its disputed presidential election.

Experts noted that dictatorships can block Internet access fairly easily when their governments already exert strong control over their domestic online service providers. This is typically carried out by enforcing strict licensing procedures over the companies' own fiber optic cables and other technologies that enable Internet connections to be maintained—or, alternatively, shut down. "I don't think there's a big red button—it's probably a phone call that goes out to half a dozen folks," said Craig Labovitz, chief scientist for Arbor Networks, an Internet security company based in Massachusetts.[38] Five days later, on Wednesday, February 2, Egypt's government allowed the country's Internet service providers to reverse the "kill switch" and restore service; observers noted that the speed in which service was restored once again confirmed that the shutdown had been coordinated nation-ally. The way Egypt's government managed to suspend Internet access so quickly—imposing a virtual blackout of online public space for almost one week—caught many analysts by surprise. As technology writer Jordan Robertson noted: "Egypt has apparently done what many technologists thought was unthinkable for any country with a major Internet economy: It unplugged itself entirely from the Internet to try and silence dissent."[39] The negative global response cut across politics and economics: Egypt's stock market fell 15 percent in the three trad-ing sessions that followed the shutdown, and ultimately, this episode had the effect of galvanizing the dissenters, many of whom immediately demanded access to Facebook and Twitter as fundamental rights and called even more forcefully for Mubarak to step down. One activist in Egypt, Wael Ghonim, a marketing executive for global Internet and communications giant Google, gave the world this fitting quotation for the early twenty-first century: "A government that is scared from [sic] #Facebook and #Twitter should govern a city in Farmville but not a country like #Egypt."[40]

Shortly after tweeting these words on Friday, January 28, Ghonim disappeared and his tweets stopped. One of Ghonim's final tweets from January 28 sounded ominous: "Pray for #Egypt. Very worried as it seems that government is planning a war crime tomorrow against people. We are all ready to die." His whereabouts were then unknown until Sunday, February 6, when a prominent Egyptian political figure told reporters Ghonim was under arrest. The next day, police freed Ghonim after twelve days in detention, and his release energized the protest movement as word spread that it was Ghonim who had anony-mously started and moderated the Facebook page "We Are All Khaled Said" and helped to organize the January 25 protests. Speaking on Egyptian television one night after his release, on February 7, Ghonim mesmerized his country and the world when he recounted his twelve days blindfolded (but not tortured) in captivity: "I am not a hero," he told Mona Al Shazly, the interviewer for Dream TV. "I only used the keyboard—the real heroes are the ones on the ground, those I can't name."[41] Then he became emotional as he was shown images of some of the three hundred people who had died in the uprising while he was in detention: "I want to say to every mother and every father that lost his child, I am sorry, but this is not our fault. I swear to God, this is not our fault. It is the fault of everyone who was holding on to power greedily and would not let it go."[42] He then stood up and walked out of the television studio. Outdoors in Tahrir Square, Ghonim electrified a massive crowd and urged the protesters to settle for nothing less than the departure of Mubarak. His interview instantly took the Internet by storm, as millions around the world watched videos posted on YouTube with subtitles in many different languages.

In clear hindsight, the decision of Egypt's authorities to detain Ghonim backfired massively: the sensation that followed his release gave the opposition movement an appealing young face—an intelligent activist with a compelling story to project in the global media and who seemed to share more in common with cosmopolitans than fundamentalists. Egypt's opposition movement, at a pivotal and historic moment, had now found a single person who, if not exactly a leader, could still embody for a global audience the dreams for democracy shared by the next generation of Egyptians and present a clear alternative to everything that Hosni Mubarak and his authoritarian regime had come to signify. Ghonim's release and public appearances inspired many Egyptians who had not yet joined the uprising to head outdoors and reinforce the growing crowd in Tahrir Square. "He's the most credible person in Egypt right now; he feels what we are all feeling," a twenty-five-year-old protester, Reem El-Komi, told a British journalist. [43]

A chorus of support and enthusiasm also resounded on Twitter. One person, identifying herself as Menna Gamal, tweeted the following: "My aunt called me crying after Ghonim's interview saying 'I'm going to Tahrir tomorrow! God Bless him! He made us proud!'" Another Twitter activist identified only as AngelSavant, wrote with excitement: "Ghonim just became the mayor of Tahrir Square!" And Egyptian-Canadian journalist Daliah Merzaban, posting on Twitter as Desert_Dals, turned to the Arabic phrase for "God willing" to capture Ghonim's impact: "Left breathless by Wael Ghonim. InshaAllah his sincerity & patriotism, beamed into Egypt's living rooms, will ignite this revolution #Jan25."[44] It was telling that Egyptians came to admire and, indeed, love Ghonim for his sense of *patriotism*, even as he appealed to universal values of liberty and democracy, traversed the world as an executive for Google—based in the Arab world's cosmopolitan hub of Dubai—and engaged with tremendous efficacy the online tools of twenty-first-century global activism. Married to an American, Ghonim could have become a U.S. citizen but affirmed during his television interview that he wanted to remain a citizen of Egypt. In April 2011, Ghonim told his Twitter followers that he had "decided to take a long term sabbatical from @Google & start a technology focused NGO to help fight poverty & foster education in #Egypt."[45]

CHRONICLING THE ARAB SPRING: MEDIA OLD AND NEW

Journalists from the world's leading news organizations swept into Cairo to cover the uprising and tapped into the same electronic communication mechanisms as the protesters—while working to overcome the same kinds of barriers. Columnist Nicholas Kristof of the *New York Times*—well known for his coverage at the forefront of the Tiananmen Square protests and subsequent massacre in Beijing in 1989, as well as his ongoing dispatches from zones of conflict, disaster, and adversity all around the world—arrived in Egypt on Sunday, January 30, when the Internet remained off-limits but mobile phones were coming back online. In classic new media fashion, and relying on his satellite phone to work at least partially around the Internet shutdown, Kristof immediately began posting updates minute by minute via Twitter, Facebook, and his blog, alongside his usual editorial columns.[46] Kristof's scores of Cairo tweets provided readers outside Egypt with immediate eyewitness accounts that hardly would have been possible outside of continuous television coverage just a few years earlier. Some of his initial tweets from Tahrir Square are noted here in sequence:

> People defying the curfew in Tahrir, and mood giddy w/ excitement there. But elsewhere, shops boarded up, no traffic, v tense.
> My taxi was stopped every 100 yds by private roadblocks, w/ tense young men w/ bats & machetes, looking for looters & cops.
> Until now, ElBaradei has been all stature, no support. But defying curfew, speaking in Sq, gives him street cred he needs.
> "What we have begun cannot be reversed."—El Baradei in Tahrir. I hope he's right, but elsewhere I've seen pop uprisings crushed.
> Fabulous, giddy mood at Tahrir. Love the campfires. But 1 troubling thought: Tiananmen was the same before the shooting.
> I find it deeply sad that #Egypt pro-democracy protesters feel inspired by Tunisia, and stymied by America.

Women in Tahrir say #Egypt democracy won't lead to oppression. They note that autocracy hasn't been so hot for them either.

Only one hostile encounter so far—a man in Tahrir who was enraged that I was asking lots of questions about the Muslim Brotherhood. He said I was focussing on dangers of democracy.

Others in #Egypt sometimes suspicious, but friendly. Even guys with clubs.

Innaharda, ehna kullina Misryeen! Today, we're all Egyptians![47]

Just a few years earlier, no one imagined that the most widely read newspaper columnists would soon be communicating in "real time" with a global audience in sentence fragments littered with abbreviations and occasional spelling errors. The social networking era has brought journalists much closer to their readers as well as their sources—and has also widened the range of their readers and their sources. For international journalists playing a key role in the shaping of global public space for information, conversation, and debate, social media tools have brought powerful new ways to maintain instant contact with readers while also gaining instant updates from people in the field. While in Cairo, Kristof crossed the milestone of one million Twitter followers, on February 9, two days before Mubarak gave up the presidency. In the end, Kristof's column published on January 31 connected the dots from these tweets and concluded that Hosni Mubarak should resign as Egypt's president while the United States should support the democracy activists in "the most exhilarating place in the world," Tahrir Square:

Many Egyptian pro-democracy advocates said they feel betrayed that Americans are obsessing on what might go wrong for the price of oil, for Israel, for the Suez Canal—instead of focusing on the prospect of freedom and democracy for the Egyptian people. Maybe I'm too caught up in the giddiness of Tahrir Square, but I think the protesters have a point. Our equivocation isn't working. It's increasingly clear that stability will come to Egypt only after Mr. Mubarak steps down. It's in our interest, as well as Egypt's, that he resign and leave the country. And we also owe it to the brave men and women of Tahrir Square—and to our own history and values—to make one thing very clear: We stand with the peaceful throngs pleading for democracy, not with those who menace them.[48]

The Arab world's premier global news organization, Al Jazeera, also found itself a natural leader in covering the story out of Egypt and continued to broadcast from Cairo even after the government ordered the network's bureau to shut down and revoked its license to broadcast from the country. The network defiantly replied that it would continue broadcasting and placed its coverage on various satellite frequencies. As the network noted in a statement: "In this time of deep turmoil and unrest in Egyptian society it is imperative that voices from all sides be heard; the closing of our bureau by the Egyptian government is aimed at censoring and silencing the voices of the Egyptian people."[49] Some called the social media revolution in the Arab world "Al Jazeera's moment," with its coverage throughout the network's fifteen-year history gradually shaping a transnational narrative against numerous dictatorships across the Arab world, many of them backed by the United States—thereby handing the protesters a broader storyline to follow. As Middle East scholar Marc Lynch has observed: "The notion that there is a common struggle across the Arab world is something Al Jazeera helped create. They did not cause these events, but it's almost impossible to imagine all this happening without Al Jazeera."[50]

Indeed, Al Jazeera coverage fueled Tunisia's Jasmine Revolution when the network hired a freelance journalist and self-described human rights activist, Lotfi Hajji, to work undercover in Tunisia at considerable personal risk, with the regime's secret police keeping close watch. When the uprising began after Mohamed Bouazizi set himself on fire, activists used Facebook to send Hajji amateur videos shot on mobile phones documenting police brutality. As one account of Al Jazeera's role put it: "Each time Al Jazeera broadcast the videos, more would flood into Mr. Hajji's Facebook account, in a cycle that blew the seeds of revolt across the country. . . . Two years ago, an amateur journalist reporting for a website was jailed for showing film of an uprising in the Tunisian city of Gafsa; with no coverage in Facebook or Al Jazeera, it never spread to other towns."[51] Ironically, as the Arab Spring catapulted Al Jazeera into the global spotlight in much the same way as the bombing of Baghdad in 1991 enabled CNN to solidify its role as a global news organization, Al Jazeera continued to languish on the margins within the United States, with only three local cable systems carrying the network as of March 2011.[52]

Some commentators, however, worried in early 2011 that the "people power" behind Internet mobilizations and social networking sites would inevitably prove no match for the coercive power of national governments and militaries. As a commentator in the *Jerusalem Post* grimly noted on February 4, after thugs loyal to Mubarak began to attack protesters, international human right activists, and journalists, and as riot police began detaining many people on the streets of Cairo:

> Will we follow their interrogation and detention on Twitter? Will Facebook find a way to ensure they get proper legal representation? While social networking sites did galvanize the protest movement, as the world saw in Iran's "Green Revolution," when the hammer finally does drop, it doesn't seem to matter if the world is watching, tweeting, blogging or hash-tagging. As in Tehran, we are seeing in Cairo that while it's great to have history and the media on your side, it's better to have bullets.[53]

Likewise, Nicholas Thompson, writing in the *New Yorker,* cautioned against jumping to conclusions that technology would—or should—always favor the activists and their followers: "Movements that center around hashtags often don't center around leaders. Who is the Václav Havel of Tunisia? Headless movements have advantages: are the charismatic people who are best at leading protests really the people you want to lead your country after the government changes? But they also have disadvantages: if a government falls, who, then, will run it?[54] These words of caution, in many respects, foreshadowed the uncertainty that would linger in Tunisia and Egypt following the departures of Ben Ali and Mubarak, as well as the brutal force that several governments across North Africa and the Middle East continued to deploy against protesters.

CONCLUSION

The Arab Spring showed the world that the Facebook and Twitter generation of political activists mobilizing on the Internet now have the power to take down dictatorships, but it isn't yet clear if they have the staying power to build up a democracy. It also isn't yet clear what kinds of democracies might emerge or whether they will be sustainable. At the start of 2012, the prospects in Egypt and Tunisia remained highly uncertain. In the months that followed Hosni Mubarak's fall from power in Egypt, critics accused the military government that took over, at least for the short term, of the same sorts of brutal police tactics, including torturing protesters taken into custody, that had prompted the uprising against Mubarak. On October 27, just one day after the controversial verdict in the Khaled Said murder case was announced, reports surfaced that a twenty-four-year-old man, Essam Atta, had been tortured to death in his prison cell, allegedly by security officials, who then dumped his body in front of a local hospital. Atta had been serving a two-year sentence for "illegally occupying an apartment," a charge disputed by his family and friends. Dozens of Atta's supporters made their way to Tahrir Square, where they joined more than twenty thousand protesters critical of the interim military government. Among them was the mother of Khaled Said, Leila Marzouk, who told the crowd as tears streamed down her face: "Sadly, I am here today to bring in another Khaled. They cannot keep killing our youth and getting away with it. My faith is in you."[55] At end of 2011, Egypt's ruling generals were accused of ordering the firing of live ammunition against protesters who filled Tahrir Square to oppose a bid by the military to retain certain key political powers permanently, rather than transfer power to democratic rule by civilians. Police were also accused of raiding the offices of several human rights and democracy organizations in Cairo. Parliamentary elections encompassing several rounds of voting began in November and were slated to be completed by March 2012, with a presidential election expected to follow by June 2012.

Meanwhile, citizens in Tunisia no longer live in fear of the secret police and portraits of Zine al-Abidine Ben Ali no longer are displayed alongside the country's national flag. But the country's credit rating deteriorated sharply in the aftermath of the uprising, tourism dried up amid the continued instability, and unemployed young adults were leaving the country in record numbers for Europe, with an exodus of fifteen thousand estimated in the weeks following the fall of Ben Ali. This made the immigration issue in neighboring Italy and France that much more contentious, as we shall see in chapter 4—while political leaders left behind worried openly that it would take a very long time to pull Tunisia into a more open and prosperous society. As one local mayor said of the migrants: "If I were their age, I would have emigrated. . . . It's an entire country that needs to be remade. It's not going to be one year, or two years, or three years. It's going to be an entire generation."[56]

The Arab Spring of 2011 illustrates the duality at the heart of this book: dynamics of globalization, and especially the new global social media platforms, certainly have opened the doors for citizens across the Arab world to organize themselves, project their voices, and spur a transnational political awakening in pursuit of basic rights and democratic citizenship. Globalization is leading to new flows of ideas across borders and enlarging the political, economic, and social aspirations for the next generation coming of age across the Arab world. At the same time, these citizens are reminded at every turn how they still remain subject to the power of national governments that can at least temporarily disable the tools of globalization and political opening, even if ultimately it comes at great cost, and use their coercive authority to crack down on protesters. In many important respects, the opposition activists in Tunisia and Egypt still remain an exception within the Arab world—and they, too, faced much state-induced violence. Elsewhere, especially in Syria, protesters have been overwhelmed by police brutality as they continue to demand political change.

While Tahrir Square became a true public space for liberation in Egypt, even as the opposition movement had to fight bitterly to retain a presence after Mubarak fell, in March army troops in Bahrain's capital of Manama took down the Pearl Monument that had become the landmark to the country's growing democracy movement and its gathering place in Pearl Square. With demolition diggers cutting away at the six bases of the monument until it collapsed, the dismantling served as a reminder that repressive governments can disfigure, if not destroy, public space, even as citizens discover new ways to create and cultivate that space. It is also noteworthy that many of the new citizen-activists often fuse together their sweeping moral visions for the future with strong and principled senses of national allegiance, belonging, and loyalty to their native countries, just as Wael Ghonim identified resolutely as an Egyptian.

The Arab Spring, while certainly driven by citizens from within particular countries, did not emerge in isolation from the rest of the world. On the contrary, external forces tied to globalization helped set the stage for the uprising, which in turn created ripple effects far beyond the Arab world. One notable external force turned out to be WikiLeaks.

The confidential U.S. State Department cables it obtained and then released in late 2010 included misgivings about practices of torture under the Mubarak government and also indicated that if Tunisia's government and military ended up in conflict, the United States would likely support the military over the Ben Ali regime. In March 2011 the cofounder of WikiLeaks, Julian Assange, told a group of students at Cambridge University that the public release of the cables, revealing the unvarnished attitudes of U.S. diplomats toward the governments of Tunisia and Egypt, made it impossible for the United States to offer anything more than tacit support to both governments once their own people turned against them. At the same time, Assange cautioned that while the Internet does set up new ways for citizens to communicate with each other and obtain transparent information about governments and corporations, it is also "the greatest spying machine the world has ever seen" and provides governments with new ways to crack down on citizens. He argued that global news coverage broadcast on television by Al Jazeera had much greater impact in Tunisia and Egypt than the global social media platforms of Facebook and Twitter:

> The guide[book] produced by Egyptian revolutionaries . . . says on the first page, "Do not use Facebook and Twitter," and says on the last page, "Do not use Facebook and Twitter." There is a reason for that. There was actually a Facebook revolt in Cairo three or four years ago. It was very small . . . after it, Facebook was used to round-up all the principal participants. They were then beaten, interrogated and incarcerated.[57]

Indeed, media reports indicated that Egypt's police used Facebook and Twitter in the days following the January 25 uprisings to track down protesters. And in China, news of the uprisings in North Africa and the Middle East created much excitement as the country's democracy activists tried to start a "Jasmine Revolution" of their own. Street demonstrations in at least a dozen cities in February 2011 prompted authorities to arrest numerous activists, attempt to block the word "jasmine" from local social networking sites and online chat rooms,[58] and interfere with international journalists trying to interview protesters—even assaulting and detaining correspondents from CNN and Bloomberg News in Beijing.[59] Still, the Internet has been catching on in China as a political lever. Even in remote provincial areas, such as Inner Mongolia, citizen-activists—some of them calling for the northern region's independence—have been mobilizing online, holding rallies, and confronting harsh security measures.[60] The long struggle for democracy and human rights in China and the campaign by WikiLeaks for greater global transparency and access to information from governments around the world have many striking parallels when it comes to globalization and citizenship; the next chapter examines these related themes.

CHAPTER 3

A TALE OF TWO CITIZENS: LIU XIAOBO AND JULIAN ASSANGE

Two global tempests converged in 2010 around two distinct political activists: Chinese literary critic and human rights activist Liu Xiaobo and WikiLeaks founder Julian Assange. The awarding of the Nobel Peace Prize to Liu in December 2010 led to greater global recognition of the long uphill struggle for democracy in China, while Assange roared out of obscurity once his "stateless news organization" gained attention from mainstream news outlets and began coordinating with some of the world's premier newspapers to release massive inventories of formerly confidential U.S. government files. Assange and Liu emerged within strikingly different spheres, and accounts of the two men suggest that they have remarkably contrasting personalities, world views, and tactics.

This chapter looks first at how Liu Xiaobo and Julian Assange each emerged on the international stage, along with their particular organizations, and then examines how they encountered legal clashes with national authorities that prompted contentious global debates. In different ways, Liu and Assange are agents as well as products of globalization, and their stories reveal how many spheres of contestation have emerged in recent years regarding the endeavors of citizen-activists, particularly those who struggle for goals such as human rights, democracy, and transparency. Their stories also offer competing perceptions of the world's most powerful national governments. The campaigns Liu and Assange have carried out through their organizations and network partners tell us a great deal about the relationship between globalization and citizenship in the present day.

Plenty of common links can be identified: both Julian Assange and Liu Xiaobo have confronted governments they consider to be authoritarian and have sought to advance fundamental rights, such as freedoms of speech and assembly, as well as the principle of democratic accountability. Both have raised their voices as publishers seeking global audiences: Liu released a manifesto calling for outright political change within China to include democracy, the rule of law, and the universal right to free expression, while Assange posted an online call for "radical transparency" as the rationale for his role in sharing official secrets with the public. Both have networked heavily with transnational populations of activists, many of them operating underground, who regularly communicate with each other across international boundaries. Another source of commonality is how different sets of authorities and commentators, especially in China and the United States, have castigated Liu and Assange as reprehensible criminals rather than as virtuous citizens, even as "enemies of the state." China continues to keep Liu in prison, after convicting him in 2009 on charges of "inciting subversion of state power," while the U.S. government has jailed a U.S. Army soldier, Bradley Manning, suspected of having provided confidential files to WikiLeaks. The U.S. government has also investigated possible charges against Assange, who is already facing charges in Sweden for the alleged rape of two women there in August 2010. The two superpowers have confronted each other over Assange, Liu, and their respective organizations, with the United States publicly calling for China to release Liu and make advances on basic human rights. China, in turn, has publicly criticized the United States for detaining Manning. Both Liu and Assange became focal points of global contestation among governments, multinational corporations, and civil society groups; at the same time that China was pressuring several national governments to boycott the Nobel Peace Prize awards ceremony honoring Liu, the U.S. government pressured, at least indirectly, some key global corporations to shut down accounts held by WikiLeaks.

Of course, differences between the two activists are also worth highlighting. Julian Assange managed to continue speaking out in public even as he waged a legal battle in Great Britain in late 2010 and 2011 to avoid being sent to Sweden, while authorities in China have effectively silenced Liu Xiaobo for the time being with his prison sentence. Assange continues to have at his disposal the tools of global media and the limited resources of his transnational organization, WikiLeaks, while Liu must rely on his supporters at home and abroad and is presumably cut off from the constant flow of global news and information that today's Internet users in the world's democracies take for granted. Their personal histories, their formative experiences, and even some of their apparent ideological leanings are also a study in contrasts: Liu has lived in China nearly his entire life and passed up several opportunities to leave the country, ultimately paying a high price to stay in his homeland, while Assange moved a reported thirty-seven times before the age of fourteen and continues to have no permanent address even as he remains, legally, a citizen of Australia.[1] Liu is often cast as a "pro-Western" actor who seeks to remake China in the image of the United States, while Assange is labeled an "anarchist" who seeks to expose, if not overturn entirely, all forms of government power to greater public scrutiny. In many respects, Liu fits the profile of a "rooted cosmopolitan" or a "cosmopolitan patriot," driven by his vision for a democratic transformation in China, while Assange comes across as rooted not to any particular local or national community but mainly to the principle of a borderless right to know what governments are doing.

THE ACTIVISTS AND THEIR ORGANIZATIONS, CAMPAIGNS, AND NETWORK PARTNERS

LIU XIAOBO: "I HAVE NO ENEMIES AND NO HATRED."

Born in 1955 in Jilin Province, in China's rural northeast, Liu Xiaobo worked in the countryside as he grew up during Mao Zedong's Cultural

Revolution; he entered his university years as Deng Xiaoping took the country into market reforms. First taking up Chinese literature at Jilin University and then shifting to Western philosophy as a graduate student at Beijing Normal University, Liu became known as a critic of China's official policies and had published two books before finishing his doctorate in 1988. Liu then traveled outside China for about a year and decided to leave a visiting post at Columbia University in April 1989 just as protests led by students and intellectuals were intensifying in Tiananmen Square. As Liu later recalled, he was changing planes in Tokyo when he heard the news that China's government had condemned the protest movement: "I even asked about flights returning to New York. But then I heard the boarding call for my flight to Beijing. I didn't have time to hesitate. I thought, what the heck, live or die, I'll just go."[2]

Liu and three other activists, including a famous pop music star at the time, Hou Dejian, began a hunger strike on June 2 in an effort to encourage fellow protesters to continue their quest for democracy and occupation of the square in the face of growing pressure from government authorities to back down, and to make their own movement more democratic as rifts grew among different factions within the protest movement. On the same day, however, leaders of China's Communist Party decided to clear Tiananmen Square by force, and army troops and citizens clashed violently in the streets of Beijing; several hundred citizens were killed as the government ultimately regained control of the city on June 4. According to various accounts, Liu and his colleagues negotiated an agreement on June 3, the day before the massacre, between army commanders and student leaders that allowed several thousand students to withdraw peacefully from Tiananmen Square without being fired upon by soldiers. On June 6, Chinese authorities arrested Liu for his activities in the protest movement, and he lost his academic position shortly thereafter—though his books soon found a new audience in Taiwan.

In 1993, following his release from prison and the end of his first marriage, Liu turned down chances to seek refugee status abroad when he briefly visited Australia and the United States to give interviews for a television documentary on the Tiananmen protests. He returned to China only to be detained again in May 1995 while organizing a citizens' petition calling for political change. One year later, in October 1996, authorities arrested him yet again for collaborating on a declaration calling for peaceful unification between China and Taiwan and sentenced him to three years of "reeducation through labor." Ironically, China signed the two leading international human rights conventions in the years that Liu served this sentence.[3] During this period, Liu married Liu Xia, a former civil servant turned painter, poet, and photographer who once told the BBC: "Now his name is unknown (in China). But one day, even if he's not regarded as a hero, he'll be thought of as a very good citizen."[4] After his release in 1999, Liu published several books circulated abroad, including a collection of poems that he and Liu Xia wrote to each other during his years in prison. He continued to have run-ins with government monitors, who in 2004 confiscated his computer while he was writing a report on human rights. While many activists from the Tiananmen Square protest movement moved on to positions in business and government, Liu kept to his roots in literature, philosophy, and activism. As one of his oldest friends, dissident writer Liao Yiwu, has described him: "Because of him, Chinese history does not come to a stop. After 1989, many people chose to forget what had happened, chose to go abroad, chose to divert themselves into doing business, or even to work with the government—but he did not."[5]

During the same year that Beijing hosted the 2008 Summer Olympics, Liu collaborated on a statement known as Charter 08 that called for a new constitution in China that would uphold basic civil rights and freedoms and also would set up an independent judiciary and an open multiparty electoral system. Inspired partly by the Charter 77 manifesto a generation ago in Czechoslovakia that foreshadowed the country's eventual emergence from communism, Charter 08 was a call for China to adopt a model of democratic citizenship and transform itself into a free enterprise system with an emphasis on private property.[6] The document has been signed by more than ten thousand people in China and around the world; most of the original three hundred signers reportedly have been harassed by authorities in China. An English translation of a key portion of the document reads as follows:

> We should make freedom of speech, freedom of the press, and academic freedom universal, thereby guaranteeing that citizens can be informed and can exercise their right of political supervision.

These freedoms should be upheld by a Press Law that abolishes political restrictions on the press.

The provision in the current Criminal Law that refers to "the crime of incitement to subvert state power" must be abolished. We should end the practice of viewing words as crimes.

For China the path that leads out of our current predicament is to divest ourselves of the authoritarian notion of reliance on an "enlightened overlord" or an "honest official" and to turn instead toward a system of liberties, democracy and the rule of law, and toward fostering the consciousness of modern citizens who see rights as fundamental and participation as a duty.[7]

Just hours before Charter 08 was to be published, in December 2008, police raided Liu's home and arrested him. Authorities put him on trial—with a hearing that lasted just two hours—and sentenced him to eleven years in prison on Christmas Day 2009, a day that seemed calculated to minimize global attention to the case. Despite being aware of the risks faced by outspoken activists in his native land, Liu Xiaobo never went underground or on the run but chose to speak out openly and embraced the vulnerability of being exposed to state crackdowns on freedom of speech under Article 105, the 1997 law in China's penal code that makes it a crime to "encourage subversion of the political power of the State or to overthrow the socialist system."[8] China's legal case against Liu focused especially on the direct call written into Charter 08 for Article 105 to be withdrawn and, as noted above, to "end the practice of viewing words as crimes."

The Christmas Day sentencing in Beijing elevated Liu's global prestige, at least within academic and activist circles, as a martyr for the universal causes of freedom, democracy, and human rights. As one popular Chinese blogger known as Beichen wrote: "China's Mandela was born this Christmas."[9] Likewise, the illustrious Chinese artist and dissident Ai Weiwei, who attended Liu's sentencing, posted later that day on Twitter: "This does not mean a meteor has fallen. This is the discovery of a star. Although this is a sentence on Liu Xiaobo alone, it is also a slap on the face for everyone in China."[10] As a journalist for the *Times of London* summarized the day in court, casting further global doubt on the legitimacy of China's government: "The guilty verdict was a foregone conclusion in a country where charges are rarely brought unless a court has already seen sufficient evidence to ensure a conviction, and where the sentence in sensitive cases is decided by the Communist Party. Only the severity of the punishment was in doubt."[11] Once news spread around the world of Charter 08's existence and Liu's arrest, some international human rights observers began to think of Liu as the "Václav Havel of China." In China, however, Charter 08 and Liu Xiaobo's sentence were not covered in the state-controlled news media, and the country's censors worked to block online references from abroad.

Similar to many global dissidents through the years who have weathered persecution and jail sentences, Liu's speeches have shown steadfast optimism and an eagerness for reconciliation with one's oppressors. In an essay titled "I Have No Enemies: My Final Statement," which he released on December 23, 2009, two days before being sentenced to prison in the Charter 08 case, Liu wrote the following appeal for universal human rights, conveying his own sense of humanity and his capacity for forgiveness:

> I stand by the convictions I expressed in my "June Second Hunger Strike Declaration" twenty years ago—I have no enemies and no hatred. None of the police who monitored, arrested, and interrogated me, none of the prosecutors who indicted me, and none of the judges who judged me are my enemies. . . . Hatred can rot away at a person's intelligence and conscience. Enemy mentality will poison the spirit of a nation, incite cruel mortal struggles, destroy a society's tolerance and humanity, and hinder a nation's progress toward freedom and democracy.

Liu also spelled out, in essence, his aspirations for democratic citizenship in China:

> I look forward to [the day] when my country is a land with freedom of expression, where the speech of every citizen will be treated equally well; where different values, ideas, beliefs, and political views . . . can both compete with each other and peacefully coexist; where both majority and minority views will be equally guaranteed, and where the political views that differ from those currently in power, in particular, will be fully respected and protected.[12]

Liu's statement and his direct approach to calling for political change within China portray not only a remarkable degree of fortitude but also a contrast with Julian Assange, who has often conveyed to his supporters and the general public the image of a man on the run from many perceived enemies. While collaborating in Great Britain with journalists from the *Guardian*, Assange on one occasion disguised himself as an elderly, hunchbacked woman in an attempt to evade possible pursuers, real or imagined.[13] When he agreed to be interviewed by an Australian news reporter during a visit to his erstwhile hometown of Melbourne, the journalist was given specific instructions by an intermediary who provided an address for the meeting place: "Don't call a cab, find one on the street; turn off your mobile phone before you catch the cab and preferably, remove the batteries."[14] While in Reykjavik, where WikiLeaks members prepared to release a video recorded from the cockpit of a U.S. military helicopter that showed American soldiers in Iraq killing at least twelve people, including civilians, Assange kept the draperies closed day and night in a small house that he called "the bunker." Two of his better known quotations are "I enjoy crushing bastards"[15] and "Capable, generous men do not create victims; they nurture them."[16]

JULIAN ASSANGE: A LIFE ON THE MOVE

Born in 1971 along the northeastern coast of Australia, Julian Assange lived for many years on Magnetic Island, located along the Great Barrier Reef off the coast of Townsville, Queensland. His mother and adoptive father, Christine and Brett Assange, ran a touring theater company for several years. Later his mother married a musician connected with a controversial New Age group in Australia, and after that marriage ended, Christine Assange entered a custody dispute over the couple's younger son, Assange's half-brother. This prompted her to take both children into hiding all across Australia for a five-year period, roughly from the time Assange was eleven until he was sixteen, when he made his first forays into computer hacking. Around 1987 he formed a group with two other hackers that they named the "International Subversives," foreshadowing Assange's later forays into global activism. The group reportedly operated under the following code of conduct: "Don't damage computer systems you break into (including crashing them); don't change the information in those systems (except for altering logs to cover your tracks); and share information."[17] In 1991, police in Australia charged Assange with hacking into the master computer terminal of Melbourne telecommunications giant Nortel, which claimed that the hacking incident cost them more than $100,000. After Assange pled guilty to twenty-five charges of hacking and related crimes, the judge handling the case released him with a fine of Australian $2,100, saying, "There is just no evidence that there was anything other than sort of intelligent inquisitiveness and the pleasure of being able to—what's the expression—surf through these various computers."[18]

Throughout the 1990s, Assange also fought to work out a custody arrangement for a child born in 1989 to a woman who was either his girlfriend or his spouse; there are conflicting accounts as to whether the couple ever married, and Assange, when asked the question directly by journalists, declines to comment. Working with his mother, Assange formed an activist group called Parent Inquiry Into Child Protection, which campaigned to make records on child custody issues more accessible to the public. During this period, Assange lived in Melbourne, contributed to a book on hacking, and created various "open source" computer programs. He registered the domain name *leaks.org* in 1999 but did not immediately create a website for this domain; later, it would become a promotional website for WikiLeaks.[19] He studied math and physics at the University of Melbourne from 2003 to 2006, when he dropped out. Toward the end of this time, Assange wrote a manifesto with the title "Conspiracy as Governance," in which he articulated his rationale for WikiLeaks: that disrupting the methods of internal communication among authoritarian governments will have the effect of reducing flows of information among them, and that as officials share less and less information with each other, conspiracies themselves will fade. In Assange's view of radical transparency, then, leaks of information to the public can play an essential role in undermining potential government conspiracies.

Calling itself "an intelligence agency of the people," WikiLeaks posted its first leaked documents in December 2006, unveiling itself to the world as an electronic venue to receive and publish top secret and highly sensitive information—word for word, without editing, rewriting, or filtering. WikiLeaks originally focused mainly on dictatorships in Asia, Africa, the Middle East, and the former Soviet Union; its first leaked document was a signed statement from a rebel leader in Somalia calling for hit men to kill government officials. The organization's

Twitter feed, which crossed the one million mark in the summer of 2011, lists its location as "everywhere," with the slogan "We open governments."[20] Its computer servers are said to be in several countries, including Belgium, Switzerland, and especially Sweden, where the organization's two most important servers sit inside an underground bunker in suburban Stockholm.[21] The *New York Times* summed up the organization's global approach: "By being everywhere, yet in no exact place, WikiLeaks is, in effect, beyond the reach of any institution or government that hopes to silence it."[22] In terms of personnel, WikiLeaks reportedly consists of a handful of about three to six unpaid volunteers supported by eight hundred to a thousand volunteers around the world who provide occasional expertise in areas such as computer programming, encryption, and writing news releases. The technology of the WikiLeaks site is said to be configured in ways that render its sources untraceable when they submit information. There is no specific WikiLeaks headquarters for government prosecutors to raid; no dedicated landlines for telephone conversations to be tapped; only computer servers and digital information in cyberspace for authorities to try to disrupt.

Like the global presence of his organization, both everywhere and nowhere, and in contrast with Liu Xiaobo who remained grounded in China, Assange himself moved frequently around the world in the first few years of running WikiLeaks, from 2006 through 2010. As an individual with no home and no daily commitments to an immediate family, and who by many accounts requires little sleep and few regular meals, Assange seemed perfectly cast to build a "bottom-up" global organization such as WikiLeaks, traveling from country to country with a backpack filled with computer hard drives and disks. In May 2010 Assange told an Australian journalist that he had four "bases" from which to operate but named only two of them—Iceland and Kenya—and said he has been particularly attracted to Kenya for its "extraordinary opportunities for reforms" as a young democracy. He added that he finds advantages in being a permanent outsider, relative to any local community: "The sense of perspective that interaction with multiple cultures gives you, I find to be extremely valuable, because it allows you to see the structure of a country with greater clarity, and gives you a sense of mental independence. You're not swept up in the trivialities of a nation. You can concentrate on the serious matters."[23]

THE RISE AND EVOLUTION OF WIKILEAKS

After publishing a smattering of material collected seemingly at random from around the world—ranging from allegations of political corruption in Kenya to the contents of Sarah Palin's personal e-mail inbox, to an incriminating internal document from a bank in Iceland just before the country plunged into financial crisis—WikiLeaks shifted its emphasis to the United States in early 2010. A single source, Bradley Manning, began feeding WikiLeaks massive and highly sensitive electronic files originating from both the U.S. Department of Defense and the U.S. Department of State. The material from the defense department included exhaustive details about combat operations, civilian deaths, and local contacts in Afghanistan and Iraq, as well as an explosive video from Iraq. The State Department cables included salacious comments written in memos from ambassadors and their deputies who, until this release, had felt secure enough within the U.S. government's in-house communications systems to convey to Washington their raw, candid impressions of the people and circumstances they encountered.

The rise of WikiLeaks opened up new ways for activists across borders to work together via Internet communication. In early 2010, WikiLeaks relied on transnational coordination among hundreds of its networked supporters to "decrypt" the U.S. military video from Iraq, using Twitter to make the following appeal: "Have encrypted videos of U.S. bomb strikes on civilians. We need super computer time." The followers of the organization responded, and WikiLeaks posted the video in April 2010 with the politically loaded headline "Collateral Murder," directly contradicting U.S. military statements about the civilian killings in Baghdad that claimed that at least two of the individuals were armed. The video showing U.S. airstrikes killing at least twelve people in Baghdad, including two journalists from Reuters, would eventually be viewed more than two million times online and broadcast within countless television news reports around the world. In some ways, this video marked a high point for WikiLeaks in gaining recognition as a clearinghouse for releasing official secrets to the public.

Increasingly wise to the extensive freedom of speech protections it can claim in many democracies as a news organization, WikiLeaks has been trying to present itself as a transparent news source, rather than its earlier phrase, "the people's intelligence agency." As one observer noted, by early 2011 WikiLeaks had "peppered its 'about' page with the words 'journalism' and 'journalist,' which appear a combined 19 times, and as a self-described 'not-for-profit media organization' lists its primary goal as bringing 'important news and information to the public.'"[24] WikiLeaks now tries to avoid the appearance of actively encouraging people to send confidential files; its website no longer lists "classified" within the description of the kinds of material it accepts, and includes this disclaimer: "WikiLeaks accepts a range of material, but we do not solicit it."[25] WikiLeaks also dropped an assertion that "Submitting confidential material to WikiLeaks is safe, easy and protected by law," and instead now makes a claim laced with caution, if not cynicism: "Submitting documents to our journalists is protected by law in better democracies."[26]

After the release of the Iraq video, the two biggest breaks for WikiLeaks came with the largest sets of leaked documents thus far. First was the "Afghanistan War Logs" in July 2010; these included more than ninety thousand classified reports from the U.S. Department of Defense that detailed the U.S. military's campaign in Afghanistan and were published verbatim by WikiLeaks as detailed news accounts in three collaborating newspapers, the *New York Times*, the *Guardian*, and *Der Spiegel*. While the disclosures showed that the war in Afghanistan had been going considerably worse for the United States than the administrations of both George W. Bush and Barack Obama had conveyed, some officials in the U.S. government also hoped that descriptions in the leaked files of connections between Pakistan's main spy agency and the Taliban might push Pakistan to cooperate more directly with the United States on counterterrorism. "This is now out in the open," said one unidentified official in the Obama administration as he leaked the White House spin on WikiLeaks to the public. "It's reality now. In some ways, it makes it easier for us to tell the Pakistanis that they have to help us."[27] Then, in October 2010, WikiLeaks posted some four hundred thousand documents, known as the "Iraq War Logs," revealing that fifteen thousand more civilians had been killed in Iraq since 2003 than had been previously reported.[28] There was also evidence that U.S. military authorities had "failed to investigate hundreds of reports of abuse, torture, rape and even murder by Iraqi police and soldiers whose conduct appears to be systematic and normally unpunished."[29]

Following the leaks of the U.S. military documents from Iraq and Afghanistan, what many considered the most sensational release of all began in November 2010. Over a series of months 251,287 diplomatic cables were released—which included scores of candid, incisive, and colorful observations of political elites around the world, often written in vivid but rather undiplomatic language. These disclosures, too, had mixed impact—with multiple dimensions of embarrassment and breached confidences, but they also articulated U.S. positions more clearly than before in some instances serving to advance U.S. interests on a variety of fronts, such as the example discussed in chapter 2 of a U.S. ambassador's ambivalence about Tunisia's autocratic government. The same mixed dynamic emerged when Julian Assange announced in December 2010 that WikiLeaks might soon publish tens of thousands of documents that could "take down a bank or two," reportedly e-mail messages from the computer hard drive of an executive at Bank of America. While many corporate officials reacted with alarm and scrambled to tighten up their internal security mechanisms, U.S. government regulators, already under public pressure to come down harder on the financial sector following the economic crisis that peaked in 2008 and 2009, wondered if a treasure trove might be headed their way. Assange later backed away from his bold claim about the bank files, apparently authorizing a leak to Reuters with his collaborators saying he could not make sense of the material. As of December 2011, WikiLeaks had still not released the files amid reports that the organization was fragmenting from within and plagued by internal strife, with some key figures within WikiLeaks turning against Assange's "siege mentality" and worrying that the massive releases of U.S. government documents during the past year had diverted the group away from its original mission as a global clearinghouse for whistleblowers. One key figure in the organization, Daniel Domscheit-Berg, left WikiLeaks in September 2010 to start a similar organization, OpenLeaks, and published a book highly critical of Assange as obsessed with money, power, and women.[30]

LEGAL TROUBLES FOR WIKILEAKS AND JULIAN ASSANGE

By the start of 2012, the U.S. government had not yet initiated any kind of legal case directly against Julian Assange, who remained under virtual house arrest in Great Britain while appealing an order to extradite him to Sweden to face accusations of rape. Washington did, however, manage to nail down a much easier target: Bradley Manning, an officer in the U.S. Army. Manning was arrested in May 2010 and shortly before the July release of the "Afghanistan War Logs" he was charged with transferring classified U.S. government data onto his personal computer and communicating to an unauthorized source U.S. national defense information. Manning remained in a U.S. military prison for all of 2011 and faced twenty-two additional charges, including "aiding the enemy," which is considered a capital offense in the United States, although prosecutors in this case are reportedly not seeking the death penalty. A pretrial hearing in his case took place in a U.S. military court in December 2011.

Born in 1987, Bradley Manning grew up first in Oklahoma and then moved to Great Britain at age thirteen when his parents divorced and his mother returned to her native Wales. His father served in the U.S. Navy, and Manning joined the U.S. Army in October 2007; he was dispatched to Iraq in October 2009 to serve as an intelligence analyst. Shortly after arriving in Iraq, Manning reportedly began accessing classified documents from his computer workstation near Baghdad. Two journalists for the *Guardian* newspaper have reported that Manning first contacted WikiLeaks in November 2009, two days after WikiLeaks posted about 570,000 intercepts of pager messages sent on September 11, 2001, the day of the terrorist attacks on New York and Washington. Before the end of 2009, Manning reportedly found, via his computer workstation, the "Collateral Murder" video of the U.S. military airstrike over Baghdad, and he allegedly furnished this to WikiLeaks in February 2010; it was released by WikiLeaks in April 2010. Manning also is suspected to have downloaded the U.S. diplomatic cables released by WikiLeaks—beginning with a "test document" (in Manning's words), a cable sent in January 2010 from the U.S. embassy in Reykjavik, Iceland; this was posted by WikiLeaks in February 2010, well before the organization began releasing the full stash of cables in November 2010. Finally, Manning is also believed to have provided the documents contained in both the "Iraq War Logs" and the "Afghanistan War Logs." Although Manning and Assange apparently never met in person, numerous reports have indicated that they corresponded online and Assange set up a special secure Internet connection for Manning to transmit electronic files of secret U.S. government documents and videos—in what would become the biggest single leak in history.[31] Without the documents reportedly supplied by Bradley Manning, it is doubtful that WikiLeaks would have generated much attention at all throughout 2010.

The way Manning landed in legal trouble serves as a textbook example of the hazards of online communication. Disenchanted with life in the U.S. military and disillusioned with U.S. foreign policy, Manning found solace in a relationship with a young man living in Massachusetts who introduced him to various computer hackers based at Boston's universities. It was through these networks that Manning encountered and began to confide in a former hacker named Adrian Lamo. Their chat logs, dating back to May 2010 and subsequently published by *Wired* magazine and in a book written by two British journalists, reveal Manning's lengthy accounts of how he had provided the "Collateral Murder" video and the U.S. diplomatic cables to "a crazy white-haired Aussie who can't seem to stay in one country for very long." They also reveal how Manning believed the public disclosures of the documents would expose U.S. government wrongdoing. The transcripts show Lamo asking brief, probing questions that managed to elicit detailed information from Manning, which he provided in rambling and sometimes tormented statements:

Lamo: How long have you helped WikiLeaks?

Manning: Since they released the 9/11 pager messages. I immediately recognized that they were from an NSA (National Security Agency) database, and I felt comfortable enough to come forward.

Lamo: So right after Thanksgiving timeframe of 2009?

Manning: Hillary Clinton and several thousand diplomats around the world are going to have a heart attack when they wake up one morning, and find an entire repository of classified foreign policy is available, in searchable format, to the public.

Lamo: What sort of content?

Manning: Uhm . . . crazy, almost criminal back-dealings. The non-PR versions of world events and crises. . . . All kinds of stuff, like everything from the buildup to the Iraq war . . . to what the actual content of aid packages is. For instance, PR that the US is sending aid to Pakistan includes funding for water/food/clothing. That much is true, it includes that, but the other 85% of it is for F-16 fighters and munitions to aid in the Afghanistan effort, so the US can call in Pakistanis to do aerial bombing, instead of Americans potentially killing civilians and creating a PR crisis. There's so much. It affects everybody on earth. Everywhere there's a US post, there's a diplomatic scandal that will be revealed. . . . It's beautiful, and horrifying, and it's important that it gets out. I feel for some bizarre reason it might actually change something. I wouldn't mind going to prison for the rest of my life, or being executed so much, if it wasn't for the possibility of having pictures of me plastered all over the world press as a boy. I've totally lost my mind.[32]

Soon after this conversation, Lamo provided U.S. Army investigators and FBI officials with transcripts of their online chats. In an interview with *Wired*, he defended his betrayal of Manning by saying he thought it was a matter of patriotic duty: "I wouldn't have done this, if lives weren't in danger. He was in a war zone and basically trying to vacuum up as much classified information as he could and (was) just throwing it up into the air."[33] While many have branded Manning a traitor, all the more since he was enlisted in the U.S. military, David Leigh and Luke Harding came to a different conclusion having read the entire chat logs: "They make it clear that he was not a thief, not venal, not mad, and not a traitor. He believed that, somehow, he was doing a good thing."[34] After receiving the testimony from Lamo, federal authorities arrested Manning in Iraq, flew him first to a military prison in Kuwait and then to the Quantico Marine Corps Base in Virginia. The original charges filed against Manning accuse him of "transferring classified data onto his personal computer and adding unauthorized software to a classified computer system in connection with the leaking of a video of a helicopter attack in Iraq in 2007," and "communicating, transmitting and delivering national defense information to an unauthorized source and disclosing classified information concerning the national defense with reason to believe that the information could cause injury to the United States."[35] In March 2011, federal authorities leveled twenty-two additional charges against Manning, and the charge sheets reportedly accuse Manning of having leaked more than five hundred thousand documents and two videos. If convicted, Manning would face life in prison and a dishonorable discharge from the military.

At Quantico, Manning was kept in solitary confinement in a 6-foot by 12-foot cell for twenty-three hours per day, with one hour of exercise each day. He was not allowed to exercise in his cell at any other time of day, forced to wake up each morning at 5 a.m., and prodded every five minutes by prison guards who asked him if he was OK, with an affirmative response required. Manning was also forced, at least initially, to strip naked each night and wear only a smock overnight; he was given no bedding and was prohibited from keeping any personal items in his cell. These conditions sparked much criticism from human rights organizations and also led to a dispute within the U.S. Department of State, ironically given that the documents allegedly leaked by Manning came from this arm of the U.S. government. Speaking to a group of students at the Massachusetts Institute of Technology in early March 2011, State Department spokesman Philip J. Crowley called the U.S. military's treatment of Manning "ridiculous, counterproductive and stupid" and then resigned two days later, under pressure from the White House. The incident prompted one blogger highly supportive of WikiLeaks and critical of Manning's detention to send a tweet that commented, "Detainee abuse is allowed, speaking out against it isn't."[36]

Crowley was hardly alone in speaking out against the conditions of Manning's detainment. In January 2011 Amnesty International sent a letter to U.S. defense secretary Robert Gates calling the restrictions on Manning "unnecessarily harsh and punitive." Two prominent law professors, Bruce Ackerman at Yale and Yochai Benkler at Harvard, took the lead in writing a letter, signed in April 2011 by at least 295 scholars, calling the treatment of Manning at Quantico a violation of the U.S. Constitution's Eighth Amendment ban on "cruel and unusual punishment" and the Fifth Amendment guarantee against punishment without trial, as well as a possible case of torture, defined as the administration or application of "procedures calculated to disrupt profoundly the senses or the personality." The letter also noted that "President Obama was once a professor of constitutional law and entered the national stage as an eloquent moral leader. The question now, however, is whether his conduct as commander-in-chief meets fundamental standards of decency."[37] The Pentagon denied that Manning's conditions were punitive and maintained they were appropriately "based on his particular circumstances as a maximum security pre-trial detainee."[38] Obama also maintained that he had checked to make sure that the treatment of Manning complied with U.S. legal standards. Nevertheless, the U.S. military, apparently in response to the mounting public pressure, transferred Manning to a medium-security prison in Kansas on April 20, 2011. There he was placed in a cell with natural light and a standard mattress, allowed some interaction with other pretrial detainees, and permitted to write whenever he wanted and keep personal items in his cell.[39]

Julian Assange, meanwhile, has tried to distance himself from Bradley Manning, both for the sake of protecting Manning as a source and also to protect himself from possible charges of conspiracy, which the U.S. government could file against him if evidence emerged that Assange had directed, helped, or encouraged Manning to send confidential U.S. government files to WikiLeaks. Citing its policy of keeping its sources anonymous, Assange and his collaborators have declined to say whether Manning provided information to WikiLeaks, though Assange has confirmed that WikiLeaks has offered to provide Manning with lawyers and also to help cover his legal expenses. In January 2011 the U.S. government sought records tracking the Twitter activity of Julian Assange and four other activists from WikiLeaks, including former spokeswoman Birgitta Jonsdottir, a member of Iceland's national parliament. Jonsdottir went public with the case, saying she had received an e-mail notification from Twitter stating that the company had received a legal request for details regarding her account—although the request did not seek the content of private messages—and that the company would have to respond unless "a motion to quash the legal process has been filed" or the matter was otherwise resolved.[40] In November a U.S. district court judge denied an appeal, filed by lawyers representing the group, to throw out the government's request for information.

The request for Twitter records is an interesting example of a national government trying to probe the activities of citizens operating well beyond its borders. The U.S. government requested records for Bradley Manning, one other American, a Dutch citizen, an Australian (Assange), and Jonsdottir—raising the possibility of objections from Australia, Iceland, and the Netherlands, who could claim that the U.S. government was trying to obstruct free communication among persons outside the United States who were not U.S. citizens. Once again, the potential emerged for channels of globalization to prompt a national government to attempt to curtail speech beyond its borders. Ms. Jonsdottir, for one, said she had not exchanged sensitive information via Twitter but would contest the subpoena because "it's just the fact that another country would request this sort of personal information from an elected official without having any case against me. . . . It is so sad. I have so many friends in the U.S., and there are so many things that I respect about it. This is not how America wants to present itself to the world."[41]

In November 2010, attorney general Eric Holder confirmed that the U.S. government was considering prosecuting Assange under the Espionage Act, a relic of the Red Scare that coincided with the end of World War I. Many analysts doubted that this approach would work, arguing that the law is exceedingly broad and that the U.S. government has never succeeded at prosecuting a member of the news media for soliciting or publishing confidential information; the United States has also never succeeded in prosecuting an organization outside the news media for soliciting or receiving classified information. Many constitutional law scholars argued that the Espionage Act would be ill-suited for prosecuting Assange, especially since it predates many Supreme Court rulings that have expanded First Amendment protections of freedom of speech and freedom of the press. Indeed, a case filed under the Espionage Act might open a window for the U.S. Supreme Court to strike down the old law as unconstitutional. Still, the possibility of prosecuting Assange under the Espionage Act also illustrated how global political activism and speech, if countered by U.S. government prosecutions, could be curtailed. However, the U.S. Justice Department would not likely succeed in prosecuting WikiLeaks without also pursuing the newspapers that had published the material. Moreover, in the Internet age individual states have expanded their definitions of the kinds of journalists—and citizens—who are protected under "shield laws" as they publish information provided by confidential sources.

Instead of facing charges in the United States related to the leaked U.S. government documents, Assange has been embroiled in two rape allegations from Sweden that have undermined his standing and credibility in global public opinion and complicated his legacy with many progressive advocacy groups seeking not only greater transparency from government but also greater rights and respect toward women. The separate incidents involving two women happened while Assange was visiting Sweden to explore the possibility of using it as a safe haven, given its reputation for press freedoms. Assange has said the timing of the rape accusations was not coincidental and that he was the victim of a smear campaign as well as an unfair European arrest warrant system in which "any person in any European country can be extra-dited to any other European country without the provision of any evidence whatsoever."[42] As of December 2011, Assange remained in Great Britain waiting for a U.K. Supreme Court decision on whether to extradite him to Sweden for questioning about the alleged rape of two women. Assange has maintained that the allegations are "without basis"; he was released from prison on £200,000 bail[43] (approximately US$310,000 at the time) but was required to wear an electronic tag and live under virtual house arrest in a countryside manor house while awaiting a hearing in the British High Court.

Just as some of Bradley Manning's supporters in the United Kingdom suggested that the government use his dual British/U.S. citizenship as a lever to protest his harsh treatment by the U.S. military, some individuals in Australia have suggested that Assange might be able to use his Australian citizenship. Clifton Fernandes, an international relations scholar at the Australian Defence Force Academy, argued that Assange would be much safer in Australia rather than overseas: "He's quite liable, if he stays away from Australia, to fall asleep in one jurisdiction and wake up in another, and all the passport and immigration documentation will be in order. But it wouldn't happen if he was here, because he's an Australian citizen and Australia is a U.S. partner and there are protocols in place to prevent that kind of snatch-and-grab operation."[44] Assange took a far more pessimistic view when he answered questions for readers of the *Guardian* during an online chat in December 2010. Asked whether he would want to return to Australia given the potential for being arrested on arrival for releasing U.S. cables relating to Australian diplomats and policies, Assange replied with the following words:

> I am an Australian citizen and I miss my country a great deal. However, during the last weeks the Australian prime minister, Julia Gillard, and the attorney general, Robert McClelland, have made it clear that not only is my return impossible but that they are actively working to assist the United States government in its attacks on myself and our people. This brings into question what does it mean to be an Australian citizen—does that mean anything at all?[45]

Of more immediate concern for Assange, Sweden and the United Kingdom each have extradition treaties with the United States. However, both countries have also placed themselves within the jurisdiction of the European Court of Human Rights, so Assange would be able to fight any possible attempt at extradition from Europe to the United States by appealing to the supranational court.

GLOBAL CONTESTATION OVER THE ACTIVISTS, THE CAMPAIGNS, AND THE SUPERPOWERS

The legal troubles faced by Liu Xiaobo and Julian Assange opened up global contestation over their specific roles as well as the stands taken by the national governments they confronted. Governments, corporations, and civil society organizations also found themselves drawn into the debate and pushed to take sides. Governments, for instance, had to calculate whether or not to attend the Nobel awards ceremony in Oslo honoring Liu, while businesses made political statements by cutting off support lines and financial conduits to WikiLeaks, especially following the publication of the U.S. State Department cables. As we shall see here, much of the debate regarding both Liu and Assange was really about which sets of actors could claim the upper hand in terms of global credibility.

CONTESTATION OVER LIU XIAOBO AND THE NOBEL PEACE PRIZE

The sentencing of Liu Xiaobo to eleven years in prison energized the international human rights movement. Liu had served as president of the Chinese affiliate of PEN International, which promotes the global right to free expression and advocates for writers around the world confronted by government censorship and repression. Almost immediately after Liu went to jail, leaders of PEN International began campaigning for Liu to win the 2010 Nobel Peace Prize. The president of the PEN American Center—Princeton University professor and noted cosmopolitanism scholar Kwame Anthony Appiah—made the case for Liu in a letter written in late January 2010 that placed Liu's domestic struggle in a global context and also underscored the importance of transnational advocacy networks for writers in China challenging a system hostile to freedom of expression:

> Since ICPC (the Independent Chinese PEN Centre) was formed in 2001, it has emerged as a leading source of information about threats

to writers and journalists . . . and it has come under increased pressure for its activities. Its meetings have been interrupted and canceled by authorities, its officers and members are regularly subject to intimidation and surveillance, and many have been detained and questioned about the center's activities. Liu Xiaobo is one of six PEN members currently in prison in China.

China wants—and needs—to be heard in the community of nations. I—and all of my PEN colleagues—believe in a cosmopolitan conversation in which we hear from every nation. But the world must let China's rulers know that we can only listen respectfully if they offer to their own citizens the fundamental freedoms we all claim from our governments. This is the right moment for the world to show those in China who do not understand that history is on freedom's side that all the world's friends of peace and democracy are watching. No signal of this would be more powerful than the award of the Nobel Peace Prize.[46]

Appiah's letter offered a ringing opening salvo in what would swell into heated contestation as transnational advocacy organizations and many of the world's democracies saw a window of opportunity opening to send China's government a message that it doesn't like to hear. Signs of this tension were evident from the immediate aftermath of Liu's prison sentencing, when diplomats representing the United States and several European countries at embassies in Beijing called for Liu's freedom, only to be rebuffed by China's foreign ministry on grounds that these statements from the West amounted to "a gross interference of China's internal affairs."[47]

As word spread in early autumn that Liu was indeed a finalist for the Nobel Prize, China warned Norway the award would damage diplomatic ties and also canceled scheduled talks on a possible free trade agreement between the two countries. China's authorities also promptly summoned the Norwegian ambassador in Beijing for an official protest when the Nobel committee announced the award on October 8, 2010, and declared that Liu and his "long and non-violent struggle" represented "the foremost symbol" of the struggle for human rights in China. Anticipating that the award would be perceived by China's government as a broadside from the West, the Nobel committee emphasized in its award citation that Liu's prison sentence illustrated how Beijing had failed to live up to its own domestic commitments on human rights, most notably Article 35 of the country's constitution, which guarantees freedoms of speech, association, and demonstration. A spokesperson for China's foreign ministry, Ma Zhaoxu, put forward a completely different view: "Liu Xiaobo is a criminal who violated Chinese law. It's a complete violation of the principles of the prize and an insult to the peace prize itself for the Nobel committee to award the prize to such a person."[48] Journalists in Beijing on October 8 noted that international news bulletins about the award to Liu were largely blocked by authorities, text messages mentioning Liu's name were difficult to send, and online conversations about Liu were "tightly controlled."[49] This continued throughout the Nobel Prize controversy; on the day before the awards ceremony, on Thursday, December 9, China's government blocked access to the websites of several global news outlets, including BBC, CNN, and NRK (the Norwegian state broadcaster), and television broadcasts from BBC and CNN went dark in Beijing as the Nobel ceremony began on December 10. Meanwhile, Chinese television news broadcasts that day led with the latest economic statistics concerning inflation, while in cyberspace some netizens in China changed their avatars on social media sites to yellow ribbons and empty chairs.

During the autumn of 2010, leaders of many democracies, such as France, Germany, and Britain reiterated their earlier calls for China to free Liu so he could travel to Norway and receive the award in person. Instead, China placed Liu's spouse, Liu Xia, under house arrest, though they did allow her to visit her husband to give him the news of his award. (Upon hearing the news, according to Liu Xia, Liu Xiaobo wept and said, "This is for the Tiananmen martyrs."[50]) China also detained numerous other democracy activists and prohibited more than a hundred friends and colleagues of Liu from traveling abroad, any one of whom could have accepted the Nobel Peace Prize on his behalf. The following list of detentions outlined the cases as of November 2010:

Guo Xianliang, an Internet writer known as the "Tianshan Hermit" has been detained in the southern city of Guangzhou for distributing leaflets referring to Liu in the city's parks and streets. Li Hai, a member of the Independent Chinese PEN Centre, was arrested on 30 October. His family has had no news of him since then. Hua Ze, a freelance journalist and human rights activist who used to work as a documentary film-maker for the government TV station CCTV, was abducted in the Beijing metro on 27 October and deported to Jiangxi, her home province, where she is now under house arrest. Human rights lawyer Teng Biao reported in a message posted on Twitter that Beijing resident Shen Minqiang was arrested while giving an interview outside Liu's home on 8 October. He has been placed under a non-judicial form of detention and it is unclear what he is charged with.[51]

China also successfully pressured eighteen other countries to join them in boycotting the awards ceremony; these included Cuba, Iran, Pakistan, the Philippines, Russia, and Saudi Arabia. Neighboring Asian democracies—such as South Korea, Japan, and India—went to Oslo anyway, where Norwegian actress and film director Liv Ullmann read Liu's "final statement" in the presence of global luminaries such as singer Elvis Costello and actor Denzel Washington. Most striking of all at the December 10 ceremony was the empty chair reserved for the laureate himself, providing a memorable symbol of Liu's absence and continued imprisonment. The chairman of the Nobel committee, former Norwegian prime minister Thorbjørn Jagland, placed the prize medal and certificate on Liu's empty chair, saying: "Liu has only exercised his civil rights. He has not done anything wrong. He must be released."[52] The award placed Liu within a distinguished collection of dissidents—Polish trade union activist Lech Walesa, Russian nuclear physicist and human rights campaigner Andrei Sakharov, and Burmese opposition leader Aung San Suu Kyi—all of whom were unable to claim their prizes in person but were allowed, at least, to send family members to pick up the awards and the prize money, which now totals US$1.4 million.[53]

China's rulers knew from observation as well as past experience that Nobel Peace Prize awards to dissidents create headaches and image problems for authoritarian governments. The 1989 awarding of the Nobel Peace Prize to the Dalai Lama, the same year as the Tiananmen Square uprising, created a global stir over China's occupation of Tibet as well as the way it crushed the democracy movement. However, to say that China's global resistance to Liu's award came primarily from its disregard of human rights would be to oversimplify the issue. As foreign policy analyst John Lee observed, China's Communist Party worried that the Nobel Peace Prize award to Liu figured into a broader global strategy, influenced mainly by the United States and its European partners, to contain China's rise not only militarily but also by trying to devalue the country's global stature:

For the Party, the attempt to contain China is not just about "guns, butter and alliances," as one prominent Chinese strategist put it to me. The leadership is convinced that the United States, Europe and American allies in Asia have stumbled upon a further, more subtle, and extremely effective two-pronged strategy. The first prong is to weaken and divide China internally. The second is to deny authoritarian China the legitimacy required for it to assume its natural place as regional leader. And this is where the Nobel Peace Prize comes in.[54]

China tried to strike back and defend its global image by declaring December 9, the day before the Nobel awards ceremony, as "Confucius Peace Day" in a hastily orchestrated attempt both to discredit Liu Xiaobo and to launch a potential Asian rival to the Nobel Peace Prize. This picked up on an idea introduced a month earlier in the newspaper *Global Times,* run by China's Communist Party. The Confucius committee set up a website casting China as a "symbol of peace" and noting that: "With over one billion people, it should have a greater voice on the issue of world peace." Implying that size matters over substance, the website also dismissed Norway as "only a small country with scarce land area and population" that was thus unable "to represent the viewpoint of most people."[55] The first named recipient of the Confucius Peace Prize was Lien Chan, a former vice president of Taiwan, who had traveled to Beijing in 2005 to meet with China's president, Hu Jintao, marking the first time the leaders of China and Taiwan had met in person since the 1949 revolution. Although news also leaked out that Microsoft founder Bill Gates and former South African leader Nelson Mandela were among the runners-up for the prize, the selection process remained far from clear—news reports said that a small group of Chinese scholars made the decision—and Mandela, Gates, and other rumored finalists appeared not to know about their possible candidacies. In the end, Lien did not show up to claim his prize; his office said Lien learned of his award only through media reports and delicately sidestepped questions as to whether he would accept. Organizers of the ceremony at a government-run hotel in Beijing handpicked a six-year-old girl, whom they described only as an "angel of peace," to take the stage and claim the glass trophy and 100,000 yuan (about US$15,000). The launch of the rival peace prize also drew further parallels to Nazi Germany, where in 1936 Adolf Hitler ordered the creation of the short-lived German National Prize for Art and Science after the Nobel

Committee awarded the 1935 Nobel Peace Prize to pacifist Carl von Ossietzky, who won the award while inside a Nazi concentration camp. He was the last Nobel laureate, prior to Liu, whose prize went uncollected.

The rising global consensus on Liu Xiaobo in December 2010 seemed to be that China's imprisonment of Liu and its attempts first to intimidate Norway and then to boycott the ceremony honoring Liu had all backfired. And yet, while many observers agreed that China's attempts at "damage control" were clumsy and heavy-handed, plenty of debate also unfolded over whether the Nobel Committee made the right call to take on China by honoring Liu Xiaobo. Many critics of Liu seized upon his comments in a 1988 interview with a Hong Kong magazine dedicated mainly to political criticism of the Chinese Communist Party. Impressed by the British colony's prosperity and political freedom, at least in comparison with mainland China, Liu said that since Hong Kong had "become like this after 100 years of colonialism, China is so big it will of course need 300 years of colonialism. . . . I have my doubts as to whether 300 years would be enough."[56] China's official Xinhua News Agency repeatedly tapped Liu's statement, which previously had received hardly any attention, as ammunition to argue that his true goal was to "make China a servant of the West." A Xinhua column also asked, rhetorically: "What qualification does someone who hails colonial history and culture have to talk big about 'democracy' and 'freedom'?" Liu's defenders argued that his comments back in 1988 were not intended to be taken literally in the present day. He Guanghua, a professor at Renmin University in Beijing, noted: "I don't believe he is advocating colonialism but only . . . a thorough change in China's national character, system and culture."[57]

Two scholars based in Hong Kong, political scientist Barry Sautman and anthropologist Yan Hairong, also called attention to Liu's past statements praising the U.S. wars in Iraq and Afghanistan and former president George W. Bush's administration.[58] Other detractors, meanwhile, noted that Liu could be viewed as a pawn in the hands of the U.S. government, since his organizations reportedly received grants totaling more than US$600,000 from the National Endowment for Democracy, a private organization funded mainly by the U.S. Congress that supports hundreds of civil society organizations around the world. Still others insinuated that Liu was not sufficiently innovative or influential to deserve the Nobel Peace Prize—that the Charter 08 manifesto was a mere offspring of the Charter 77 document produced a generation earlier by Václav Havel and his colleagues in Czechoslovakia, and that Liu would have remained in obscurity had China's government not thrown him in jail and unwittingly elevated his stature. Nick Young, a British international development consultant, argued that a better choice for the Nobel Peace Prize would have been Liang Congjie, a veteran environmental campaigner "whose non-confrontational style contributed significantly to opening space for environmental NGOs and creating two-way communication between government and activists."[59]

The Nobel Peace Prize presented Liu's adversaries in the Chinese government with a new kind of challenge: considerable segments of the country's estimated Internet users, which numbered close to five hundred million in late 2010, would learn about Liu through news of the award. The impossibility of concealing the story, given the permeability of global media platforms, left the government combining attempts to minimize news coverage at home while also casting aspersions on Liu's character and credentials—and trickiest of all, trying to discredit Liu in ways that would not arouse greater public interest in him. China managed to walk this tightrope, to an extent, within the country's borders—even going as far to emphasize that Liu had been convicted by China's criminal justice system without making any mention at all about the Charter 08 democracy manifesto.

An official Chinese survey of an unspecified number of university students taken immediately after the awarding of the Nobel Peace Prize found that 85 percent of them reported not knowing about Liu or Charter 08; however, it is possible that many students surveyed simply would not admit to knowing about Liu or Charter 08. On the campus of Beijing Normal University, where Liu had studied and taught before being banned from academia, a professor told his students that China needed to win a Nobel, but not the kind of prize Liu won and that Liu did not merit the award. One woman who reflected much of the mainstream public opinion in China, with citizens taking the safer path of buying into the denunciations of Liu and the Nobel committee relayed by government news outlets, told a reporter that she assumed Liu had done something to harm the country: "I think this year's prize is a little bit unfair," she said. "From what I can tell, its purpose is to humiliate China."[60]

Chinese dissidents watching the spectacle from afar, though, seemed to think the government's efforts to suppress Liu's story would pique public curiosity, at least within the younger generation and especially among Chinese citizens who regularly use special computer software to climb over the so-called Great Firewall of China: "The more the dictatorship bashes the Nobel Prize and Liu Xiaobo, the more people will want to know what they're talking about," said Xu Wenli, a democracy activist who spent sixteen years in prison in China and now teaches at Brown University in Rhode Island. "And in the age of the Internet, that's a war they cannot win."[61] Some younger citizens back in China seemed to prove Xu correct; for example, Xiang Yu, a recent university graduate, told a journalist from the Associated Press that when she learned Liu had won the Nobel Peace Prize, her first reaction was to try to find out firsthand what Liu had to say. While she found nothing when searching for books and did not appear to know about Charter 08, she did manage to find online an essay written by Liu after the Tiananmen Square demonstrations. Inside a bookstore in Beijing's university district, Xiang asked the journalist in hushed English why Liu was now in prison: "Was it something he wrote? Is it true he opposed the government?"[62] Despite the censorship and low public recognition, the Nobel Peace Prize had the effect of bringing Liu Xiaobo to the forefront in China—and within the more influential segments of an enormous population.

One of the most widely read public statements from Nobel laureates past, calling for the Chinese government to release Liu Xiaobo and Liu Xia in advance of the Nobel awards ceremony, came from Czech dissident turned president Václav Havel and retired South African archbishop Desmond Tutu, who together serve as the honorary cochairs of Freedom Now, a group that advocates for prisoners of conscience around the world. In a commentary published in the *Observer* and picked up by scores of newspapers, Havel and Tutu argued that the decline of economic and political power among Western nations represents "an encouraging shift and one that is bringing greater equality and prosperity to the world," but that China's political repression at home, as well as the government's support of dictatorships such as Myanmar, North Korea, and Sudan continued to forestall its rise as a genuine global leader:

The world must strenuously object to the Chinese model for development which decouples economic and political reform by unapologetically asserting that anything, including domestic and international oppression, can be justified if it is viewed to enable economic growth. International scrutiny of the Chinese government's widespread violation of fundamental rights at home and abroad is not meddling in its "internal affairs"; it flows from its legal commitments to respect the inherent dignity and equality of every person.[63]

The specific point from Tutu and Havel that sparked the most debate concerned the question of credibility. As Tutu and Havel commented: "The Chinese government's willingness to assert itself internationally shows its increasing confidence on the world stage, but its extreme sensitivity to criticism demonstrates its lack of confidence domestically. This lack of confidence ultimately only serves to further undermine the credibility of the government among its people." While Havel and Tutu seemed to focus mainly on the credibility of China's government with its own citizens, many readers around the world who posted comments debated whether China's government had any credibility left to lose in the first place and also whether the Nobel committee itself could claim the upper hand in global credibility. One reader, identified as "Alex65," wrote: "China has been demonized to the extent that Beijing just does not care about 'credibility' anymore. . . . Granted Mr. Liu Xiaobo represents the best China has to offer to humanity. Maybe in hopefully [the] not too distant future the general Chinese public [will] get to learn about him and share the pride. Until then the Chinese will have to help themselves to gain more political freedom from the authoritarian government." Still another reader, "Clunie," wrote that "China really doesn't have any credibility to lose and its regime is likely to be indifferent at best—and will probably be making great capital out of Western governments' current attempts to repress all things WikiLeaks (without mentioning the info revealed about itself there, of course)." On the other hand, an obvious supporter of the Chinese government's position seized upon the funding that Liu had received over the years from the National Endowment for Democracy in the United States:

Beijing would ONLY lose credibility if it succumbs to the unreasonable foreign demands. . . . The fact is that in his '08 Charter, Liu viciously

attacked the Chinese Constitution, openly calling for the abolition of
the form of government expressly mandated in the Constitution. . . .
If Beijing releases Liu, it'd be ceding to foreigners the right to punish
criminals that threaten the very being of the legitimate government of
China—it would be no different from having to turn over the right to
collect Customs duties to the West during the Qing Dynasty. WHY in
the world would Beijing do that? What the Norwegians did with the
Nobel and Liu is nothing less than an obscenity to the Chinese. Those
who support or celebrate this obscenity would be nothing less than
open enemies of China and the Chinese.

This writer echoed the language of China's foreign ministry, which
described the award to Liu as an "obscenity" when the announcement
came from Norway on October 8. Still others questioned the credibility
of the Nobel committee and its cumulative choices of Nobel laureates
through the years—and indeed, the Nobel Peace Prize selections do
generate much global public debate on a yearly basis. A reader identified as "Howard" with an avatar showing an amalgam of the Chinese
and American flags—with the red People's Republic of China flag
shown in place of the blue field of stars in the U.S. flag—took a sweeping shot at Nobel laureates Barack Obama, Mikhail Gorbachev, Liu
Xiaobo, the Dalai Lama, and Yasser Arafat:

> Do you think the Nobel Peace Prize still has any credibility, when the
> Prize was awarded to a state leader who is fighting two wars at the same
> time? Let's look at if there is any credibility for "PEACE"?
> A former Soviet leader who ruin [sic] his homeland into pieces?
> A Chinese traitor who want his motherland to be colonized for
> 300+ years to achieve westernization?
> A Chinese Tibetan monk who fleed [sic] his homeland, talks in
> English, and later claimed himself an Indian?
> A Palestein [sic] leader who fight his whole life for an independent
> country, later called HAMAS?
> The prize will gain its credibility if it can stop itself to be seen as
> Cold War barking dogs.

Others weighing in emphasized that credibility was just part of the issue and defended the Nobel committee's right to take on China's dictatorship in its annual political statement in the form of the Peace Prize.
As a reader identified as "Dravazed" put it: "Anyone who would credit

the word of the mafia-family style government of mainland China has no more sense than those who trust the word of [British political leader Nick] Clegg or think Sarah Palin is a sharp customer. There's a hell of a lot more than 'credibility' at stake; what is at stake is whether the world is going to continue pretending that the mainland's government is other than a vicious tyranny."

At the very least, the Nobel committee's decision to call attention to Liu Xiaobo in late 2010 opened up a contentious global moment that "reinvigorated the clash of ideas between the human rights and democracy agenda promoted by most developed countries and China's authoritarian model that has produced rapid and sustained economic growth."[64] And the Nobel committee did so at a time when many governments around the world, and especially the United States in light of its dependence on China's vast purchases of its government bonds, were downplaying human rights concerns in their official dealings with China given their tight economic interlinkages with Beijing. A few weeks after the Nobel announcement, fifteen Peace Prize laureates signed a letter calling for the G-20 member nations to apply pressure on China at the upcoming economic summit in Seoul, South Korea, to free Liu Xiaobo and Liu Xia. Instead, however, these countries pressured China to raise the value of its currency, the yuan. As noted previously by U.S. secretary of state Hillary Rodham Clinton (according to a diplomatic cable released in November 2010 by WikiLeaks): "How do you deal toughly with your banker?"[65]

CONTESTATION OVER JULIAN ASSANGE AND WIKILEAKS

Three main spheres of global contestation raged over WikiLeaks amid its massive release of U.S. State Department cables at the end of 2010. One realm of contestation centered on the leaks themselves and the tactics of Julian Assange and his collaborators: Were they spies or journalists; were they enlightened global activists or rogue cyber scofflaws, even cyber terrorists? Were they valiantly advancing an essential global right to information or stealing appropriately secret files? And would the world be better off with less official secrecy than before? The second realm of debate revolved around the rape allegations against Assange, with some of his supporters insisting that the accusations from Sweden were politically motivated while many others, friends as well as foes of WikiLeaks, saw things quite differently. The third realm of contestation, already discussed in this chapter, centered on the detention of Bradley Manning in the United States.

WikiLeaks, of course, had generated plenty of controversy even before its largest release of classified documents in November 2010, and the Washington political establishment fired full throttle as the U.S. State Department files became public, portraying Julian Assange as a criminal and a terrorist much in the same fashion as China's government was castigating Liu Xiaobo. Sarah Palin, herself a former target of WikiLeaks, took aim at the Obama White House for not managing to thwart WikiLeaks and posted the following condemnation on Facebook:

> Assange is not a "journalist" any more than the "editor" of al-Qaeda's new English-language magazine *Inspire* is a "journalist." He is an anti-American operative with blood on his hands. His past posting of classified documents revealed the identity of more than 100 Afghan sources to the Taliban. Why was he not pursued with the same urgency we pursue al-Qaeda and Taliban leaders?[66]

Likewise, U.S. senator Joseph Lieberman called the "outrageous, reckless, and despicable" leaks "nothing less than an attack on the national security of the United States" and argued that they would put the lives of Americans and people around the world at risk.[67] Republican Newt Gingrich, the former Speaker of the House in the U.S. Congress and a 2012 presidential hopeful, argued that Assange should be classified as an "enemy combatant." Even more heated rhetoric surfaced north of the border from Tom Flanagan, a former campaign manager and adviser to Canadian prime minister Stephen Harper. Flanagan told a CBC television interviewer: "I think Assange should be assassinated, actually. I think Obama should put out a contract and maybe use a drone or something."[68] Flanagan later apologized for his remark, while Assange told participants in an online forum sponsored by the *Guardian* that "Mr. Flanagan and the others seriously making these statements should be charged with incitement to commit murder."[69]

Assange, in turn, took aim at U.S. secretary of state Hillary Clinton, who had called the releases of the diplomatic cables "an attack on the international community," by calling for her to resign in light of revelations in the cables that she had ordered U.S. diplomats to spy on top

U.N. officials based in New York, including Secretary-General Ban Ki-moon. And in direct response to the claims that WikiLeaks had either compromised U.S. national security or put lives around the world at risk, Assange replied that throughout the four-year publishing history of WikiLeaks, "there has been no credible allegation, even by organizations like the Pentagon, that even a single person has come to harm as a result of our activities. This is despite much attempted manipulation and spin trying to lead people to a counterfactual conclusion. We do not expect any change in this regard."[70]

While many of the harsh words from politicians targeting WikiLeaks amounted to sheer hyperbole, actual retribution came as several global corporations, under heavy political pressure from Washington, severed ties with WikiLeaks by canceling financial accounts tied to WikiLeaks and removing the group from its web servers. Online retail giant Amazon.com removed WikiLeaks files from its cloud servers on December 1, just a few days after WikiLeaks had rented server space and relocated its U.S. State Department cables there after struggling with denial-of-service attacks on its servers in Sweden; Amazon pulled the plug on WikiLeaks after receiving a request from the U.S. Senate Committee on Homeland Security, chaired at the time by Joe Lieberman. While Amazon issued a statement that WikiLeaks had violated its terms of service, the company did not explain further, and WikiLeaks reportedly moved its files back to a server in Sweden, and then to a server in Switzerland.

Online payment service PayPal followed suit two days later, on December 3, freezing the account of a German foundation accepting donations for WikiLeaks, once again claiming an unspecified violation in the company's terms of service. This move amounted to a more severe obstruction as the PayPal account had been the conduit for most of the contributions WikiLeaks had received in 2010, totaling US$1 million. Next came MasterCard, which on December 6 stopped transferring payments to WikiLeaks saying that the company's rules "prohibit customers from directly or indirectly engaging in or facilitating any action that is illegal."[71] Visa made a similar move on December 7, leaving supporters of WikiLeaks to make donations through a web page hosted by a Swiss-Icelandic company, DataCell.com. For a short time it seemed as if a Swiss bank account Julian Assange had opened up with PostFinance, the financial arm of the country's postal service, would provide an alternative funnel for donations, but this, too, did not last: PostFinance shut down the account (which reportedly contained 31,000 euro, or about US $43,000) on December 6, saying that Assange had "provided false information regarding his place of residence" by listing Geneva as his domicile. The bank also made it clear how Assange's noncitizen status would disadvantage him even in Switzerland: "[Mr.] Assange cannot provide proof of residence in Switzerland and thus does not meet the criteria for a customer relationship with PostFinance. For this reason, PostFinance is entitled to close his account."[72] In addition, Bank of America announced later in December 2010 that it would stop processing payments intended for WikiLeaks.

Supporters of WikiLeaks then fought back with their own global campaign led by members of the transnational group "Anonymous"— an informal and diffuse group of "cyber-anarchists" around the world, who meet and talk with each other in multiple online forums and chat rooms. Billed as "Operation Avenge Assange," against the detractors of WikiLeaks, the group called for cyberattacks targeting the companies cutting off services to WikiLeaks and for the creation of "mirror sites" to host exact copies of the content on the original WikiLeaks websites in a global effort to overcome censorship in any particular country. "The reason is amazingly simple: We all believe that information should be free, and the Internet should be free," said Gregg Housh, one of the Anonymous activists who organized the campaign—making a rare public statement for a group whose leaders normally stay in the shadows.[73] Members and supporters of Anonymous responded immediately by creating more than two hundred mirror sites in the first week of December. "Cut us down, and the stronger we become," declared a posting on WikiLeaks' Twitter feed.

In the days that followed, thousands of netizens connected with WikiLeaks and Anonymous targeted specific corporate and U.S. government websites by "bombarding" them with Internet traffic that made them temporarily inaccessible. One news account reported that as many as three thousand sympathizers of WikiLeaks used a computer program called Low Orbit Ion Cannon to install a "bot"—an online software application that runs automated tasks—capable of sending twenty million connect requests an hour to specifically targeted websites in "denial of service" attacks, thereby making the targeted computers or web servers temporarily unavailable.[74] Media reports noted that the Twitter account identified with the Anonymous movement was posting messages with terse instructions such as "Fire Now," and some civil libertarians advocating for truly open access to information on the Internet likened the strikes to the 1775 early skirmishes of the American Revolution: "This is kind of the shot heard round the world—this is Lexington," said John Perry Barlow, a cofounder of the Electronic Frontier Foundation.[75] The cyber strikes managed to briefly knock out the MasterCard, Visa, and PostFinance websites, though online transactions at these companies were not necessarily disabled. WikiLeaks supporters also targeted the websites of Joseph Lieberman, Sarah Palin, and several other politicians at odds with the organization. The entire spectacle lent itself to a twenty-first-century adaptation of the nineteenth-century maxim by Prussian military theorist Carl von Clausewitz: "Cyber war is the continuation of cyber politics by other means."

As this contentious state of affairs peaked in December 2010, many institutions that were officially neutral with regard to WikiLeaks found themselves taking defensive stances just the same. Columbia University warned its students that having an electronic record of connecting to WikiLeaks might undermine their future chances of getting hired by the U.S. State Department and other government agencies. U.S. military personnel were told WikiLeaks was off-limits, and even those not officially forbidden or unofficially discouraged from accessing WikiLeaks found the website difficult to access amid all the multidirectional cyberattacks. As the world famous linguist and critic of U.S. policy Noam Chomsky quipped in an e-mail to a colleague: "I can't get any access to WikiLeaks in the land of the free."[76] International relations scholar Scott Burchill noted the irony that the Washington political establishment and corporate America were on the side of limiting free speech in this particular cyber war: "The Chinese must be getting a real thrill out of this—they will be sitting back and saying: 'We were always wondering when the cyber war would start; now it's begun among yourselves. We were going to do it.'"[77]

The online campaign by Anonymous coincided with the arrest and detention of Julian Assange at a London police station on rape allegations from Sweden. The case became a point of contention as to whether Assange had been set up and persecuted, with the possibility that the U.S. government was covertly pulling the strings, or whether he truly had behaved in ways ill-suited to a global campaigner trying to position his organization on the moral high ground in public debates over free-dom of speech, transparency, and access to information in the Internet age.[78] Two of Assange's supporters, Israel Shamir and Paul Bennett at the political newsletter *Counterpunch*, wryly described the charges against Assange as a conspiracy, in an essay written shortly after they first surfaced in August 2010: "In order to frame Julian in Singapore, they would have to fit him up with drugs. To frame Julian in England, they might have to report he had skinned and roasted cats or at least dumped a kitten in a trash bin. To hang a frame on Julian in Sweden only required reporting sex between consenting adults."[79] But other activists highly supportive of Assange's notion of "radical transparency" and his advocacy of Internet freedom were gravely troubled by the rape allegations. Johanne Hildebrandt, a columnist for the Swedish tabloid newspaper *Aftonbladet*, noted that, initially, Assange impressed people the world over as "an internet freedom of speech hero," but the rape allegations changed everything:

> I personally think WikiLeaks is a great thing, but with the rape charges, Julian Assange lost all credibility. I have worked as a war correspondent for 20 years, in very corrupt countries where people are right to be afraid. What's he afraid of in Sweden? What's he hiding? In my view, Julian Assange was a priest who turned into a clown when he started criticising the system here. A freedom of speech priest who wanted to reveal everything but his own story.[80]

Many people in Sweden and around the world also worried about the "flood of hatred" directed at the two accusers from die-hard fans of Julian Assange and supporters of WikiLeaks.

And then, still others, especially those steeped in old-school diplo-macy, questioned whether Assange's goal of radical transparency would be such a good thing, especially in the Internet age, and that some segments of global public space still require discretion, even secrecy. Italy's foreign minister, Franco Frattini, likened the releases of the dip-lomatic cables to the "9/11 of diplomacy" and feared it would "blow up the trust between states," a statement that implies that trust between states, behind the scenes, matters more than public disclosures and ac-countability to citizens. Commentator David Brooks echoed this point of view in somewhat more nuanced tones, essentially arguing that there must be a better way to provide truthful information to the public than massive releases on the magnitude of electronic filing cabinets:

> The WikiLeaks dump will probably damage the global conversation. Nations will be less likely to share with the United States. Agencies will be tempted to return to the pre-9/11 silos. World leaders will get their back up when they read what is said about them. Cooperation against Iran may be harder to maintain because Arab leaders feel exposed and boxed in. This fragile international conversation is under threat. It's under threat from WikiLeaks. It's under threat from a Gresham's Law effect, in which the level of public exposure is determined by the biggest leaker and the biggest traitor.
>
> It should be possible to erect a filter that protects not only lives and operations but also international relationships. It should be possible to do articles on specific revelations—Is the U.S. using diplomats to spy on the U.N.? What missile technology did North Korea give to Iran?—without unveiling in a wholesale manner the nuts and bolts of the diplomatic enterprise. We depend on those human conversations for the limited order we enjoy every day.[81]

One skeptic of radical transparency, identifying himself as a former British diplomat (but not by name), put this question directly to Assange in an online chat in December 2010:

> In the course of my former duties I helped to coordinate multilateral action against a brutal regime in the Balkans, impose sanctions on a renegade state threatening ethnic cleansing, and negotiate a debt relief programme for an impoverished nation. None of this would have been possible without the security and secrecy of diplomatic correspondence, and the protection of that correspondence from publication under the laws of the UK and many other liberal and democratic states. An embassy which cannot securely offer advice or pass messages back to London is an embassy which cannot operate. Diplomacy cannot operate without discretion and the protection of sources. . . .
>
> In publishing this massive volume of correspondence, WikiLeaks is not highlighting specific cases of wrongdoing but undermining the entire process of diplomacy. . . . My question to you is: why should we not hold you personally responsible when next an international crisis goes unresolved because diplomats cannot function?

Assange chose to duck the question with this one-sentence response: "If you trim the vast editorial letter to the singular question actually asked, I would be happy to give it my attention."[82]

Other pundits and former diplomats were much less pessimistic about the possible negative effects of WikiLeaks and argued that, as one observer noted, "diplomats would continue their long tradition of politeness in public and brutal honesty in the reports back home."[83] Sir Christopher Meyer, a former British ambassador to the United States, put it this way: "This won't restrain dips' [diplomats] candor. But people will be looking at the security of electronic communications and archives. Paper would have been impossible to steal in these quantities."[84] Michael Cox, a U.S. foreign policy expert based at the British think tank Chatham House, offered a similarly balanced view of the leaked cables, suggesting that the real winners would be historians with a "treasure trove" of first-hand accounts to comb through: "It is a sign that in the information age, it is very difficult to keep anything secret. But as to whether it is going to cause the kind of seismic collapse of international relations that governments have been talking about, I somehow doubt. Diplomats have always said rude things about each other in private, and everyone has always known that."[85] The more dispassionate commentators also pointed out that for all the hand-wringing in the United States about Julian Assange and his immediate collaborators, the game has changed in the global information age and that leaks of electronic files will ultimately force governments to be more honest in communicating with the public and more forthright in actions and policies. As Robert Wright noted:

> For the United States to respond wisely to the WikiLeaks fiasco, American policymakers will first have to realize that Assange himself isn't all that important. If he had never been born, they would still eventually have to adapt to the age of transparency, to a world in which expedient lies to cover expedient collaborations with dubious regimes are a long-term threat to our national security. Sooner or later, America was bound to wake up to the implications of modern technology. Julian Assange just made it a particularly rude awakening.[86]

CONCLUSION

After all the dust settled in the months following the initial release of the U.S. State Department cables and the awarding of the Nobel Peace

Prize to Liu Xiaobo, matters on all sides seemed to revert into a holding pattern. Julian Assange remained in Great Britain as WikiLeaks continued to fragment and as the U.K. Supreme Court prepared to consider an appeal from Assange to a High Court decision in November approving Sweden's request for his extradition. Liu Xiaobo, meanwhile, remained in jail as his story, and his life's struggle, faded from the headlines, while countless lesser known Chinese political activists continued to face harassment and roadblocks in their campaigns for democracy. As Tunisia's Jasmine Revolution swelled into the Arab Spring, China's president, Hu Jintao, and the country's domestic security chief, Zhou Yongkang, both gave speeches in early 2011 advocating tighter Internet censorship, with Zhou calling upon Internet censors to "strive to defuse conflicts and disputes while they are still embryonic" and Hu proposing to "establish a system of public opinion guidance on the Internet,"[87] a development that would seem to run entirely against what both Liu Xiaobo and Julian Assange have been fighting for when it comes to freedom of expression and access to information. While observers noted that political jokes in China were now being exchanged via "microblogs" rather than the dinner table,[88] many democracy activists themselves continued to languish in a state similar to the underground democracy movements in Eastern Europe that operated in the shadows of the Cold War. As Murong Xuecun, a popular Chinese Internet author, noted ruefully: "Our mother tongue has been cut into two parts: one safe, and the other risky."[89] The possible long-range impacts of Julian Assange and Liu Xiaobo remained clouded: it seemed that awarding the Nobel Peace Prize to Liu, in many respects, made more of a splash on Chinese expatriates and human rights organizations around the world than within China itself, while WikiLeaks as of late 2011 had yet to follow up its spectacular releases of 2010 with anything comparable as its members continued to splinter.

The global media dramatically heightened the profiles of both Liu Xiaobo and Julian Assange, amplifying their voices and highlighting the campaigns and struggles waged by their organizations and network partners. Globalization also figured heavily into the clashes that emerged between activist groups and the national governments of the United States and China, with both governments losing face in different ways over the ways they responded to Liu and Assange. China's imprisonment of Liu and the U.S. government's harsh detainment of Bradley

Manning alongside all the rhetoric aimed at suppressing WikiLeaks dented the global images of both countries. When U.S. secretary of state Hillary Clinton gave a speech in February 2011 on Internet freedom, in the midst of the Arab Spring, her affirmation that the United States would stand with cyber dissidents around the world was ironic: the very government agency at the center of the most voluminous WikiLeaks revelations would now begin funding small-scale initiatives to help bloggers around the world work around government censorship and notorious barriers such as the Great Firewall of China.[90] The announcement came at the same time as the State Department launched Twitter feeds in Arabic and Farsi, and Clinton promised further Twitter feeds in local dialects to reach out to people living in China, Russia, and India. As Clinton noted—in comments that could easily be taken, out of context, as a ringing endorsement of WikiLeaks and a warning to the U.S. government: -

> We believe that governments who have erected barriers to Internet freedom—whether they're technical filters or censorship regimes or attacks on those who exercise their rights to expression and assembly online—will eventually find themselves boxed in. They will face a dictator's dilemma, and will have to choose between letting the walls fall or paying the price to keep them standing—which means both doubling down on a losing hand by resorting to greater oppression, and enduring the escalating opportunity cost of missing out on the ideas that have been blocked.[91]

Not to be mistaken, however, as a supporter of Julian Assange, Clinton framed a distinction in her speech between dictatorships that suppress criticism from political opponents and the U.S. government's confrontation with WikiLeaks and its detention of Bradley Manning. As Clinton said, referring to Manning's alleged forwarding of the confidential documents: "The WikiLeaks incident began with a theft just as if it had been executed by smuggling papers in a briefcase. The fact that WikiLeaks used the Internet is not the reason we criticized it. WikiLeaks does not challenge our commitment to Internet freedom."[92] Julian Assange took a very different view; in an online conversation published in June 2011 on the WikiLeaks website he criticized the "extraordinary hypocrisy from the entire White House with regard to the importance of the freedom of speech, and, on the other hand, a betrayal of those statements—an awful betrayal of the values of the US Revolution."[93]

The cases of Liu Xiaobo and Julian Assange also reveal how new spheres of global contestation have emerged in recent years. One realm of contestation involves the superpowers and whether the United States and China will respond affirmatively to multiple sets of public demands for basic human rights and greater openness and transparency. Another realm of contestation involves the activists and their organizations, and the balance between civil society organizations and nation-states. Not so long ago, many international relations scholars and practitioners were speculating that the new balance of power in the early twenty-first century would be between the United States, as the world's sole national superpower, and civil society organizations challenging American-led economic globalization and foreign policy. The cases of Julian Assange and Liu Xiaobo show us that the fault lines in contemporary world politics are becoming more complex, not only given China's rise over the past several years but also with the Internet and social media platforms opening up new ways for citizens to make their voices heard. The lines of contestation will likely become even more complex down the road as more power centers emerge among nation-states, multinational corporations, and transnational civil society, especially as more and more civic groups emerge and build momentum in the Global South.

As the relationships between citizens, civil society actors, and national governments take on new dimensions, it is interesting to note how the idea of global credibility is gaining ground. What counts as global credibility is very much in the eye of the beholder, but the case studies in this chapter provide many perspectives from public officials, political and social activists, journalists and commentators, and everyday people as to what would—or would not—count as globally credible behavior from all sorts of institutions and individuals. The lines of disagreement over WikiLeaks and Liu Xiaobo had a great deal to do with credibility on all sides—whether China has any credibility left to gain in light of its imprisonment of Liu and suppression of so many other democracy activists; whether the United States has been losing credibility through its concerted efforts to undermine WikiLeaks and its harsh detainment of Bradley Manning, as well as its troubled military occupations in Iraq and Afghanistan and diminished civil liberties at home; whether Liu Xiaobo does not have as much credibility as the Nobel Committee claimed given some perceptions that he is too enamored of colonialism and the West; and whether Julian Assange's personal conduct has cost him credibility as an activist fighting for public accountability and transparency. For activists and governments alike, global credibility matters even more than before, and this is one important way our collective experiences of citizenship and political community are evolving and expanding public spaces for debate and deliberation. In other ways, however, citizen groups have been fighting to narrow their visions of national public space, especially when it comes to immigration, and it is to these kinds of cases that we will now turn.

CHAPTER 4

EUROPE'S INWARD TURN: THE RETRENCHMENT OF PUBLIC SPACE

At first glance, Europe might appear fortuitously positioned at the vanguard of globalization, leading the world when it comes to political, economic, and cultural interconnectedness across national borders. Torn apart for centuries by national conflicts and imperial rivalries, devastated in the twentieth century by two world wars, and divided by the Iron Curtain into rival spheres of influence as the United States and the former Soviet Union battled for global supremacy during the Cold War, today's Europe has made a decisive break from the past and evolved into the world's leading venue for international collaboration. In the eyes of some observers, Europe serves as a forerunner of how a more advanced model of global governance might one day emerge. The European Union, with its single economic zone across twenty-seven member states, a common currency shared by seventeen of these countries, a supranational court with the power to strike down national laws, and an elected parliament complete with transnational coalition politics and recently acquired key legislative powers, has ushered in a new era of interdependence in which a "de facto solidarity," as envisioned in one of the EU's founding documents, the Schuman Declaration, seems to have rendered conventional war "unthinkable" as well as "materially impossible."[1] This is true not only between France and Germany, which initiated the first steps toward economic and political integration following World War II, but also across the entire continent, with the possible exception of the fractured republics of the former Yugoslavia. As journalist Keith Richburg heralded the rise of Europe's borderless Generation E:

> While bureaucrats in Brussels, the headquarters of the European Union, toil away at highly technical regulations aimed at forging a single, more integrated Europe—with rules on everything from aviation to how to store fresh cheese—a new society is being created much faster on the ground, by people in their twenties and thirties for whom the ability to live, work and study anyplace on the continent is now taken as a birthright. . . . A 28-year-old Finnish pediatrics nurse who is working in Dublin and buying a home there says she has no intention of ever returning to Finland. A 22-year-old French student with an Italian mother began playing rugby while on an exchange program in Oxford, and now feels comfortable speaking three languages and spending time in various countries. A 21-year-old Italian student, whose girlfriend is half-Finnish and half-Greek, says: "My passport is Italian. I am more and more European."[2]

In fact, his Italian passport is already European, as it isn't only the loosening of internal border restrictions within the European Union that has made it easier for younger, cosmopolitan Europeans, who tend to be more affluent and educated than their peers, to travel across the continent. European Union citizenship, which took effect in 1993, has also made it simpler to live and work across the member states—not only for Europeans but also for growing numbers of Americans, Australians, and Canadians seeking dual citizenship in the countries of their European ancestors, gaining access to a continent's worth of job opportunities, and widening their cultural horizons in ways that would have been impossible not so long ago. One massive dividing line persists, though: legally speaking, European Union citizenship is available only to the citizens of its twenty-seven member states. People who are not citizens of the member countries are cast as outsiders in Europe, even if it has become easier to move around and thrive within the "postmodern utopia" of the European Union. Because EU citizenship is dependent upon national citizenship and the workings of the European Union tend to involve political and business elites much more than everyday people, the nation-state still prevails over European citizenship, all the more so considering that member states are permitted to establish their own immigration policies. And because many of the "third country nationals" who in recent generations have migrated to Europe happen to be from the Middle East, North Africa, and South Asia, tensions surrounding differences in ethnicity and religion have increased. Many Europeans who feel left out by economic globalization or believe that their immediate interests are threatened by European integration as well as the global reach of the United States, vent their frustration on the growing communities of immigrants, especially Muslims, and call for harder-line policies, including deportation.[3]

The limits of European Union citizenship have led to political tensions over the past twenty years and have given voice to far-right, hard-line nationalist parties, launching new waves of anxiety and xenophobia and sharp denunciations of "multiculturalism" from growing numbers of European elites, including the leaders of Italy, Germany, and the United Kingdom. In many important respects, globalization's mixed political legacy in contemporary Europe involves forward-looking innovations such as the institution of European Union citizenship, but as well a heightened emphasis across the continent on tightening national citizenship as a fortress against perceived threats posed by the increasing economic, political, and cultural interconnectedness. For all the interest in European Union citizenship as a possible harbinger of cosmopolitan citizenship, the borders of the European continent are far more restrictive now than in centuries past. This chapter examines the juxtaposition of European Union citizenship on the one hand, and the recent anti-immigration politics on the other. First we will look at how the European Union has expanded the content and scale of citizenship within its enlarged borders. Then we will turn to a series of cases that illustrate how citizenship and immigration policies have been tightening within the member states, and in some instances, have severely compromised the basic rights of immigrants and minority groups. We will also examine how several national leaders in Europe, pressured by rising far-right, anti-immigrant political parties, have been turning against multiculturalism in recent years, essentially calling for the retrenchment of public space into national realms more restrictively defined.

CITIZENSHIP AND FREEDOM OF MOVEMENT IN THE EUROPEAN UNION

European Union citizenship, as set forth in 1992 in the Maastricht Treaty, confers upon citizens of member states the right to live, work, vote, and run for office in local and EU parliamentary elections anywhere in the European Union.[4] Citizens also have the right to hold many national civil service positions within any member state and to receive diplomatic protection when seeking assistance outside the European Union if their respective home countries do not operate an embassy or consulate in the country in question. Alongside the institution of European Union citizenship, the Treaty of Lisbon ushered in a new Charter of Fundamental Rights for the European Union, proclaimed in 2000 by the key European Union institutions and affirming a wide range of political, economic, and social rights. Moreover, all twenty-seven European Union member states, as members of a separate organization, the Council of Europe, have ratified considerable portions of the European Convention on Human Rights. The convention dates back to 1950 and affirmed many fundamental rights and freedoms, opening the door for anyone who believes his or her rights have been violated by one of the member countries to take a case directly to the European Court of Human Rights. The court's judgments are binding on the member governments, just as the decisions of the European Court of Justice are binding upon member states of the European Union.

Freedom of movement within the European Union has also eased greatly in recent decades, thanks to the Schengen Agreement, which was signed in 1985 and set up a zone essentially free of internal border controls that now encompasses twenty-two EU member states, plus four nonmember countries, Switzerland, Liechtenstein, Iceland, and Norway. (The United Kingdom and Ireland opted out and three of the most recent EU entrants—Romania, Bulgaria, and Cyprus—are still waiting to join.) However, at an EU summit held in the summer of 2011, the member states were debating the possibility of rolling back Schengen and relaunching internal border controls in response to growing public hostility over immigration, especially in the wake of unusually heavy migration from North Africa prompted by the Arab Spring. European Union treaties, meanwhile, leave it up to each member state to decide its own immigration and citizenship policies and "to lay down the conditions for the acquisition and loss of nationality."[5] This leaves European Union citizenship derivative upon national citizenship, and it reinforces an image of citizenship as a sorting device in which insiders are included but outsiders remain vulnerable to exclusion. Although the European Union functions in many respects as a postnational model of political community—and provides an illustration, on a regional scale, of how global governing institutions might continue to evolve alongside market globalization—its member states continue to reinforce the inherent limitations and restrictions of national citizenship. This tension between dynamics of globalization and forces of national citizenship is especially striking when examining how countries such as France, Greece, and Italy have been cracking down on migrant populations, for whom European Union citizenship means very little.

In contrast with migrant laborers who struggle to gain even the right to live and work as guestworkers abroad, many professionals are able to empower themselves on their citizenship status—and their preferred venues for living and working. One recent trend associated with globalization has been the upward trend of U.S. citizens with family roots in European countries claiming European Union citizenship—thereby expanding their range of options far more than their European ancestors would have dreamed. While the U.S. government warns Americans that they could lose overseas diplomatic protection from the United States when they hold passports from other countries, Americans who choose to take up citizenship in another country still retain their U.S. citizenship; the U.S. government does not keep track of how many Americans are dual citizens. On the European Union side, the exact citizenship requirements of the member states vary from country to country, and it is easier to gain citizenship in some European countries than others. Most European countries require the applicant to provide documentation that at least one of his or her parents was a native-born citizen of the country, while some countries, such as Ireland and Italy, allow descendants to draw upon the citizenship histories of their grandparents and even great-grandparents.

During the past decade the European Union has expanded into the formerly communist countries of Central and Eastern Europe, and the combination of EU enlargement with EU citizenship has opened the doors for citizens living outside the European Union whose parents and grandparents emigrated from these countries decades ago. Until Romania joined the European Union in 2007, Florida resident Suzanne Mulvehill never would have had the opportunity to permanently live and work in any European Union member state. After Romania's entry, Ms. Mulvehill, who runs a company that trains entrepreneurs and whose mother was born in Romania but emigrated to the United States, completed the extensive paperwork required to become a citizen of Romania, spending $750 in government fees in the course of three years. She visited the Romanian consulate in Washington, D.C., but was not required to visit Romania, and told a news reporter quite frankly that she did not seek Romanian citizenship out of any desire to settle in that country. Instead, she said, she wanted the freedom to work across the European Union: "I recognized for the first time in my life that being American had limits, and that if I really wanted to become what I call a global citizen, then I needed to tap into all my resources to expand my ability to serve entrepreneurs . . . not just in Florida or in America or North America, but on the globe."[6]

Globalization, then, is the motivating force for those with the initiative, the resources, and the good luck of matching up with European countries, owing to their family histories, that will accept them as citizens while demanding virtually nothing from them beyond the initial "membership fees" to obtain the desired passport. North Americans who seek European passports are usually driven to do so by the potential and promise of having internationally mobile career paths and lifestyles, not out of a sense of patriotic sentiment or political responsibility for the European country they are eligible to join. Instead, the notion of "going global" takes center stage in their minds, even if in reality they are going European or going French. Lauren Berg, for example, obtained Greek citizenship, thanks to a connection with her grandfather, shortly after graduating from the University of Michigan, but she actually planned to move to Paris to learn French and gain international business experience: "It's definitely a really good thing to have on your résumé with business going so global. I probably never would have done it if it wasn't for the EU, but at the same time I've always been extremely proud of my Greek heritage."[7] Many Americans seeking dual citizenship benefit from the fact that several European countries still confer citizenship based on blood ties, or *jus sanguinis*, rather than conferring citizenship based only on *jus soli*, or being born within the country. Eric Hammerle, a Florida resident whose father was born in Germany, gained German citizenship for himself and his son simply by taking the required birth, marriage, and death certificates to the German consulate in Miami and paying an $85 fee. "The whole process took about 20 minutes. They read over the documents, came back and said, 'Congratulations, Germany has two new citizens.'"[8]

CITIZENSHIP BARRIERS IN THE EUROPEAN UNION'S MEMBER STATES

While many Americans with no previous direct ties to Europe are finding it easy to become European Union citizens, many people who live and work in European Union member states as immigrants have run into barriers. Germany, which had long recognized nationality only by blood ties, reformed its citizenship laws in 2000 to make it possible for immigrants living there since the early 1960s to become citizens— most notably more than 2.3 million Turkish residents. Still, however, barriers persist: in 2009 a German court denied citizenship to a Turkish immigrant granted permanent residency, after receiving asylum in 1993, on grounds that he was illiterate; the court ruled that an ability to speak limited German was not enough for citizenship.[9] As of January 2011, Denmark had denied citizenship to several stateless Palestinians born in the country, despite a UN convention that requires the granting of citizenship in such cases; the immigration minister involved subsequently lost her job. Spain blocked a 2007 citizenship request from longtime resident Darling Velez, originally from Colombia, because her given name violates a Spanish law forbidding the use of names that do not clearly indicate gender; in this case, Velez's citizenship application was accepted by the Spanish government in 2006, but Velez was unable to complete the process of becoming a citizen by registering her name.[10] In March 2006, the Netherlands immigration minister denied an application for fast-track citizenship to soccer superstar Salomon Kalou, a native of Ivory Coast, on grounds that he had failed a Dutch language and culture test; the minister also pointed out that Kalou had lived in the Netherlands for three years, rather than the five-year period normally required by law. The decision meant that Kalou could not play on the Netherlands World Cup team despite his status as a player for the team Feyenoord Rotterdam. Kalou ended up playing for Ivory Coast during the 2006 World Cup, alongside his brother Bonaventure, and left the Netherlands shortly thereafter to join the British football club Chelsea. Such cases underscore the limits of Europeanization, let alone globalization, when it comes to how European Union member states approach citizenship and political membership.

Authorities in the United Kingdom, meanwhile, denied a citizenship application from the Canadian spouse of a British soldier, telling her in a February 2008 decision that she needed to apply for "entry clearance" into Britain from overseas (not upon entering the country, as she had done) and would have to return to Canada and wait for several months before she could return under a different visa and apply again for British citizenship. Britain's Home Office, in this case, reversed its decision one month later and allowed Samantha Crozier to obtain a residency visa, which allowed her to stay with her husband and two toddlers, ages two and one (both British citizens). This came after the news media, including Britain's most widely read tabloid newspaper, the *Sun,* played up her concern that she and her two young sons would be uprooted at the same time as her husband prepared to leave for either Iraq or Afghanistan, fulfilling the ultimate civic duty of military service. Ms. Crozier voiced her frustration by saying: "I think it is disgraceful. I came here to start a new life with my husband and my two wonderful little boys. My husband is very patriotic and would gladly fight for his country, but it seems his country won't fight for him."[11]

Several members of parliament, however, were willing to fight, and they called for the Home Office to change its rules on entry clearance for military families. A soldier's advocacy group helped the couple confront the bureaucracy, and a Facebook group, "Operation Keep Sami in U.K.," with more than a thousand members rallied behind the family. Not everyone, though, welcomed the Home Office's reversal of its decision. As one person commented on a celebratory news article in the *Sun*: "Being a serving soldier and having had to go through the immigration process to get my Canadian wife into (the) UK, this decision makes a mockery of the system. I was serving in Iraq and still managed to find out the complete process to get my wife to the UK."

The British government, meanwhile, has also considered denying citizenship to immigrants who do not speak English and immigrants who take part in allegedly "unpatriotic activities" such as protesting against the country's military policies.

CITIZENSHIP RESTRICTIONS IN FRANCE: MUSLIM ATTIRE IN A SECULAR SOCIETY

More so than any other European country, France has wrestled with the question of "who belongs" as a growing population of Muslim immigrants transforms a society that professes to be secular. In a case that opened up tremendous debate about the requirements for political belonging and what behavior should be expected of citizens in the public spaces of contemporary Europe, France's highest administrative court upheld a June 2008 denial of citizenship to Faiza Silmi, a Muslim woman from Morocco. Silmi is fluent in French, and her husband and four children are French citizens, but the court cited her "insufficient assimilation" in light of the country's tradition of laïcité, meaning a commitment to a secular society. The negative decision followed a social worker's report that Ms. Silmi had shown up for meetings wearing a dark facial veil known as a niqab. (In contrast with the burqa, which covers the body from head to toe, a niqab covers only the face, though many Muslim women who wear the niqab also wear other full-length garments.) While France had previously refused to grant citizenship to several Muslims linked with Islamic extremist circles, this marked the first case in which citizenship had been denied to a Muslim because of a personal religious practice.

In its exact wording, the ruling from the Council of State said that Ms. Silmi, by wearing the niqab, "has adopted a radical practice of her religion, incompatible with essential values of the French community, particularly the principle of equality of the sexes."[12] A social worker whose testimony led to the rejection of the citizenship application reported that Ms. Silmi "has no idea about the secular state or the right to vote. She lives in total submission to her male relatives. She seems to find this normal and the idea of challenging it has never crossed her mind."[13] Her lawyer has argued that the Council of State acted arbitrarily as French law specifies two tests of assimilation, knowledge of the French language and the absence of a criminal record—both of them unrelated to dress.

Since this case emerged in 2008, the French government has gone further and has forbidden women from wearing the niqab in public. While France's highest administrative body stated in March 2010 that an outright ban would violate both French law and the European Convention on Human Rights, France's National Assembly voted 335 to 1 in July 2010 to ban the niqab, and the Senate overwhelmingly passed the law 246 to 1 in September 2010. (In both houses, almost all members of the minority Socialist party abstained from voting, with many lawmakers saying that they would rather oppose the veils through political debate, not compulsory legislation.) The new law—the first of its kind worldwide—took effect in April 2011, with mandatory fines of €150 (about US$200) imposed on anyone caught wearing the niqab—although the law faces a likely challenge in the European Court of Human Rights. While crackdowns on traditional Islamic dress have been widely supported by far-right political parties that typically run on platforms hostile to immigration, the idea for a ban in France first came from a communist mayor and parliamentarian as a necessary defense of France's republican values of liberty and equality, dating back to the 1789 Declaration of the Rights of Man and the Citizen. The niqab ban also gained support by a leading advocacy group on behalf of women's rights, Ni putes Ni Soumises, or Neither Whores Nor Submissives, on grounds that wearing Islamic veils can leave women vulnerable to disempowerment and abuse.

The new law came as several European countries struggle to navigate a path in balancing norms of human rights and cultural diversity in postmodern Europe with increasingly visible displays of Islamic faith as the continent's Muslim population continues to grow. France's recent interpretation of its secular political tradition as justification for banning Muslim garments had intensified since 2004, when the government passed a law banning Islamic headscarves and other conspicuous religious symbols from public schools, and public debate leading up to France's niqab ban invoked heated language related to citizenship. France's president, Nicolas Sarkozy, appealed to the idea of citizenship to justify restrictions on the niqab, arguing in a May 2010 cabinet meeting: "Citizenship should be experienced with an uncovered face. There can be no other solution but a ban in all public places."[14] Sarkozy has also called for a French ban on the burqa and received extended applause in a June 2009 speech, before both houses of the national assembly, when he framed the burqa as an affront to gender equality: "In our country, we cannot accept that women be prisoners behind a screen, cut off from all social life, deprived of all identity. . . . The burqa is not a religious sign, it's a sign of subservience, a sign of debasement—I want to say it solemnly. It will not be welcome on the territory of the French Republic."[15] Faiza Silmi, who does not wear a burqa but covers her body with three different layers of clothing when she walks outdoors, expressed a different view to a journalist from the *New York Times* shortly after being turned down for French citizenship: "They say I am under my husband's command and that I am a recluse. They say I wear the niqab because my husband told me so. I want to tell them: It is my choice. I take care of my children, and I leave the house when I please. I have my own car. I do the shopping on my own. Yes, I am a practicing Muslim, I am orthodox. But is that not my right?"[16]

The changing population in France, then, has brought about tremendous national debate over questions such as what it means to be French and how the country should respond to cultural change brought on by recent immigration, itself a product of globalization. Some of France's religious activists outside Islam oppose bans on Islamic garments and suggest that such restrictions will turn France into "the laughingstock of democracies," in the words of sociologist Raphael Liogier, for violating basic rights to freedom of religion and freedom of expression.[17] Daniele Lochak, a French law professor not involved in the case, told *Le Monde* newspaper that it was "bizarre" to deny citizenship on the basis of excessive submission to men: "If you follow that to its logical conclusion, it means that women whose partners beat them are also not worthy of being French."[18] On the other hand, France's urban affairs minister as of 2008, Fadela Amara, herself a practicing Muslim of Algerian heritage, cast the garments as "a prison" and a "straitjacket" corrosive to democratic values: "It is not a religious insignia but the insignia of a totalitarian political project that promotes inequality between the sexes and is totally lacking in democracy."[19]

Several leaders of Muslim organizations in Europe have, in fact, supported bans on garments that prevent others from identifying the person wearing them. As Taj Hargey, chairman of the Muslim Educational Centre in Oxford, England, told a journalist from Al Jazeera: "Muslims need to adjust and adapt to Western society. There is no reason why women should cover their faces because it is not an Islamic requirement.

If we enter a public domain, we need to follow the public rules and that means showing our faces."[20] France's Muslim leaders have walked a tightrope on the issue, saying that although Islam does not require women to wear the niqab or the burqa, outright bans on the garments run the risk of creating public stigmas against Muslims. The majority of French citizens, meanwhile, worry that the clothing opens the door to radical Islam and undermines the standing of women in French society; public opinion surveys in France showed overwhelming support across the country's political spectrum for the court ruling against Ms. Silmi's citizenship application.

The controversy over the niqab, at its heart, also reflects disagreement as to whether people have a right to identify other people they see in public spaces—and whether people have corresponding duties as citizens to make their identities public and to communicate face to face. "Showing one's face is a question of dignity and equality in our republic," said France's justice minister, Michèle Alliot-Marie, as members of France's Senate debated the issue before passing the niqab ban almost unanimously in September 2010. This issue also became the focal point of an interesting exchange in print between a supporter of the niqab ban—Jean-François Copé, the majority leader in the French National Assembly—and Ronald Sokol, the American lawyer and a resident of France who has been representing Faiza Silmi pro bono in her appeal before the European Court of Human Rights. Mr. Copé, who also serves as mayor of Meaux, home to the world's most renowned Brie, argued that the niqab should not be classified as an article of clothing but as a mask "making identification or participation in economic and social life virtually impossible." As he continued in a commentary published May 2010 in the *New York Times*:

> This face covering poses a serious safety problem at a time when security cameras play an important role in the protection of public order. An armed robbery recently committed in the Paris suburbs by criminals dressed in burqas provided an unfortunate confirmation of this fact. As a mayor, I cannot guarantee the protection of the residents for whom I am responsible if masked people are allowed to run about. The visibility of the face in the public sphere has always been a public safety requirement. It was so obvious that until now it did not need to be enshrined in law. But the increase in women wearing the niqab, like that

of the ski mask favored by criminals, changes that. We must therefore adjust our law, without waiting for the phenomenon to spread.[21]

Mr. Copé further argued that the niqab ban could be reconciled with France's republican principles of liberty, equality, and fraternity, and that without such a ban, the country ran the risk of throwing these three values out of balance. In his view, Muslim women wearing niqabs in France are essentially abdicating both their rights and responsibilities to exist as individuals, at least in the eyes of their fellow citizens:

> Individual liberty is vital, but individuals, like communities, must accept compromises that are indispensable to living together, in the name of certain principles that are essential to the common good. Let's take one example: The fact that people are prohibited from strolling down Fifth Avenue [in New York City] in the nude does not constitute an attack on the fundamental rights of nudists. Likewise, wearing headgear that fully covers the face does not constitute a fundamental liberty. To the contrary, it is an insurmountable obstacle to the affirmation of a political community that unites citizens without regard to differences in sex, origin or religious faith. How can you establish a relationship with a person who, by hiding a smile or a glance—those universal signs of our common humanity—refuses to exist in the eyes of others?[22]

The lawyer representing Ms. Silmi in her ongoing appeal rejected Mr. Copé's arguments. Ronald Sokol noted that no evidence exists that women wearing the veil pose a public safety problem and disputed Copé's view that citizens have rights and duties when it comes to showing their faces in public:

> I know of no such right. Copé will not find it in the Declaration of the Rights of Man, nor in the European Convention of Human Rights. When walking down the Champs Elysées, I have no right to see the face of passersby. Nor do I want such a right. While Copé may want a passerby to give him a glance or a smile, he has no right to demand it. Yes, the veil may be antisocial, but, fortunately, in a democratic, pluralistic society there is no legal duty to be social. Monsieur Copé may be right in calling the veil a "mask making participation in economic and social life virtually impossible." He may be correct in thinking that participation is desirable. But he is profoundly wrong in thinking there is a legal duty to participate.[23]

Ultimately, this debate about the obligations of citizens in France's changing public space—a new incarnation of the debate between liberals and communitarians, as noted in chapter 1—just might be resolved by the European Court of Human Rights, where an appeal by Faiza Silmi remained pending at the end of 2011. Similar debates over face-covering garments have been brewing in Belgium, the Netherlands, and beyond. In December 2011, the government of Canada decided that Muslim women attending ceremonies to become Canadian citizens must remove niqabs and burqas before taking the oath of citizenship.

FRANCE'S TOUGHENING IMMIGRATION POLICY

Alongside the vexing questions related to "who belongs" as citizens, Europe's member states have been trying to figure out how to manage ever-present streams of undocumented immigrants passing through the continent's most heavily traveled gateway zones. The area surrounding the French port city of Calais, for example, overlooking the narrowest point of the English Channel at the northern tip of France, has become a hub for undocumented immigrants from South Asia making their way into the United Kingdom. Even though the British government stops approximately twenty thousand migrants each year as they try to enter the country, thousands of people—mostly from Afghanistan, Iraq, and several East African countries—continue to attempt the crossing from Calais. Often they are men in their twenties who have already paid huge sums of money and have taken great risks to reach Calais, and they are not inclined to turn back whatever the dangers. Many of the migrants believe Britain, which in contrast with many continental European countries has no national identity card system, offers plentiful job opportunities and comparatively generous social welfare provisions for undocumented workers.

The routine for the migrants is familiar: head for the rest stops and refueling stations where trucks stop just before crossing from France to Britain, climb once or twice a day—often in broad daylight—onto a truck that appears to be headed for Britain; once discovered, a quick trip to the police station to receive a written warning; an occasional court appearance; and then freedom to make another try. Many people make dozens of attempts before finally crossing successfully. Tragedies often occur; the worst incident happened in 2000 when fifty-eight migrants from China suffocated to death in the back of a truck traveling from Calais to Dover. In early 2009, twelve migrants from Afghanistan and Kosovo were found huddled inside the back of an empty chemical tanker not realizing it was about to be filled with industrial acid; moments before workers at a chemical plant in Calais turned the switch to fill the tanker, one worker heard muffled cries inside and stopped just in time. "A few seconds more and they would have been burned to the bone," the company's director told a British journalist.[24] Another scare occurred in May 2010 when five people believed to be from Afghanistan managed to break out of a frozen foods truck after a child fell unconscious as the temperature plunged to minus 25 degrees Celsius, or minus 13 degrees Fahrenheit. Although the migrants had set out hoping to evade government authorities, they ended up placing a frantic emergency call to police, begging for assistance. Officers used GPS technology to locate their mobile phone at a camp inhabited by refugees, where they had returned after escaping from the truck.

The presence and persistence of undocumented migrants has created controversy in French politics. The government tries to discourage migration and increasingly has been dispatching riot police equipped with tear gas to raid encampments, while charities commonly affiliated with local churches run soup kitchens and provide migrants with clothing and medical services. For three years, the Red Cross operated a refugee camp near Calais in the small village of Sangatte, from which as many as sixty-eight thousand undocumented migrants made their way to Britain before the French government closed the camp in November 2002; this came under orders of then interior minister Sarkozy amid growing public criticism, in both France and Britain, that Sangatte seemed like an open invitation for migrants to enter Britain illegally. The closing of the camp coincided with the opening of British border control posts on the French side of the English Channel, near the entrance to the undersea tunnel terminals. The British government estimated that the total number of undocumented migrants entering Britain by way of Calais fell from ten thousand in 2002 to about fifteen hundred in 2006. On the French side, however, thousands of migrants have continued to flock to Calais, just as before, but with no designated shelter.

For several years after Sangatte was closed, as many as one thousand migrants at any given time camped illegally in a wooded area outside Calais that became a makeshift shanty town known as "The Jungle," littered with garbage and lacking beds or bathroom facilities. This, too, was closed and torn down by the French government in September

2009 as Sarkozy, now the country's president and himself the son of a Hungarian immigrant, cracked down on undocumented migrants in an effort to appeal to his conservative base. The three hundred migrants who remained at "The Jungle" until the end were detained by police when French authorities moved in to demolish the camp, and many Afghan men expressed fear about being returned to their native country. BBC journalist Emma Jane Kirby visited the camp just a few days before the bulldozers arrived and found herself surrounded by migrants eager to talk. As Kirby observed:

> Each of the Afghan men here is keen to make me understand that returning home for him would be a death sentence. One is wanted on suspicion of selling state secrets, another is hunted by his brother-in-law in the bloodiest of feuds. Others fear the Taliban has put a price on their heads. There is a dark rumour that the French police briefly, but deliberately, weakened their port surveillance systems to allow a few immigrants to slip through the net to Britain.
>
> Beside me there is a heated argument going on in Pashto between two Afghan men and the interpreter from the United Nations refugee agency. The UN worker has been explaining to the men how the asylum process works in France, but the men are angrily listing the names of scores of their friends who have already been rejected by the French system.
>
> I put the question to Helene, one of the volunteers at the charity Salaam, while they are serving an evening meal to long lines of illegal immigrants near the Calais port. She shrugs: "You can close 'The Jungle,' but look at all these people—do you think they can just disappear?"[25]

Advocates of refugees and asylum seekers called the bulldozing and subsequent detainments "horrific" and inhumane but also argued that the camp should not have existed in the first place: "They should never have been allowed to rot there like this," said Sandy Buchan, the leader of the British-based group Refugee Action, calling for France to grant asylum to those migrants needing protection while helping the others return to their native countries. "It's appalling neglect and has allowed false expectation to be built up."[26] France's immigration minister, Eric Besson, defended the destruction of the camp, saying the government had to deter human smugglers charging migrants the equivalent of US$1000 to $2000 to help them sneak on trucks without getting caught. In Besson's words: "The law of the jungle cannot last eternally. A state of law must be re-established in Calais."[27] In the end, France's immigration ministry said that approximately 170 of the migrants uprooted from The Jungle in its final days applied for asylum in France, another 180 agreed to return to their native countries, and those who did not agree to leave France were expelled to Greece, the point from which most of the migrants had first entered the European Union. This decision by France also generated controversy, with human rights groups in France arguing that expelling the migrants would merely disperse them elsewhere. What is more, the demolition of The Jungle did not deter migrants from gathering elsewhere. After authorities razed the site, some twenty new camps surfaced in the area around Calais. Such standoffs between people asserting rights to freedom of movement as they desperately try to improve their lives and states asserting control over borders are emblematic of the current tension over migration in the dual dynamic between globalization and citizenship.

BACKLASHES AGAINST MIGRANTS IN GREECE

Positioned as the gateway from the East into continental Europe, and harboring multiple points of entry given its 227 inhabited islands in the Mediterranean Sea, Greece has unusually porous borders. Authorities estimate that more than one hundred thousand undocumented migrants enter Greece each year, and many of these migrants used to end up in a camp in an olive grove on the outskirts of the port city of Patras, biding their time until smuggling themselves onto trucks and shipping containers headed for Italy. Iraqi Kurds built the squatter camp around 2002, and many of the shacks gradually took on the character of shabby but semipermanent homes; some even included satellite televisions. As migration flows to Europe changed from 2005 to 2010, refugees from Afghanistan took over the camp, most of them young men and boys arriving by boat from Turkey, as well as growing numbers of Africans and Roma migrants. As many as two thousand migrants lived in Patras at any given time throughout much of the past decade, but conditions deteriorated, and Greek authorities bulldozed and burned the camp in June 2009.

The demolition of the camp did not steer migrants away from Patras. Instead, throughout late 2009 and 2010, they set up plastic shelters that became known locally as the "Afghan Jungle"—a chilling parallel with the situation in France. Police in Greece consistently have been trying to drive out the migrants by arresting residents and tearing down their huts, but the migrants tend to stay until they can find their way to other destinations in Europe. Some choose to remain indefinitely, even though the "jungle" lacks even the most basic amenities such as running water and public toilets. Authorities in Greece have also tried to crack down on migrants leaving the country for other European Union member states—most commonly Italy, by way of ferry boats that leave Patras daily—but such efforts have not substantially reduced the immigrant population in Greece, as new migrants continue to arrive each day.

The Greek government has promised to build more detention centers as holding stations for undocumented migrants, but the government's demolition of the squatter camp, as in France, sparked controversy at home and abroad. The country's opposition parties, along with international human rights groups, have been quick to call attention to how the poor living conditions in Greece's detention facilities violate the basic human rights of the migrants. In the words of Georgia Trismpioti, the director of the Greek branch of Amnesty International: "It's not a solution to have more and more detention centers. It's not a solution to the migration or refugee problems. They did not commit any crime. Their only 'crime,' so to say, is just to enter another country to find political asylum or to find a better condition of life."[28]

Greece stepped up its attempts to tighten immigration controls as the country's economic prospects soured amid a public debt crisis that forced Greece to obtain two bailout packages worth more than US$300 billion from the European Union and the International Monetary Fund.[29] At the start of 2011, Greece announced it could no longer handle the inflow of migrants and would upgrade the Greek Coast Guard and build a fence eight miles long along its border with Turkey, in the northeastern part of the country. As Greece's public order minister, Christos Papoutsis, posted on his website, framing the issue as a matter of the state upholding duties exclusively on behalf of its own national citizens: "Greek society has exceeded its limit in its capacity to accommodate illegal immigrants. This is the hard reality and we have an obligation to the Greek citizen to deal with it." Greece's decision came as Frontex, the European Union's border agency, reported that about 90 percent of all illegal immigration into the European Union was coming through Greece, with an average of 245 undocumented migrants esti-mated to have entered into the EU through Greece every day in October 2010. As the Greek government announced its intent to build the bor-der fence, some fifty thousand migrants—many of them refugees from Afghanistan and Iraq—were waiting for asylum in Greece.

Greece is also the entry point into the European Union for a dispro-portionate number of refugees—who then apply for political asylum in Greece. Under the Dublin Regulation, adopted in 2003 by the member states and one of the only uniform guidelines regarding European Union immigration policy, migrants seeking asylum are required to apply for asylum and remain in the first member state they entered while they wait for a decision. The conditions faced by refugees and asylum seekers in Greece, as well as the Dublin Regulation that forces so many migrants into Greece, have come under increasing criticism. In September 2010 the Council of Europe's commissioner of human rights and a representative from the United Nations High Commis-sion on Refugees both made unprecedented appearances before the European Court of Human Rights in the case of an asylum seeker from Afghanistan, identified only as "MSS," who appealed his transfer in June 2009 from Belgium to Greece, on grounds that he feared "deten-tion in appalling conditions in Greece" and the prospect of being sent arbitrarily back to Afghanistan. In the end, the asylum seeker, who reportedly had survived a murder attempt by the Taliban after having worked as an interpreter for U.S.-led forces, ended up homeless once he arrived in Greece.

The Council of Europe's human rights commissioner, Thomas Hammarberg, supported the Afghan migrant and told the human rights court that asylum seekers transferred to Greece run a high risk of be-ing returned to their home countries, regardless of the dangers. Mr. Hammarberg also said he would support a proposal by the European Commission, not yet implemented, that would suspend transfers of asylum seekers within the European Union and give states such as Greece at least temporary relief from the constraints under the Dublin Regulation.[30] On January 21, 2011, the court ruled that both Belgium and Greece had violated the man's rights, ordered both countries to compensate him in damages, and also ordered Greece to process his asylum claim without delay. As the court stated in its decision: "In spite of the obligations incumbent on the Greek authorities . . . he spent months living in extreme poverty, unable to cater for his most basic needs—food, hygiene and a place to live—while in fear of being attacked and robbed."[31]

In calling for more help and coordination from the European Union regarding the country's heavy inflow of migrants, Greek foreign minister Dora Bakoyannis has appealed to the idea of solidarity, saying: "In order to be able to manage this in Greece, we need European solidarity."[32] It is not clear, at this point, what European solidarity on immigration policy might look like: whether it will involve more member states, particularly those northern and central European countries insulated from the European Union's external borders, taking initiatives to accommodate migrants arriving into countries such as Greece, Italy, and Spain; or whether European "solidarity" will merely amount to an increase in coordinated restrictions that block the flow of outsiders into the European Union.

The need for greater collaboration and collective responsibility has been obvious to human rights advocates, who have noted that the only visible European coordination when it comes to asylum seekers has been for all member states to send applicants back to the countries they first entered. Bill Frelick of Human Rights Watch has criticized the existing system under the Dublin Regulation: "If a person who passes through Greece applies for asylum in Sweden or Germany, their fingerprints show up on what's called the eurodoc system, and they're kicked back to Greece, and Greece has proven itself completely incapable of handling this problem, and they've gotten precious little support from the EU member-states."[33] At the end of the day, international human rights advocates, officials from the European Union, and authorities in Greece have agreed on one thing: the planned border fence separating Greece and Turkey will not address the root causes of the influx of migrants into Greece or the inability of the European Union to better accommodate migrants. Greece might well be left to handle continuing global migration on its own national terms. Moreover, European solidarity on immigration might essentially wall off the continent more sharply from its immediate neighbors as well as the broader concerns surrounding global migration.

ITALY'S ANTI-IMMIGRANT POLITICS

One reason why growing numbers of migrants have been entering the European Union via Greece despite the poor conditions there is that circumstances in a more popular neighboring Mediterranean gateway have deteriorated since July 2009. That summer Italy's parliament passed a new immigration law, billed as a "security package," making unauthorized immigration a criminal offense punishable by fines ranging from €5000 to €10,000 (about US$7000 to $14,000) as well as a three-year prison term for anyone caught housing undocumented migrants. (In April 2011, the European Court of Justice struck down a provision within the law calling for prison terms of one to four years for undocumented immigrants who remained in Italy after being ordered to depart.[34])

Since hardly any undocumented migrants are in a position to pay fines totaling thousands of euro, the new law meant that authorities would now have stronger legal backing to detain and deport migrants. Under the Schengen Agreement, member states are allowed to deport undocumented migrants after they have been arrested twice; the new law enables Italian authorities to first arrest migrants for being in the country illegally and then to arrest them a second time for not paying the fine. The new law also extended detention periods for undocumented immigrants to six months before they can be sent back to their countries of origin and allowed Italian citizens to start street patrols looking for migrants to turn into authorities. Widely criticized by several of Italy's opposition parties, the Roman Catholic Church, and Italian prosecutors who worried that active enforcement of the law would overload the domestic legal system, the law also made it a criminal offense to force children to beg on the streets, a provision that was viewed as targeting gypsies and Roma migrants.

The law took effect less than two months after Italy began intercepting—in international waters—boats carrying hundreds of migrants from North Africa aiming to reach the country's southernmost Mediterranean island of Lampedusa, located about 130 miles south of Sicily and 60 miles north of Tunisia. After stopping the boats, Italian authorities turned them back to their points of departure, mostly in Libya, before they could claim asylum; the crackdown came after an estimated thirty-six thousand migrants landed on Italy's shores during 2008, an increase of about 75 percent over the year before. While Italy's interior minister called for the European Union to adopt the Italian government's new practice of intercepting boats filled with migrants at sea and sending them back to their ports of departure, rather than their countries of origin, critics, including the United Nations High Commission for Refugees, argued that Italy has been violating international law by denying refugees the right to seek asylum. Just one month before the crackdown on boats from North Africa, Italy and Malta fought publicly over which country should accept about 120 African migrants, most of them from Nigeria, rescued from two rubber dinghies in the Mediterranean by sailors on board a Turkish cargo ship. After a four-day standoff, Italy allowed the migrants to enter the country.

The political instability in Tunisia and the civil war in Libya amid the Arab Spring in early 2011 triggered an unusually high flow of migrants from North Africa to Italy. Halfway through the year, more than thirty-two thousand migrants had landed in Lampedusa since the start of 2011, about double the usual rate of arrivals. Most of the Tunisian migrants told authorities they hoped to make their way to the homes of relatives in France, but the French government turned out to be far from receptive, especially in light of rising polling numbers for the far-right National Front party just one year before the country's next presidential election. When Italy asked both France and the European Union to help the migrants settle beyond Italy—a move that would involve making changes to the Dublin Regulation, which requires that they remain in the first country they entered—France temporarily closed its border with Italy to Tunisians who wanted to enter; Denmark also closed its internal borders despite accusations that it might be violating European law. The snubs prompted Italy to threaten in April to leave the European Union, and the negative responses to immigration across the continent threw the future of the Schengen Agreement and its provisions for the free movement within the internal borders of the European Union into doubt. As one of Lampedusa's six thousand residents, Paola la Rosa, pointed out, it all signaled an element of hypocrisy with regard to immigration policy: "Europe and the West got really enthusiastic about revolutionary movements seeking freedom in Arab countries. But one of the freedoms these people want is the freedom to move, the freedom to seek a better life elsewhere. The West doesn't like that so much. They want them to be free, but at home."[35] Said the mayor of Lampedusa, Bernardino de Rubeis: "We will continue welcoming people here in Lampedusa. But Europe must do the same."[36]

Far from settling domestic public debate on immigration, Italy's 2009 law intensified public debate, with critics arguing that the law has the effect of keeping many migrants from taking their children to doctors or enrolling them in schools out of fear of being reported to the police and detained. In March 2010, supporters of immigrants held a one-day strike in advance of regional elections, as the country's restrictive immigration policies continued to be a central issue. Comparable boycotts have taken place in several other European countries and the United States to make the point that international workers, whether or not they hold the relevant legal papers, make essential contributions to national economies; in Italy, immigrants make up an estimated 10 percent of the country's labor force. As Jorge Carazas, who moved to Italy from Argentina in the year 2000, declared in a speech on the day of the strike: "We are the country's new citizens and we want to send politicians a clear message. No matter what racist tones the government chooses to adopt, we're not going anywhere. This is our home."[37]

In response, the country's prime minister at the time, Silvio Berlusconi, accused his critics of "wanting an invasion of immigrants," while campaign posters for Berlusconi's main coalition partner, the far-right Lega Nord,[38] were even more inflammatory and fraudulent. One poster depicted a Native American Indian chieftain with the slogan: "They put up with immigration, now they live on reserves."[39] Tougher enforcement measures that have accompanied the twists and turns in public sentiment are not lost on the immigrants: "These days on the streets, you see a lot of policemen, sometimes in plain clothes, stopping people and demanding their documents," a thirty-one-year-old woman from Peru who takes care of an elderly Italian woman told a journalist from the *New York Times*: "If they stop me, then what will I do?"[40] Given Italy's stagnant population trends (with only the elderly population growing in the country with Europe's lowest birthrate), immigrants fill important gaps in the national economy by taking on jobs that Italians otherwise avoid. Italian families increasingly depend on domestic help—hired from abroad—to care for children and elderly parents; Italy's construction industry also relies heavily on immigrants. As noted by Maurizio Ambrosini, a sociologist at the University of Milan: "Many Italians are convinced that immigrants are a burden, but in fact they have a very positive effect on our welfare system. If anything,

Italy constantly needs new waves of immigrants."[41] One year later, in local elections held during May 2011, the voters of Milan and Naples seemed to change direction. They turned away from right-wing parties, despite aggressive campaigning by Berlusconi, in favor of mayoral candidates from more progressive parties. Berlusconi himself stepped down as prime minister in November 2011, after losing his majority in parliament as Italy became ensnared in Europe's widening debt crisis.

The heated rhetoric coupled with occasional clashes between ethnic Italians and migrants feeds chronic tension in Italy, where immigrants account for about 7 percent of the population. Street violence between groups of immigrants and Italian locals broke out in Milan about a month before the March 2010 strike, and chaos erupted in the small southern Italian community of Rosarno, which is surrounded by citrus groves along the western coast of Calabria. In this town of fifteen thousand along the "toe" of the Italian peninsula, in a region where about eight thousand immigrants from Africa earn their living by picking fruits and vegetables, hundreds of African migrants rioted in January 2010 by throwing rocks at local residents and police, smashing shop windows, and burning cars. They were said to be retaliating after three Africans were beaten with iron bars by a gang of white youths and, in an earlier incident that the migrants also blamed on racism, a legal immigrant from Togo suffered minor injuries from pellet gunshots fired by local police. Schools were closed; people stayed indoors; and Italian state television showed video of local residents calling for the migrants to leave town. They interviewed a young mother, with a bruise under an eye and a bandage on the side of her head, who described how a group of migrants smashed her car and then set it on fire moments after she narrowly escaped with her two small children. According to media reports, local Italian residents beat many of the migrants at random with metal bars and wooden clubs, and one white resident fired gunshots into the air.

Immediately after the riots, police shipped more than a thousand African workers living in Calabria to immigrant detention centers and made arrangements to deport them back to their countries of origin. Local authorities then sent bulldozers into their makeshift encampments to destroy the shacks where many of them had slept; some immigrants had lived in an abandoned factory lacking electricity or running water. Many Italians were appalled when they learned of the incident; a junior minister in Italy's previous, center-left government, Luigi Manconi, noted with irony that Rosarno had now become "the only wholly white town in the world. Not even South African apartheid obtained such a result." He then followed up by asking: "Who now will pick the oranges?"[42]

Leaders of advocacy groups on behalf of immigrants were quick to point out that the migrant workers in Calabria toil in conditions close to slavery in a local economy dominated by organized crime syndicates. Human rights organizations have also reported that many African immigrants are lured to Italy by what appear to be legal offers of temporary agricultural work during harvest season—and often pay smugglers as much as US$10,000 for help in reaching Italy, a country that offers very few work visas—only to find upon arrival they have no choice but to work illegally from dawn to dusk for the rough equivalent of US$30 per day. Flavio Di Giacomo, the spokesman for the International Organization for Migration in Italy, says conditions of "semi-slavery" are the norm for African migrant workers in southern Italy: "Many Italian economic realities are based on the exploitation of low-cost foreign labor, living in subhuman conditions, without human rights."[43] Italian author Roberto Saviano—who wrote the best-selling book *Gomorrah*, depicting organized crime and gang wars near Naples—went even further to raise the possibility that the initial attacks against the migrants that provoked the riots came from the mafia: "Immigrants are always braver than we are against the clans," Mr. Saviano said in a newspaper interview.[44]

Such destructive clashes and images have added to anti-immigrant leanings in European politics and prompted some top officials to go out of their way to debunk the idea of "multiethnic" or "multicultural" societies, in a sense shifting the center of European politics in a reactionary direction. In May 2009, shortly after Italy began to send boats full of migrants from Libya back to that country, Silvio Berlusconi defended his government's unfolding crackdowns on immigrants, saying that Italy's previous, more left-leaning governments "opened the doors to clandestine migrants coming from other countries, with an idea of a multi-ethnic Italy," but that this kind of society was "not our idea."[45] Supporters from the prime minister's main coalition partner, the far-right Lega Nord, applauded Berlusconi's statement, while opposition leaders reacted with alarm. As a member of the center-left Partito Democratico (Democratic Party), Giovanna Melandri said at the time: "Yes, Mr. Premier, we have a different idea of Italy: multi-ethnic, pluralistic, free . . . a country in which the color of your skin, or race or religion doesn't matter, but, rather, honesty and sincerity of heart do."[46] Dario Franceschini, leader at the time of the Democratic Party, argued that Italy would continue to become a multicultural society just the same: "It's not for me or Berlusconi or anyone else to decide, for this will be the century of multi-ethnic societies. France, Great Britain and Germany are European nations with far more immigrants than us but they've worked for integration."[47]

And yet, France, Germany, and Great Britain have been turning inward, too. In Germany, where citizens with immigrant backgrounds make up 10 percent of the country's population and "foreign" residents make up another 9 percent, Chancellor Angela Merkel told a gathering of young members of her conservative Christian Democratic Union (CDU) party that Germany had failed in its attempts to build a multicultural society since guestworkers began migrating into Germany as the country's economy took off during the 1960s. In Merkel's words, "We kidded ourselves for a while that they wouldn't stay, but that's not the reality. . . . Of course the tendency had been to say, 'let's adopt the multicultural concept and live happily side by side, and be happy to be living with each other.' But this concept has failed, and failed utterly."[48] Merkel's remarks, which did not explain any further what she meant by "failed utterly," immediately received a standing ovation from her audience; her speech in October 2010 came a few days after a think tank study affiliated with Germany's center-left Social Democratic Party found that more than 30 percent of people in Germany believe the country is "overrun by foreigners" seeking generous social welfare benefits. The survey by the Friedrich Ebert Foundation also found that 13 percent of Germans would welcome a "Führer"—a German word for leader that is explicitly associated with Adolf Hitler—to run the country "with a firm hand," that 17 percent think Jews have too much influence, and that about 60 percent think Germany should "restrict the practice of Islam" among the country's four million Muslims.[49]

Even in the affluent northern regions of Italy, xenophobia persists—sometimes in digital media fashion. As of October 2009, a Facebook group with the title "Let's invade Zingonia and kill them all" had reached seven hundred members. Zingonia is Italy's most notorious ghetto, a neighborhood conceived during the 1960s as a planned district of Milan but has since degenerated into a slum; it was first inhabited by migrants from Italy's poorer southern regions and is now inhabited by immigrants mainly from Morocco and Pakistan. Police routinely raid the decaying apartment towers in the district as early as 5 a.m. An Italian woman who teaches English in Zingonia, Miriam Franchina, told a journalist that her students, many of them undocumented migrants, avoid officially registering for her classes: "They're just there, ghosts with a life-story to whisper and the fear of being chased after by the police."[50] As more immigrants have moved into Milan, more Italian voters have gravitated to Lega Nord. During Italy's 2008 election, Lega Nord ran a campaign "to clean out Zingonia, before it infects the nearby towns," setting up an election stall in the middle of Piazza Affari, the central plaza in the district that ironically is named for Milan's stock exchange but in reality is a trading center for drugs and prostitution. An article in the *European Union Times* described the "eccentric anti-immigrant measures" advocated by local and regional Lega Nord officials across northern Italy:

> Kebab shops have been banned from Capriate. In the north-eastern region of Friuli Venezia Giulia, the Lega has pushed for ambulances not to be made available to non-citizens. Their deputy, Matteo Savini, has gone as far as to demand that the seats on the Milan metro be reserved for the Milanese. Wearing of the so-called "burkini," the swimming costume that preserves Islamic modesty, is punishable by a 500 euro fine in Verona.
>
> When questioned about the law, the mayor, Gianluca Buonanno, commented that "Muslims can choose to swim in their own bathtubs." Giancarlo Gentilini, one of the Lega's most well known members, expressed a wish for the "elimination" of "gypsy children" and the "ethnic cleansing" of "faggots." In September 2008, he called for a "revolution against those who want to open mosques, phone centres and foreign shops." Such outbursts have done nothing to dent his popularity with the electorate; he served the maximum two terms as mayor of Treviso and is now the deputy mayor. As mayor, he is notorious for his decision to remove all the benches from the local park to "stop immigrants from gathering on them." The water and electricity of the Treviso mosque was cut off on the first day of Ramadan in 2009.[51]

The city of Treviso is a center of Islam within Italy, and Muslims living in the metropolitan area have increasingly reported harassment and intimidation by police when they attend services at local mosques, with police officers photographing Muslims walking into prayer services and also stopping Muslims outside mosques demanding to see their legal papers. The Italian government has also singled out Islam by refusing to provide mosques in Italy with government subsidies handed out each year to religious organizations representing a variety of other faiths, including Jewish, Hindu, and Buddhist temples, Greek Orthodox churches, and Jehovah's Witnesses centers. The government provides about 8 percent of income tax revenue each year to Italy's established churches—with the lion's share of the money going to Roman Catholic churches—but the government has refused to grant Islam legal recognition as one of Italy's established churches. Lawmakers from the ruling conservative coalition have cited radical clerics, polygamy, and limited rights for women as obstacles to official recognition of Islam. The lack of legal recognition sends a clear message of exclusion to the 1 million to 1.5 million Muslims now estimated to be living in Italy.

SWITZERLAND'S MINARET BAN

Far-right political parties have been rising across Europe for the past twenty years, appealing especially to citizens who worry that they—and their respective countries—are no longer in control of their destinies. Even in tiny Switzerland, stereotyped by many outsiders as a cosmopolitan haven for international institutions and discreet banks, voters have been turning against the rising immigrant population, especially the four hundred thousand Muslims who call Switzerland home and now make up about 5 percent of the country's population. In a November 2009 referendum sponsored by the far-right Swiss People's Party, the country's most popular political party, voters caught many political observers by surprise when they decided to ban the construction of new minarets in the country. The referendum called for adding a sentence to the country's constitution stating, in simple and stark terms, that "the construction of minarets is prohibited." Four minarets already attached to mosques in Switzerland were not affected by the referendum. The controversy that led to the ballot question dated back to 2006, when city officials in the town of Langenthal gave permission to a Muslim congregation to build a minaret atop the town's existing Islamic center, on condition that the traditional Muslim call to prayer would not be issued from the building. Switzerland already has some hundred and fifty mosques, four of which have minarets, and Muslims in Switzerland generally keep a low profile; many are guestworkers originally from Bosnia, Kosovo, and Turkey. Canton officials in Bern, however, opposed the decision, ostensibly because of local zoning problems, even as minarets in several other Swiss cities were already standing and the Swiss High Court had ruled that Muslims living in Switzerland had the right to build mosques with minarets.[52]

This was one of just two minarets being planned at the time in Switzerland, but it was enough to prompt the Swiss People's Party to initiate the referendum campaign with the help of a second political party, the Federal Democratic Union. Together, the two parties and their supporters argued that minarets are symbols of rising Muslim political and religious power that could eventually turn Switzerland into an Islamic nation. A majority of the country's voters backed up these arguments, with 57.5 percent of voters favoring the referendum even after the Swiss government objected that the ban would violate religious freedom and human rights in the country and would have the unintended consequences of provoking Islamist radicalism and harming Switzerland's global image. Amnesty International, for one, warned that a ban on minarets would contradict Switzerland's obligations to freedom of religious expression. "That Switzerland, a country with a long tradition of religious tolerance and the provision of refuge to the persecuted, should have accepted such a grotesquely discriminatory proposal is shocking," said one of Amnesty International's top European leaders.[53] At the same time, anyone familiar with the power of scare tactics in campaigning would not be surprised to see that many Swiss voters responded to fear-mongering: campaign posters by supporters of the referendum showed a Swiss flag sprouting black, missile-shaped minarets alongside a woman wearing a niqab to conceal her face. Such images played to prejudice and fear by fueling a perception within Swiss society, however false, that Muslim immigration posed a threat to the country.

Leaders of the Swiss People's Party used rather chilling language to describe their rationale in calling for the minaret ban: "We do not forbid Islam—we forbid the political symbol of Islamization, and this is the minaret," said Ulrich Schüler, a member of Switzerland's national parliament and a leader of the anti-minaret referendum campaign. Schüler noted repeatedly that he did not object to the construction of new mosques—only minarets—because of how he interpreted their symbolism:

> As a structure, the minaret has no religious character. It is not even mentioned in the Koran, nor in any other Islamic religious texts. Rather, the minaret is far more a symbol of the religious-political claim to power and dominance, which threatens—in the name of alleged freedom of religion—the constitutional rights of others. This is why the claim contradicts the constitution and rule of law in Switzerland.[54]

Other political and civic groups in Switzerland—many of them church-affiliated—made it clear that they saw the *ban* on minarets more threatening than minarets in themselves. The Swiss Council of Religions, which represents Protestant, Muslim, and Jewish religious leaders in the country, opposed the ban and during the campaign emphasized that its congregations support "integration instead of exclusion, as every human being is a divine creation from the point of view of Judaism, Christianity, and Islam. Ways must be found to deal with differences and to live together in peace and mutual respect for each other and for each other's beliefs." The church group also criticized the initiative as a huge step backward for freedom of religion and social inclusion in Switzerland:

> The minaret initiative does not solve any problems. On the contrary, it only contributes to suspicion, mistrust, and aggression against people of Muslim faith. The prohibition of minarets, moreover, would constitute a legal step backwards, as the Swiss people have already removed all religious exceptions from the federal constitution. Switzerland enjoys a long liberal tradition, one that seeks out dialogue and works towards a common learning process. The country recognizes that the true challenge lies in finding ways for all of the society's members to live together despite any differences among them.[55]

The leader of the Muslim congregation in Langenthal, Mutalip Karaademi, flatly rejected Ulrich Schüler's characterization of the minaret as a symbol representing conquest or domination. As he told a television interviewer: "It's just a symbol, nothing more. It's nice to see a house of God with minarets or church steeples or cupolas on synagogues. The architecture isn't as important as the campaigners make out." Karaademi also disagreed with the view that minarets on mosques would somehow restrict the integration of Muslims into Switzerland:

> The stop-the-minaret committee is waging a dirty campaign. . . . They call us terrorists; they call us radicals; they call us the Taliban, so many different labels, all of them wrong. We are fully integrated in Switzerland. We love this country almost more than our own. Our children were born here. They're more Swiss than Albanian. It's not true what they say. We're not as radical as they think, and I repeat, it's a scandal—they're waging a dirty campaign.[56]

Switzerland's minaret ban also placed democracy in direct tension with cosmopolitanism. After all, the referendum is normally a measure of citizenship as democratic empowerment and participation, but as often happens with ballot questions around the world, the referendum ended up sending a message of disrespect and intolerance to a segment of the country's population. In Switzerland, any proposal receiving more than 100,000 signatures from citizens becomes a ballot question with the potential to amend the country's constitution, and in this case, about 115,000 citizens signed papers to put the question on the ballot. A strong democratic outpouring on behalf of the ballot question emerged with the express purpose of narrowing public space in Switzerland. And once supporters of the ballot question launched their campaign, many everyday people and civic groups who opposed the referendum assumed it would fail and didn't refute its far-right supporters aggressively enough. As Swiss novelist Peter Stamm noted in a newspaper commentary after the referendum passed:

> Some consideration was given to having it declared invalid on the grounds that it was unconstitutional as well as a violation of the European Convention on Human Rights, but in the end the government agreed to allow the referendum to go forward, probably in the hope that it would be roundly defeated and thereby become a symbol of Swiss open-mindedness. So certain were the politicians of prevailing that hardly any publicity was fielded against the initiative.[57]

After the referendum, the country's largest newspaper, *Le Temps*, captured the political sentiment of critics by calling the vote a "brutal sign of hostility" to Muslims that was "inspired by fear, fantasy and

ignorance."[58] Government officials also expressed their shock and outrage, with the country's justice minister calling the result "undeniably
a reflection of the fears and uncertainties that exist among the population—concerns that Islamic fundamentalist ideas could lead to the
establishment of parallel societies."[59] Abdel Majri, the president of the
League of Swiss Muslims, told news reporters that his group had not
expected the ballot question to pass: "This is another step toward Is-
lamophobia in Switzerland and Europe in general."[60] Because voters in
more than half of Switzerland's cantons approved the measure—in fact,
the referendum won in twenty-two of the twenty-six cantons—the outright ban on minaret construction was added to the Swiss constitution.
The government had no immediate choice but to uphold the decision
of voters, and the European Court of Human Rights in July 2011 turned
down two appeals filed by Swiss Muslims contesting the ban. But the
altered constitution, even if it has constrained public space for Muslims
living in Switzerland, has not shut down public spaces for contestation
and debate over this question. Consider these lyrics by the country's
most popular rapper, Stress, himself an immigrant from Estonia, who
makes a career out of challenging the far right:

> My Switzerland sees its future in multiculturalism.
> My Switzerland doesn't see mosques and minarets as a threat.
> My Switzerland is open, pro-European
> And she doesn't make a fuss about granting citizenship to foreigners.
> For Switzerland, that's down and dirty political rap.[61]

CONCLUSION

In some respects, the struggles many European countries now face
over how to respond to migration and multiculturalism might seem
like domestic matters—or at most, common continental concerns—
operating at arm's length from more pronounced dynamics of globalization. The actual picture, however, is closely intertwined with
globalization in several important ways. First is the impact of the
current wave of migration on Europe's multilayered political systems,
as people from all across Africa and Asia continue making their way to
Europe. The presence of the European Union alongside the member
states has left the continent with a more intricate bureaucratic landscape of regulating immigration than ever before. The member states,

the European Union, and the European Court of Human Rights are still trying to sort out what kinds of laws and policies should be set as well as how responsibilities for accommodating immigrants and enforcing border controls should be distributed. The institution of European Union citizenship has cleared the way for nationals of the member states to live, work, and run for certain political offices in other member states and also encompasses the rights of citizens, at least in theory, to exert direct influence over European Union decision makers in Brussels and Strasbourg and hold Europe's supranational institutions accountable. Likewise, interest group activity has increased in Europe's hubs of governance. At the same time, access to the continent from beyond is tightening and lines of distinction between insiders and outsiders are hardening. Globalization has opened more opportunities for some, built more walls for others, and created additional restrictions for everyone. Calls from national leaders for European "solidarity" on immigration policy might very well result in formidable barriers separating Europe from the rest of the world, thereby restraining a thin version of solidarity to the European Union itself as an emerging but bounded polity writ large, rather than as a prototype of a truly cosmopolitan or globally embracing approach to solidarity.

Second, from the vantage point of Europe's immigrants themselves, those who manage to migrate to the European Union are often doing so based on the allure of what they perceive as universal aspects of *global* culture rather than any particular national or European culture. Many immigrants hoping to make the crossing from France into Britain seek to become part of the "global city" of London and tap into educational and professional opportunities for themselves and their children that are out of reach in their home countries. Consider the mother of a five-year-old girl, who had made her way to Calais from Eritrea; when asked by a news reporter if the journey was just too long and dangerous she responded: "Of course, but what else can I do? I want to go to England not for me, but for my baby. There are good schools there. I want her to learn English."[62] Europe's border zones such as Calais, Patras, and Lampedusa are not only key gateways in global migration, but are also flash points for international advocacy groups concerned about the rights of immigrants, refugees, and asylum seekers and venues of interest for global news organizations that situate personal stories of migrants into the global context of immigration debates; thus the stories of Europe's migrants feed into a broader global narrative.

With regard to the ongoing interplay and tension between globalization and citizenship, Europe's inward turn reminds us that despite an upsurge in transnational activism and allegiances within some segments of the population, overall public space in Europe has been retreating into national realms narrowly defined, neither widening nor deepening, and remains a far cry from the cosmopolitan principle that the dignity and well-being of each human person warrant equal moral concern and priority. The construction of fences, the bolstered patrols along external borders, the increase in deportations, the electoral victories for ultranationalist, anti-immigrant political parties, the sweeping denunciations of "multiculturalism" coming from key political figures, the success of ballot questions that discriminate against and disrupt the lives of immigrants, and draconian new laws that essentially reduce many immigrants and cultural minorities to second-class citizens—and sometimes exclude them entirely from politics and society—all remind us that reactionary politics often emerge as counter dynamics within globalization, as part of the push and pull between centralizing and localizing forces, between integration on the one hand and fragmentation on the other. Europe's predicament can be compared with the political situation in the United States, where anxieties about globalization and immigration have also emerged and intensified. The next chapter, then, shifts to the other side of the Atlantic.

CHAPTER 5

IMMIGRATION POLITICS AND THE CONTESTED AMERICAN DREAM

As the world economy crashed in late 2008 and early 2009 and the U.S. unemployment rate reached 10 percent nationwide, anti-immigration sentiments intensified in the United States—sentiments that had been rising even before as the country's real estate bubble burst and nearly destroyed the banking sector. The crisis eased only when the U.S. government stepped in with bailout funds and rock-bottom interest rates and decided to print money and take on higher levels of public debt. In such a severe economic climate—which laid bare the limits of the prevailing "market globalist" creed of neoliberalism and its orthodoxy of deregulation, privatization, and free trade—immigrants often became easy scapegoats for the country's economic troubles. This held fast despite reality: similar to Europe, immigrants in the United States contribute to the nation's economy by taking on low-wage, highly unstable, and dangerous jobs largely shunned by native-born Americans and—in contrast with parts of Europe—have kept the population of the United States growing at a time when birthrates otherwise would have fallen. The recent crest of American-style economic globalization has been accompanied by a growing backlash against immigrants. Regardless of which political party has control of the White House or Congress at any given time, populist political movements and state legislatures have increasingly been setting the agenda and driving the debate on immigration.

The United States ushered in the new century by repositioning its official immigration system more decisively within the enlarged security and counterterrorism apparatus of the government, and thereby reframing immigration issues primarily as security concerns rather than as public service ones, although the United States has long enforced varying degrees of border restrictions. Following the terrorist attacks in New York and Washington on September 11, 2001, the George W. Bush administration folded many U.S. government agencies into a new cabinet-level Department of Homeland Security—with the term "homeland security" signifying a marked turn inward and a view of outsiders as inherently threatening. As part of this reorganization, the federal agency handling immigration policy and new citizenship applications—the former Immigration and Naturalization Service—took on a new identity as it moved from the U.S. Department of Justice and into the new "homeland security" matrix. In contrast with its predecessor, the new Bureau of Citizenship and Immigration Services no longer polices border zones—in 2003 the former agency's "border security" functions were handed over to a newly created agency, the Directorate of Border and Transportation Security. Instead, the new citizenship bureau gained additional powers to detain and question immigrants and visa holders suspected of being connected to terrorist organizations. Previously, periods of detention were limited to twenty-four hours, but after 9/11 these were extended to indefinite lengths of time on a case-by-case basis.

The current state of affairs is a contrast from the very first U.S. immigration agency that opened its doors in 1864, at a time when the United States had a largely "open door" policy, despite a history of social exclusion and discrimination directed toward immigrants and outright legal exclusion of immigrants from China under a law passed in 1882. By the 1890s, immigration restrictions began to creep into the system, although the U.S. government still did not require new arrivals to carry passports or visas. That changed in 1924, when a new and comprehensive Immigration Act imposed quotas on the numbers of immigrants from specific countries and regions. Outright bans were placed on countries across the Asia-Pacific region, including China, Japan, Korea, the Philippines, India, Thailand (then known as Siam), and Malaysia. The United States also prohibited the entry of certain groups of people, such as men practicing polygamy as well as those suffering from contagious diseases and conditions diagnosed as mental illnesses. Many immigrants who landed in these sorts of categories never made it past the holding centers at Ellis Island in New York Harbor, which operated as the gateway for most of the twenty-three million Europeans who arrived in the United States from 1880 to 1930, a half century in which the country's population more than doubled.[1] As the country recovered from the Great Depression, the U.S. government combined immigration and naturalization functions into a single agency in 1933. The new agency operated within the U.S. Labor Department but shifted over to the Department of Justice when the outbreak of World War II created a political climate similar to the post-9/11 era, with immigration and security interlinked more closely than before in American public policy. Most European refugees who fled Nazi Germany were not able to enter the United States.

The most dramatic step forward in U.S. immigration policy came in 1965, when Congress abolished the quota system of 1924 that had favored white immigrants from European countries. By the year 2000, 85 percent of the immigrant population in the United States came from outside Europe, compared with 40 percent in 1970. As recently as 1990, the prevailing political currents favored permitting greater numbers of immigrants to strengthen the country's economic base alongside an aging population. That year, President George H. W. Bush signed legislation that increased legal immigration quotas by 40 percent to accept 700,000 new immigrants per year, compared with 500,000 before the new law took effect. Just a few years later, a commission on immigration reform appointed by President Bill Clinton in a very different political climate proposed reducing the quota of legal immigrants to 550,000, though the quota remains at 700,000 per year. American public opinion began to turn sharply against immigration precisely as the effects of economic globalization were becoming more visible, with growing numbers of manufacturing jobs moving overseas. Once the North American Free Trade Agreement took effect in 1994, it became infinitely more attractive for American businesses to hire cheap labor in newly opened factories in cities just across the border in Mexico.

While the Statue of Liberty became the gateway to the United States during the peak of European immigration to the United States a century ago, in this century the icon of the times might be the "border fence" that is actually a series of barriers totaling about seven hundred miles along the border between Mexico and portions of Texas, New Mexico, Arizona, and California. Spurred by rhetoric that the borders ought to be "secured" to stop illegal immigration, the George W. Bush administration cast the construction of the barriers as so urgent that Michael Chertoff, the administration's head of the Department of Homeland Security, decided to waive more than thirty federal laws that he said could interfere with swift construction along the border. These included numerous laws intended to protect the natural environment and many wildlife and endangered species—including America's national symbol, the bald eagle—as well as the gravesites of Native American Indians who never regarded the territory where the United States and Mexico now meet as signifying a valid legal or geopolitical border of any kind. When the U.S. Congress approved the construction of the border fence in 2005, not only did lawmakers give Mr. Chertoff unprecedented power to void any federal law that could be viewed as impeding the project, but they also prohibited the federal courts from ruling on whether Mr. Chertoff's decisions were legal or appropriate. As one skeptic noted: "So long as Mr. Chertoff is willing to say it is necessary to void a given law, his word is final."[2] Two environmental groups sued in federal court to stop construction of the border fence, arguing that Congress violated the U.S. Constitution by handing over such sweeping powers to the executive branch while at the same time denying the judiciary any opportunity for oversight. However, a federal court ruled against the lawsuit and in June 2008 the U.S. Supreme Court declined to hear the case.

While some proclaim that globalization heralds a world without walls, in the United States these new barriers piecing together the border fence underscore how new kinds of walls have been rising—quite literally, in the country that continues to set the agenda for economic globalization. The George W. Bush administration also set forth plans to install a "virtual fence" with a series of networked cameras, sensors, radar, and communications gear intended to enable officers from the U.S. Border Patrol to catch illegal immigrants and smugglers more quickly. However, the U.S. government has found that foolproof immigration controls along a land border of about two thousand miles are not easy to implement, even in the age of high technology. The construction of the virtual fence encountered many technical problems and the Obama administration, after initially supporting the plan, announced in March 2010 that it would halt the project immediately, after two pilot projects in Arizona failed to work.

The end of the program marked the third time that the U.S. government gave up on an effort to use innovative technology to tighten the border. Between 1998 and 2005, the government reportedly spent $429 million on surveillance initiatives that the *Washington Post* reported "were so unreliable that only 1 percent of alarms led to arrests."[3] Just as skeptics warned in early 2011 that Greece would find it difficult to develop an airtight system to deter immigrants even after building a fence along its border, the United States has learned this lesson through trial and error. The cases that we will focus on in this chapter—a highly controversial state immigration law, proposals to curtail or even abolish the tradition of "birthright citizenship," and ongoing efforts to pass national legislation that would help the children of undocumented immigrants eventually gain U.S. citizenship—all serve to illustrate how the broader immigration debate in the United States today is closely intertwined with globalization and its effects.

THE CONTESTED ARIZONA IMMIGRATION LAW

The single most powerful salvo in the recent immigration debate in the United States has been a controversial law enacted in April 2010 by the border state of Arizona. The law was temporarily blocked, for the most part, by a judge in U.S. District Court on July 28, 2010, just one day before it was slated to take effect, and its fate ultimately will be decided by the U.S. Supreme Court. Known officially as Senate Bill (SB) 1070, the most contested provisions of the Arizona law make it a crime for immigrants to be present in the state without carrying documents confirming their legal status; the new law awarded local and state police officers broad powers to detain anyone in Arizona suspected of being in the United States illegally. The law also allows citizens to sue government agencies that fail to enforce immigration laws and bans employers from hiring undocumented migrants for day labor or knowingly transporting them. (An earlier Arizona measure, passed in 2007 after an effort in the U.S. Senate to reform the immigration system fell apart, prohibits employers from hiring undocumented immigrants for permanent jobs; this law was upheld by the U.S. Supreme Court in May 2011.) The 2010 Arizona law became a prime example of how regional political actors—in this case a state government—have recognized that many of their citizens are increasingly worried about a loss of control over their destinies, in an era of global interdependence and interconnectedness, and in response have taken assertive new measures to "circle the wagons," sending their constituents and the rest of the world strong messages that local decisions can still leverage power in the face of globalization.

The law entered the books at a time when 11.9 million people were believed to be living without proper documentation in the United States—with an estimated 460,000 of them in the state of Arizona. Supporters of the law argued that it defended national laws that U.S. government immigration officials have not enforced: "The reason Arizona passed this bill . . . is because the federal government wasn't doing its job," said U.S. Rep. Trent Franks, a Republican from Arizona. "Arizona is just trying to do the things that the federal government failed to do. All we've done here is to put in law in Arizona what was already federal law."[4] The law was passed shortly after a sensational crime in March 2010 in which a fifty-eight-year-old member of one of the best-known ranching families in southeastern Arizona was found shot to death on his ranch just after making a radio call to his brother saying that he was aiding someone he believed to be an undocumented migrant. Shortly after that call, Robert N. Krentz, Jr., went missing. Several hours later, police found his body in his all-terrain vehicle, as well as footprints leading to the Mexican border twenty miles away. Police suspected a drug smuggler might have shot him; the case prompted many politicians from Arizona and its neighbors across the Southwest to call for the U.S. government to dispatch National Guard troops to the border and tilted the political climate more favorably toward the tighter restrictions in SB 1070.

If it were to be implemented in full, the Arizona law would represent the most sweeping crackdown targeting U.S. immigrants in a generation.

Fiery public debate has targeted the law itself as well as several copycat bills proposed in other states. On the same day that Arizona's Republican governor, Jan Brewer, signed the bill into law, President Barack Obama sharply criticized the law while speaking at a naturalization ceremony for a group of active-duty military officers in the Rose Garden at the White House. Obama called upon Congress to put through an overhaul of U.S. immigration laws, warning that "our failure to act responsibly at the federal level will only open the door to irresponsibility by others." Taking a rare step for a sitting president to criticize a state law, Obama added that Arizona's new law threatens "to undermine basic notions of fairness that we cherish as Americans, as well as the trust between police and their communities that is so crucial to keeping us safe."[5]

Hours later, Arizona's governor fired back during a news conference held at the state's National Guard headquarters. Jan Brewer told reporters it was not the job of the state governments to secure the border "but we have no other choice" in the absence of stronger restrictions from the federal government: "Those who have failed to protect us have shown only weakness and delay," Brewer said, accusing the Obama administration of having "simply turned a blind eye to the issues that Arizona is being overrun by illegal immigration, terrorizing the citizens. No matter the cost, no matter the sacrifice, we cannot shirk government's [principal] responsibilities to the citizens we serve to provide safety and security."[6] Insisting as she signed the bill into law that she would not tolerate racial profiling or racial discrimination in the enforcement of the law—and noting how she worked with state lawmakers to insert additional language in the interests of respecting civil rights of all persons—Brewer invoked the idea of citizenship along with the right of Arizona to protect its interests and its citizens:

> Border-related violence and crime due to illegal immigration are critically important issues to the people of our state, to my Administration and to me, as your Governor and as a citizen. There is no higher priority than protecting the citizens of Arizona. We cannot sacrifice our safety to the murderous greed of drug cartels. We cannot stand idly by as drop houses, kidnappings and violence compromise our quality of life. We cannot delay while the destruction happening south of our international border creeps its way north. We in Arizona have been more than patient waiting for Washington to act. But decades of federal

inaction and misguided policy have created a dangerous and unacceptable situation. . . . Today, with my unwavering signature on this legislation—Arizona strengthens its security within our borders.[7]

In providing a rationale for the law based on a sense of responsibility from the government to its citizens, Brewer seemed to rely on a very narrow definition of "citizens" as those under the legal jurisdiction of a particular government. Using language strongly indicating a desire for Arizona to empower itself amid widely perceived vulnerability to globalization in general and migration in particular, Brewer added that the new law "represents another tool for our state to use as we work to solve a crisis we did not create and the federal government has refused to fix—the crisis caused by illegal immigration and Arizona's porous border."[8] Although Brewer justified the new law citing concern about crime and violence, local media reported that the statistics actually show an improving public safety picture in Arizona, with the statewide violent crime rate dropping every year since 2004, murders in the state's largest city, Phoenix, down 50 percent since 2003, and illegal border crossings down by 49 percent since 2004. Moreover, Brewer's campaign chairman and policy adviser for her 2010 election bid also worked as a lobbyist for the largest private, profit-making prison company in the United States, which had a U.S. government contract to detain undocumented immigrants picked up in Arizona.[9] In fact, the concern about cross-border crime is at least as pressing on the Mexican side of the border, as police in Mexico have confiscated tens of thousands of guns from Arizona that had supplied drug cartels in Mexico. Some of the guns were purchased legally in Arizona at gun shows under a loophole allowing private individuals to sell guns without asking buyers for identification and without running criminal background checks on the buyers.[10]

Following the signing of the new law, numerous civic and advocacy groups filed lawsuits in Arizona's federal courts, including the American Civil Liberties Union, the National Coalition of Latino Clergy and Christian Leaders, as well as various individuals who argued that their rights would be violated. For example, a Washington, D.C., resident and U.S. citizen, Roberto Javier Frisancho, filed a lawsuit in April 2010 just days after Brewer signed the bill, saying he planned to visit Arizona in September 2010 to conduct research and worried about how he would be treated; his lawsuit stated that the new law "establishes a crime of being Hispanic."[11] Likewise, a Tucson police officer, Martin Escobar, filed a lawsuit saying he would not be able to carry out the new law in a race-neutral way and that law enforcement officials were now forced "to actively engage in racial profiling to detain, question, and require every Hispanic" to prove their legal status.[12] Police associations in the state were divided on the new law; the Arizona Association of Chiefs of Police opposed the law, while the Phoenix Law Enforcement Association, which represents rank-and-file police officers in Arizona's largest city, supported the measure.

Religious groups also diverged on the new law, creating a tricky situation especially for the Church of Jesus Christ of Latter-day Saints, the Mormons. The coauthor of the bill, Arizona state senator Russell Pearce, is Mormon and claimed that SB 1070 followed the Mormon teaching of obedience to the law. However, the Mormons have worked aggressively to recruit Latino members to the church, and church elders avoided taking an official position on the law.[13] On the other hand, the National Council of Churches and the U.S. Conference of Catholic Bishops denounced the law. One of the most direct and blistering critiques of the new law came from Los Angeles cardinal Roger Mahony, who posted an entry on his blog calling the measure "the country's most retrogressive, mean-spirited, and useless anti-immigrant law." In his words:

> The tragedy of the law is its totally flawed reasoning: that immigrants come to our country to rob, plunder, and consume public resources. That is not only false, the premise is nonsense. . . . The law is wrongly assuming that Arizona residents, including local law enforcement personnel, will now shift their total attention to guessing which Latino-looking or foreign-looking person may or may not have proper documents. That's also nonsense. American people are fair-minded and respectful. I can't imagine Arizonans now reverting to German Nazi and Russian Communist techniques whereby people are required to turn one another in to the authorities on any suspicion of documentation. Are children supposed to call 911 because one parent does not have proper papers? Are family members and neighbors now supposed to spy on one another, create total distrust across neighborhoods and communities, and report people because of suspicions based upon appearance?[14]

The cardinal added that the real solution, from his point of view, would be national immigration reform that would acknowledge the country's dependence on immigrant labor. Noting the contradictions inherent in the current state of affairs in the United States, Mahony wrote in his post: "We have built a huge wall along our southern border, and have posted in effect two signs next to each other. One reads, 'No Trespassing,' and the other reads 'Help Wanted.' The ill-conceived Arizona law does nothing to balance our labor needs."[15]

Similarly, a wide range of critics lambasted the new law for trampling on basic civil rights and civil liberties and argued, contrary to Governor Brewer, that Arizona police officers would now be terrorizing the public if pressed into enforcing the new law. Mexico's president, Felipe Calderón, condemned the new law as opening the door to "intolerance, hate, discrimination, and abuse in law enforcement," and Mexico's government issued an official travel warning for Arizona stating that "all Mexican citizens could be bothered or questioned without motive at any moment."[16] However, commentators were quick to point out that Mexico has its own Arizona-style law requiring local police to check the immigration status of persons suspected of being undocumented migrants, and that police officers in Mexico engage in racial profiling and routinely harass migrants from Central America. According to a report by Mexico's National Human Rights Commission, nearly ten thousand migrants were kidnapped in Mexico and held for ransom, some of them with the direct involvement of police officers, who are known for routinely stopping undocumented migrants and shaking them down for bribes. As Melissa Vertíz of the Fray Matías de Córdova Human Rights Center in Tapachula, Mexico, noted with skepticism: "The Mexican government should probably clean up its own house before looking at someone else's."[17]

In August 2010 the statewide newspaper, the *Arizona Republic,* published a list of cities officially boycotting the state, including Berkeley, Boston, Los Angeles, Oakland, St. Paul, and Seattle, among many others; typically these boycotts amounted to travel bans and prohibitions on buying any items made in the state. Travel boycotts and conference cancellations came from dozens of organizations such as the Leadership Conference on Civil and Human Rights, the National Alliance of Black Educators, the United Food and Commercial Workers International Union, and the World Boxing Council. Most notably, just hours after Governor Brewer signed the bill into law, board members for the American Immigration Lawyers Association voted unanimously to cancel its national convention scheduled for September 2010 in Scottsdale. The National Urban League canceled its 2012 conference in Phoenix, and the high school girls' basketball team from Highland Park, Illinois, canceled a trip to play in a basketball tournament amid speculation that at least one of the players might have been an undocumented immigrant.[18] Interestingly, the protests and boycotts targeting Arizona seem to have originated mainly from the United States rather than overseas— the 3,412 signatures (as of January 2012) on the "Boycott Arizona!" page of one of the more popular online petition sites were nearly all from U.S. citizens.[19] Likewise, one of the most common epithets against the Arizona law decried it as "un-American," underscoring how the rhetoric against the law seemed to work more effectively through the prism of the American political creed rather than its accompanying universal principles.

In general, however, public opinion seemed to side with the supporters of the Arizona law. One week after Brewer signed the bill, *Gallup* reported that more than 75 percent of Americans had heard about it, and 51 percent of these people supported the law while 39 percent were opposed.[20] *Rasmussen Reports* focused more narrowly on Arizona voters and found that 70 percent of likely voters approved of the law, although 53 percent of its respondents thought the law would end up violating the civil rights of some U.S. citizens.[21] Another nationwide survey conducted in late May 2010 by *Angus Reid Global Monitor* found even stronger support—67 percent of respondents agreed with the idea that police should arrest people unable to provide documentation to prove they are in the United States legally.[22]

Advocates of immigrants, on the other hand, argued that public opinion polling has limited value in helping the U.S. government shape immigration policy: "Very few people understand the complexities of immigration law, and there is a lot of confusion about how and why people are here illegally," said Ben Johnson, the director of the American Immigration Council. "The deeper questions are whether people are OK with citizens and legal residents being stopped by police and asked to prove their status, and how far police can go to creating the reasonable suspicion."[23] Political scientists, meanwhile, noted that the public opinion data seemed influenced by the downturn in the American economy. In the words of Barbara O'Connor, the director of the Institute for the Study of Politics and Media at California State University, Sacramento: "History has a way of showing that when times are tough, people lash out more strongly against what they feel is beyond their control—in this case, immigrants."[24] Illustrating this point, in a sense, a man who identified himself as Jon Spencer from Tucson, Arizona, posted on the *New York Times* discussion boards that he genuinely felt he had lost his freedom to live peacefully in his home state:

> Yeah, OK, conservative Arizona flipped out on this one. But when are we going to militarize the border so that illegal immigration is stopped? East coast liberals, and liberals everywhere, are opposed to militarizing the border. It offends them and all their sensibilities of what the USA should stand for. But I am a scientist who has worked outdoors in Arizona for 28 years, and last year I started carrying a pistol. Why? Because the desert is being overrun by immigrants, drug runners, car theifs [sic], and criminals of various sorts, any of whom I might encounter in the middle of nowhere, without cell phone contact for miles, etc. This is my land too! I feel ripped off by feeling that I have to carry a gun to do my job anywhere within 40 miles of the border. I say "build the wall." Then we won't need national ID cards, and liberals can find some other global catharsis zone for their bleeding hearts.

Another commenter on the discussion boards—with a different point of view—connected the dots to the North American Free Trade Agreement and its impact upon Mexico:

> This is a bunch of chickens coming home to roost. The border can never be sealed without draconian measures unless one of the main driving forces for migration is dealt with. I'm talking about so-called free-trade agreements which are more about the freedom to move capital than to move goods, to the benefit only of the "haves." NAFTA destroyed the livelihoods of many small farmers in Mexico, who flooded the cities which were unable to support them, so naturally they looked north of the border. The ones that got here compete for service jobs with Americans whose manufacturing jobs were exported and whose communities were hollowed out by NAFTA. The architects of NAFTA have much to answer for.

These were among the 559 comments posted by readers of the *New York Times* in response to a scorching commentary, titled "Breathing

While Undocumented," by Linda Greenhouse, the longtime Supreme Court correspondent, now a senior fellow at Yale Law School. Known for her usually dispassionate analysis of the nation's constitutional debates, Greenhouse minced no words in blasting SB 1070:

> I'm glad I've already seen the Grand Canyon. Because I'm not going back to Arizona as long as it remains a police state, which is what the appalling anti-immigrant bill that Gov. Jan Brewer signed into law last week has turned it into. What would Arizona's revered libertarian icon, Barry Goldwater, say about a law that requires the police to demand proof of legal residency from any person with whom they have made "any lawful contact" and about whom they have "reasonable suspicion" that "the person is an alien who is unlawfully present in the United States?" Wasn't the system of internal passports one of the most distasteful features of life in the Soviet Union and apartheid-era South Africa?[25]

Activists on behalf of Latinos in the United States joined forces to criticize the new law, and many political observers noted that the law could well backfire for the Republican Party in its efforts to court Latino voters as a key swing voting bloc, now that large numbers of Latinos view the law as opening the door for racial and ethnic profiling. A key Latino civil rights group, the Mexican American Legal Defense and Educational Fund, accused Governor Brewer of having "caved to the radical fringe" and launching Arizona "into a spiral of pervasive fear, community distrust, increased crime and costly litigation, with nationwide repercussions."[26] More significantly, the organization promised to challenge the new law in court, on grounds that states do not have authority to implement, on their own, measures regulating immigration that conflict with U.S. government policy and the Constitution itself. The U.S. Department of Justice did just that in early July 2010, when it filed a lawsuit asking a federal court in Phoenix to issue an injunction that would stop the law from taking effect as scheduled on July 29, 2010.

The suit argued that the law violated the U.S. Constitution by taking away control over immigration reserved exclusively for the U.S. government, and that federal law enforcement officials would be forced into the "detention and harassment of authorized visitors, immigrants and citizens."[27] Rather than anchoring the case on allegations that the new law would lead to racial profiling, U.S. attorney general Eric Holder instead emphasized that the law would interfere with the authority of the U.S. government and argued that government resources would be wasted pursuing individuals who posed no threat to the country's security, thereby preventing the government from focusing adequately on more substantial threats. In his words: "Arizonans are understandably frustrated with illegal immigration. But diverting federal resources away from dangerous aliens such as terrorism suspects and aliens with criminal records will impact the entire country's safety."[28]

By the time the U.S. Justice Department filed its suit, several civil rights groups, including the American Civil Liberties Union and the Mexican American Legal Defense and Educational Fund, had already filed similar lawsuits of their own. Taken together, these lawsuits were meant not only to stop Arizona's new law but also to stop at least twenty other states considering similar laws at the time. As stated in the Justice Department's lawsuit: "The Constitution and the federal immigration laws do not permit the development of a patchwork of state and local immigration policies throughout the country."[29] At the same time, in the summer of 2010 there seemed to be little support for a genuine immigration reform measure similar to a bipartisan initiative proposed earlier in the year by two U.S. Senators, Democrat Charles E. Schumer of New York and Republican Lindsey Graham of South Carolina—which Obama supported in his July speech on immigration.

Under the plan from these two senators, immigrants without the required documentation would be required to admit that they had broken the law—either by entering into the United States illegally or by staying past the expiration of a visa—and then pay fines and back taxes, pass background checks, prove they could speak English, and then "go to the back of the line" to gain permanent residency into the United States. The two senators also called for an employment verification system requiring biometric Social Security cards to make it more difficult for undocumented immigrants to find jobs.[30] As of December 2011, this proposal still had not moved forward in the U.S. Congress, and critics pointed out that its proposed remedies were highly problematic. Biometric cards pose privacy and reliability issues, and many consider it callous and unrealistic to force undocumented immigrants to apologize and pay fines, and then expect them to go "to the back of the line," which, in practice, would mean they would have to leave the United States—and their families here—and wait as long as twenty years to reach the front of the line for permanent residency.[31]

On July 28, 2010, just one day before the Arizona law was scheduled to take effect, U.S. District Court judge Susan Bolton ruled to block its most controversial sections: one that required police officers in Arizona to check a person's immigration status while enforcing other laws, and another that required immigrants in Arizona to prove they had legal documents authorizing their presence in the United States or risk facing state charges. In the text of her decision, officially classified as a "preliminary injunction" to block these aspects of the new law until a final ruling emerged, Bolton agreed with the logic employed by the U.S. Justice Department and ruled that Arizona could not make it a "state crime" for immigrants to be in the state without documents proving their legal status. She also blocked provisions of the new law that allowed police to detain anyone arrested for any crime until the person's immigration status was determined. As Judge Bolton wrote: "Requiring Arizona law enforcement officials and agencies to determine the immigration status of every person who is arrested burdens lawfully present aliens because their liberty will be restricted while their status is checked."[32] The ruling basically placed the central aspects of the new law on ice, at least temporarily. The U.S. Supreme Court announced in December 2011 that it will consider the state of Arizona's appeal to the ruling.[33]

Scholars who focus on immigration were skeptical that Judge Bolton's ruling to invalidate key provisions of the Arizona law would necessarily address the underlying public frustration over immigration. Some wondered if it would have the effect of pushing the public for more severe immigration policies at the national level. As law professor Peter Spiro wrote in response to Judge Bolton's ruling:

> Congress has dropped the ball on immigration reform and now we have the courts telling the states that they can't pick it up. Anti-immigrant activists will redouble their efforts to mandate more effective enforcement at the federal level and to block anything that smacks of amnesty. What comes out of this new mix may not serve immigrant interests. . . .
>
> It might have been better if Arizona's law had been allowed to die a natural death. Arizona's image has already taken a major hit. If S.B. 1070 had gone into effect, it would have taken a toll on the state's economy in the form of lost tourism and business boycotts, from here and abroad. Implementing the law (a messy one that would have been prone to variable application) would inevitably have produced stories making the state look even worse. In the end, Arizona would probably have backed down on its own, in a way that would have better

demonstrated the error of its ways. . . . As it is, today's ruling increases the chances of similarly unfortunate legislation at the national level.[34]

DEBATE OVER "BIRTHRIGHT CITIZENSHIP"

At the start of 2012, the most controversial aspects of Arizona's immigration law remained in a state of suspension. The national debate over immigration, however, took a new turn when a group of mostly Republican lawmakers from fourteen states, including Arizona, joined forces to propose bills in their respective state legislatures to create two kinds of birth certificates: one for children of citizens and permanent legal residents, and another one for children of immigrants whose parents were unable to provide documents confirming either their residency or citizenship in the United States. Some of the lawmakers also proposed creating a new definition of state citizenship, alongside national citizenship, that would specifically exclude babies born in their states to families in which both the mother and father were unauthorized immigrants. "We are here to send a very public message to Congress: We want to bring an end to the illegal alien invasion that is having such a negative impact on our states," said Daryl Metcalfe, a Republican state representative from Pennsylvania, at a news conference of state lawmakers as the U.S. Congress opened a new session with the Republican Party in control after four years in the minority.[35] Confrontations at the news conference underscored the tempestuous immigration debate in the United States: supporters clapped and cheered while protesters interrupted the speakers four times and carried posters that accused the lawmakers of intolerance and racism.

The motivation for this campaign comes amid growing interest among some American political actors in trying to undo the citizenship provisions in the U.S. Constitution's Fourteenth Amendment, adopted in 1868 to protect the citizenship status of former slaves born outside the United States and freed during the Civil War. The opening statement to the amendment reads as follows: "All persons born or naturalized in the United States, and subject to the jurisdiction thereof, are citizens of the United States and of the state where they reside. No State shall make or enforce any law which shall abridge the privileges or immunities of citizens of the United States; nor shall any State deprive any person of life, liberty, or property, without due process of law; nor deny to any person within its jurisdiction the equal protection of the laws."[36] The Fourteenth Amendment essentially struck down an 1857 U.S. Supreme Court decision in the infamous case of *Dred Scott v. Sandford*, which stated that persons of African descent could never be American citizens; the ruling contributed to conditions that deteriorated into the Civil War in 1861. In 1898, exactly thirty years after the Fourteenth Amendment took effect, the U.S. Supreme Court decided in *United States v. Wong Kim Ark* that the language in the amendment extended U.S. citizenship to a child born in the United States to a Chinese immigrant couple—at a time when Chinese immigrants to the United States were prohibited from entering the country and Chinese adults already living in the United States were not allowed to become naturalized citizens. Ever since, the language in the Fourteenth Amendment has usually been interpreted to mean that any children born on American soil, regardless of whether their parents are U.S. citizens, are "subject to the jurisdiction" of the U.S. government and are U.S. citizens. The U.S. Supreme Court reinforced this view even further when the justices affirmed in a footnote within a 1982 decision, *Plyler v. Doe*, that undocumented immigrants are indeed subject to the jurisdiction of the United States.

As the immigration debate in the United States has heated up in recent years, the Fourteenth Amendment and its provision of birthright citizenship have come under attack in two different ways, first by claims that unauthorized immigrants and their children should *not* be regarded as subject to the jurisdiction of the United States, and second by calls for changes in the amendment's language. Rather than propose a new constitutional amendment—which would require ratification by thirty-eight of the fifty states—some state lawmakers seeking to modify the birth certificates of children born to undocumented immigrants hope to enact measures that could eventually lead to a U.S. Supreme Court decision reinterpreting the amendment with regard to birthright citizenship. Those behind such proposals maintain that abolishing birthright citizenship is not as extreme as it might seem. "Only a handful of countries in the world grant citizenship based on the GPS location of the birth," said John Kavanagh, one of the Arizona legislators involved.[37] For the most part, however, constitutional law scholars believe that the Fourteenth Amendment and the current model of birthright citizenship will withstand any potential legal tinkering, that the U.S. Supreme Court would refuse to hear these kinds of cases, given its previous decisions, and that it is more likely that the court would strike down any attempts by state governments to tamper with the granting of birth certificates. In the words of Gabriel J. Chin, a law professor at the University of Arizona and the grandson of a Chinese immigrant who came to the United States during the ban on Chinese immigration. "This is political theater, not a serious effort to create a legal test. It strikes me as unwise, un-American and unconstitutional."[38]

Other scholars maintain that the language of the amendment can be kept intact and interpreted in ways that would modify birthright citizenship but stop short of abolishing the tradition entirely. Law professor Peter H. Schuck has pointed out that when Congress debated the amendment back in 1868 and when the Supreme Court issued its related decision in 1898, no one considered the possibility of U.S. citizenship for children of undocumented immigrants, because there were no federal laws at the time requiring immigrants to hold any specific resident legal status. Despite the Supreme Court's 1982 reference in *Plyler v. Doe* that affirmed that the Fourteenth Amendment protects children of undocumented immigrants, Schuck has argued that Congress retains the right to regulate the citizenship of children born in the United States to parents who are not permanent "resident aliens," meaning visitors to the United States as well as undocumented immigrants. In Schuck's view, Congress could resolve the issue by making birthright citizenship conditional on completing a certain number of years in American schools; around the age of ten, children of undocumented immigrants and visitors to the United States could apply to become U.S. citizens regardless of their parent's legal status. Schuck argues it would be a mistake to abolish birthright citizenship outright because it would increase the number of undocumented people in the United States, especially children who would run the risk of being "legally stranded, perhaps even stateless, in a country where they were born and may spend their lives."[39]

Despite the protection that birthright citizenship offers children born in the United States, the U.S. government retains the power to deport undocumented immigrants even if they are raising children who are U.S. citizens; their children must wait until they turn twenty-one before they can file papers to sponsor their parents for legal immigration to the United States. The rise of the populist Tea Party movement in the United States has prompted some elected officials to argue that children born in the United States to undocumented immigrants should be deported with their parents. "And we're not being mean," said U.S. Rep. Duncan Hunter, a Republican from San Diego, California, who also called the controversial Arizona immigration law a "fantastic starting point" while speaking at Tea Party rally in April 2010. "We're just saying it takes more than walking across the border to become an American citizen. It's what's in our souls."[40] At the time Hunter also supported a bill in the U.S. House of Representatives—that was not passed—calling for an end to "birthright citizenship" for children of undocumented immigrants. His vague comment about "what's in our souls" received a stern reply from a Connecticut resident who wrote a letter to the *New York Times:* "I would argue that risking one's life in the hopes of making a better life for oneself and one's child in a new and unwelcoming country is the very definition of what is in the American soul. Precisely what does Mr. Hunter think the Pilgrims were?"[41] Many Latino elected officials in the Republican Party expressed dismay that their party was moving toward challenging birthright citizenship as a central element of its immigration policy: "Rather than attacking babies born in the United States and the Constitution, we demand they target our suffering economy," said Deedee Garcia Blase, a spokeswoman for Somos Republicans, a Texas-based organization of Latino Republicans critical of their party's position on immigration.[42]

The derisive term "anchor babies" in American political rhetoric sometimes conflates two very different groups into a single category. One group is the children of undocumented immigrants, who often suffer from considerable poverty but live in the United States for extended periods of time, even on a permanent basis despite their lack of legal status. Another group is the children of people around the world—many of them quite wealthy—who fly to the United States for brief visits specifically to endow their children with U.S. citizenship, and opening the door for their children, once they reach the age of twenty-one, to sponsor other family members for legal immigration to the United States. While total births in the United States rose by 5 percent in the six-year-period from 2000 to 2006, according to the National Center for Health Statistics, the total number of births in the United States to "non-resident mothers" rose by 53 percent during the same period.[43] The current wave of globalization undoubtedly has increased the trend of "birth tourism" to the United States in ways that the architects of the Fourteenth Amendment probably never envisioned in the nineteenth century. It highlights the irony that national citizenship status matters more than ever in the current global era, with an informal hierarchy of the most desirable or coveted national citizenships in the eyes of the global public.

The countries currently generating the most attention for birth tourism include South Korea, Turkey, and increasingly, China, as these countries grow more prosperous. Growing numbers of families from South Korea, for example, see U.S. citizenship as easing the way for their children to access American schools and universities, gain international employment opportunities, and, in the case of boys, avoid the country's two years of mandatory national military service. The trend in South Korea—a country very mindful of pecking order and hierarchy—goes back to the start of the new century, as the country made a solid recovery from the Asian financial crisis. A growing professional class began to realize that U.S. passports would provide their children with an alternative to South Korea's pressure-cooker educational system; they also realized the legal system in the United States poses no obstacles for visitors on short-term B-2 tourist visas, commonly with a duration of six months, to give birth at hospitals in the United States as long as they have the money to pay their medical bills.

South Korean families target the United States—and to a lesser degree, Canada—because these two countries continue their traditions of birthright citizenship, in contrast with other popular English-speaking countries, such as Great Britain, Australia, and New Zealand. The women typically stay in the United States for much less than six months, flying back home to their affluent neighborhoods in Seoul as soon as they receive local birth certificates and U.S. passports for their newborns. Journalist Barbara Demick from the *Los Angeles Times* looked closely at this trend in its early years and profiled a Korean "birth tourist" who was preparing to spend about US$20,000 in early 2002 to cover an airline ticket and medical expenses that normally would have been covered by South Korea's national health insurance had she given birth in Seoul:

> Among several expectant mothers who talked about their plans for giving birth in the United States, Kim Jeong Yeon was unusual in that

she was willing to be named. Elegant even in her eighth month of pregnancy, Kim wore pearls over a fashionable navy blue maternity dress and high-heeled sandals as she stepped out of a BMW convertible. She is not bashful about having money and what it can do for her.

"If they could afford it, all my friends would go to the United States to have their babies," Kim said. "My biggest complaint about Korea is the educational system. In high school, you have to study past midnight or else you fall behind the others and can't get on with your life. And since the baby is a boy, I thought it would be a big gift for him not to be burdened with military service. We're also thinking about immigration, so all in all we thought it would be better if the baby is an American citizen."[44]

Ms. Kim added that the price tag of her child's American birth would have cost her even more than $20,000 if she was not lucky enough to have a grandmother to stay with in Los Angeles.

Health officials in Korea have estimated that as many as 1 to 2 percent of all South Korean births now take place in the United States, and a transnational industry has sprouted up to serve these parents. Doctors for expectant mothers based in Seoul run affiliated centers in metropolitan Los Angeles, complete with elegant facilities where Korean women can easily follow their native custom of resting for one month after giving birth, and eating a special diet, heavy on seaweed soup believed to help them recover from the loss of blood during childbirth, before returning to Seoul. The centers also assist the mothers in obtaining U.S. Social Security numbers and U.S. passports for their little ones.

Besides the advantages of access to educational and professional opportunities and evasion of the military draft for boys, many parents are also motivated by the possibility that their child, once grown, will help them immigrate to the United States and make it easier to open international bank accounts. As noted by a doctor in Seoul's wealthy and hyper-status-conscious Gangnam district, who himself went to medical school in the United States and sent his children to American prep schools: "Most of these people are really rich. They don't want to feel like they are trapped by Korea. Some of it I just think is social pressure. Others are doing it and people want to keep up with the Joneses."[45] As many as ten thousand South Korean women travel each year to give birth in the United States, according to Korean domestic media accounts, but in recent years some official challenges to birth tourism have unfolded within South Korea. In 2005, the government passed a law requiring young men who hold South Korean citizenship but were born outside Korea to complete their mandatory military service before they can renounce Korean nationality at age twenty-two, but this law reportedly has had little effect on reducing the number of so-called anchor babies among South Korean citizens.

The practice of birth tourism, while perfectly legal in the United States and also a source of revenue for American hospitals, has recently prompted some critics, who view birthright citizenship as a loophole in the U.S. immigration system, to call for constitutional changes in which the United States would follow the lead of other countries and move away from universal birthright citizenship. Mark Krikorian, the executive director of the Center for Immigration Studies, says the United States should also reject tourist visa applications from pregnant women, even if it might seem "outrageous," with very few exceptions granted. In his words: "Do you really think that's right that somebody here visiting Disneyland should have their children be U.S. citizens, which they'll then inevitably use to get access to the U.S.?"[46] Others argue that such measures would send degrading messages and detract from what the United States is supposed to stand for. As Ali Noorani, the executive director of the National Immigration Forum, puts it: "What is the State Department going to do? To fill out a visa application have a woman pee on a stick? If we're a country that cares about families and family values, then why are we blaming the children for a decision the parents made? Their only decision was to take a first breath."[47]

Birth tourism to the United States has also been rising in Turkey, where growing numbers of parents have been turning to companies that facilitate travel to the United States in the weeks before their children are born. Like their Korean counterparts, the travelers from Turkey tend to be from affluent segments of the population and pay cash at American hospitals for medical services that would be covered back home. Companies in Turkey that sell "birth packages"—which typically include flights, hospital expenses, several months of accommodation, and tours of local attractions in cities such as New York, Los Angeles, Chicago, and Orlando—say that as the country's population has become wealthier, more segments of the population, seeking what they consider better educational opportunities for their children, are paying anywhere from US$25,000 to more than $40,000 on travel and medical expenses abroad. One Turkish hotel chain, the Marmara, has opened up a birth tourism package that includes accommodation at its facility on the Upper East Side of Manhattan; the price tag as of March 2010 was US$45,000 per family for a two-month stay. Selin Burcuoğlu, who gave birth to a little girl in 2009, told a journalist from a daily newspaper based in Istanbul that she wanted to make her daughter's life more comfortable: "I don't want her to deal with visa issues—American citizenship has so many advantages. . . . We found a company on the Internet and decided to go to Austin for our child's birth. It was incredibly professional. They organized everything for me. I had no problem adjusting and I had an excellent birth."[48]

A PERENNIAL DREAM DEFERRED: THE DREAM ACT

While children born in the United States to undocumented immigrants are automatically granted U.S. citizenship, it's another story for children who enter the United States by making illegal border crossings with their parents or who stay, along with their parents, past the expiration dates of their visas. These young people remain undocumented and have no obvious route toward U.S. citizenship. Ever since 2001, Congress has repeatedly stopped short of passing legislation intended to help hundreds of thousands of children of undocumented immigrants in the United States escape this quandary by opening the door to permanent residency and eventual U.S. citizenship.

Nicknamed the Dream Act, the proposed law, if enacted, would provide a path toward U.S. citizenship for young adults (under age thirty-five) who were born outside the United States—and accompanied their parents to the United States before the age of sixteen—on the condition that they either attend college or university for two years or complete military service for two years.[49] The Dream Act (or the Development, Relief and Education for Alien Minors Act) amounts to a greatly watered-down version of what many advocates for the eleven million undocumented immigrants in the United States had hoped for when U.S. president Barack Obama took office in early 2009. Throughout his presidential campaign in 2007 and 2008, Obama made promises especially to Latino voters that he would work to ease the way for all undocumented immigrants to gain legal status, but once in office Obama stopped short of proposing broader legislation, recognizing the slim chances of passing immigration reform in Congress. The Dream Act, as a partial reform measure, would have reached out to hundreds of thousands of teenagers and young adults who have lived in the United States for most of their lives but find their lives severely restricted, as young people without legal status are blocked from serving in the U.S. military as well as ineligible for college and university scholarships funded by the U.S. government.

The 2010 version of the Dream Act received wide and passionate support from immigrants and their advocates. However, the bill died at the end of the year as hostility toward immigrants without legal status continued to prevail in American political debate and Democrats lost control of the U.S. House of Representatives in the November 2010 election. The bill passed the House by a fairly narrow margin, 216–198, in early December 2010—as the Democratic majority prepared to hand power to the Republicans. The bill also won a majority vote in the U.S. Senate, with a vote of 55–41 in December but 60 votes were needed in the Senate to move the bill beyond a parliamentary tactic—known in the United States as a filibuster—that blocked debate of the bill. Obama called the defeat at the hands of a Senate minority "incredibly disappointing" and noted in a written statement—rather than a public speech: "The DREAM Act is important to our economic competitiveness, military readiness, and law enforcement efforts. . . . It is not only the right thing to do for talented young people who seek to serve a country they know as their own, it is the right thing for the United States of America."[50]

Supporters of the Dream Act, however, noted scornfully that the Obama administration has not managed to pass any new laws helping immigrants. Instead, Obama has taken a two-pronged approach to immigration policy, supporting legislation (but neither proposing nor wholeheartedly championing legislation) that would ease the way for undocumented immigrants to gain legal status, while also toughening up on immigration enforcement. Indeed, the U.S. government deported a record number of 390,000 undocumented immigrants in 2010.[51] As one immigration lawyer noted ruefully after the Dream Act died in Congress:

> President Obama has deported more people than President Bush. Period. The theory for the Obama Administration is that if we just enforce the law enough the Republicans will support comprehensive

immigration reform. And advocacy groups allowed President Obama to get away with this strange, irrational theory of enforcement. . . . President Obama is opening more private prisons and putting non-criminal foreign nationals in detention centers far removed from their families, lawyers and the real world in an effort to get these folks to give up and not fight their removal. President Obama is unwilling to put forward a working plan for immigration reform, leaving it up to the anti-immigrant crowd to provide Congress draft legislation for doing so.[52]

Lawmakers who voted for the Dream Act emphasized that the legislation would mainly help young people who have come of age in the United States and no longer have meaningful ties to family members in their native countries. As U.S. representative Eliot Engel, a Democrat from New York, argued moments before the House vote in December 2010: "These children came here, they didn't decide to come here; they know no other country. Some of them don't even know the language of the country in which they were born, and they deserve to have a right as free Americans."[53] Critics, on the other hand, argued the "Dream Act" would lead to a nightmare by flooding the country with more undocumented immigrants lured by the easier path to citizenship for their children. As a sign of the weak political backing for the legislation, only eight Republican House members joined Democrats in favor of the Dream Act, while nearly forty Democrats, worried about the possibility of extending any further latitude to immigrants—and the chances of retribution from voters at election time, broke with their party leadership and voted against the bill.

Opponents of the Dream Act played down the emphasis on extending to these young people the rights normally conferred upon those living in the United States and framed the argument by defining "we" in narrow and exclusive terms. Consider the words of California Republican Dana Rohrabacher just before the House vote: "It is not being cold-hearted to acknowledge that every dollar spent on illegal immigrants is one dollar less that's spent on our own children, our own senior citizens and for all those who entered this society who played by the rules, who paid their taxes and expect their government to watch out for their needs before it bestows privileges and scarce resources on illegals."[54] In this statement, Rohrabacher seemed to avoid acknowledging that the children of unauthorized immigrants had no real choice but to follow their parents to the United States—or remain in the United States if their parents did not leave after their visas expired—and that aside from their lack of legal residency, the overwhelming majority of these young people *do* play by the rules of contemporary American society.

From coast to coast, the students supporting the Dream Act showed the American public that even if they did not hold legal status as citizens or even as permanent residents, they were ready to participate in political and social causes they viewed as important. Increasing the risk of deportation by making their illegal status public, thousands of students across the country "came out" as undocumented immigrants and lobbied for Congress to pass the Dream Act, often holding sit-ins just outside, or in some cases, inside the offices of lawmakers seen as pivotal. Students at the University of Texas went on a hunger strike—eating only fruits and vegetables and drinking water fortified with salt—in an effort to persuade one of the key swing voters, U.S. senator Kay Bailey Hutchinson, to support the bill. The Texas Republican supported legislation proposed in 2007 and similar to the Dream Act, but did not support the bill in 2010. In late November 2010, several activists were arrested during a nonviolent sit-in at her office. One activist involved in the hunger strike was Benita Veliz, a graduate of St. Mary's University who as of late 2010 was facing deportation after police questioned her immigration status during a traffic stop a year earlier. "There has been an ideological shift," Veliz said of the student movement. "It used to be hush-hush—just be normal and go to class. Now it's like, let's come out and be done with it. Life without papers is not life anyway. The American dream is worth risking everything."[55] In several college towns across the country—from Boston to Berkeley—undocumented immigrants donated blood on their university campuses as a way of making the point that their contributions to American society are accepted regardless of their legal residency status. In New York, students wearing T-shirts saying "Starved 4 Dream"—and posting tweets under the user name *starved4dream* on Twitter—held a hunger strike outside the offices of Sen. Charles Schumer as part of an effort to push the New York Democrat to support the Dream Act as a stand-alone bill rather than attach it to other legislation and slow down its consideration in Congress.[56]

Online readers of the *Latin America News Dispatch* posted comments detailing their protests, and provided a microcosm of public opinion on the Dream Act. Some, such as a person identified as Janet, commented with cynicism and mockery:

> These people are mostly 20 percent and over normal bodyweight. This hunger strike is a terrific idea. It will allow them to get back to normal bodyweight prior to their return to their home countries and resumption of earning their own living through manual labor. They have been fattened up at the expense of the US taxpayers, but the Big Chump has about run out of patience now with all the freeloaders.

And some, such as Kathleen, were more direct in their criticism:

> The sense of entitlement aggressively and consistently displayed by illegal aliens only serves to further alienate American citizens. They demand rights and services which they are not entitled to nor deserve. We owe them one thing: an order of deportation. Their home countries can educate them. We have far too many deserving American citizens in need of educational assistance. Charity begins at home.

Others, like Stephen, responded with messages of support for the protesters and frustration toward the critics:

> The overwhelming majority of these protesters are undocumented through no fault of their own; this is the only country they've ever known. Deportation will not send them "home," it will effectively turn them into people without a country. And they are NOT asking for money; they are asking for the documentation everyone says they should have in the first place. They're probably contributing to the economy now through paying taxes for benefits they may never receive.
>
> I'm always amazed at the comments section of these things. I'm not sure which is worse: the ignorance or the cruelty. If this country is destroyed, it won't be destroyed by the people who come here; it will be destroyed by the people who were born here and are living under the delusion that this makes them more deserving than any other human being on the planet.

On the day the 2010 version of the Dream Act died in the U.S. Senate, several hundred Latino men and women—many of them undocumented immigrants themselves—sat in the Senate chamber galleries holding hands and wearing graduation caps and tassels as a way to show their support for the bill. Journalists observed that the young people looked stricken as the bill failed to get the sixty votes needed to become law. After the vote, they held a prayer vigil in the basement of the U.S. Capitol and then spoke to reporters: "They did not defeat us, they ignited our fire," said Alina Cortes, a nineteen-year-old Mexican-born immigrant from Texas who hopes to join the U.S. Marine Corps should she eventually receive legal status.[57]

As the Dream Act continues to falter in Washington, accounts of some high-achieving undocumented immigrants at the most elite universities in the United States remind us that deportation cases are not hypothetical for young people who accompanied their parents to the United States. Harvard University sophomore Eric Balderas, who entered the United States illegally at the age of four with his mother as she fled from domestic violence, was nearly deported when he tried to board a domestic flight to Boston using his Harvard student identification card and a Mexican consulate card, saying that he had misplaced his Mexican passport. Airport authorities detained the molecular biology major and aspiring cancer researcher, who was on his way to Boston in June 2010 to begin a summer research internship after visiting his family in San Antonio. Balderas was handcuffed, fingerprinted, and detained for five hours by Immigration and Customs Enforcement officials before being assigned a date for an immigration hearing and released. As one commentator noted: "In an instant, he went from representing the promise of the country's future to being threatened with deportation to Mexico, a country that he has no recollection of."[58]

Harvard students turned to social media to rally behind their classmate, launching a Facebook page titled "Keep Eric Home" that quickly gained fifty-five hundred supporters; university officials forwarded statements to the news media supporting the Dream Act in general and Eric Balderas in particular. Similar to just about all American universities, Harvard has no citizenship requirement for enrollment, and about 20 percent of Harvard's students are from outside the United States. After considerable lobbying from Sen. Dick Durbin, the sponsor of the Dream Act, the Immigration and Customs Enforcement agency backed away and said it would not deport Balderas. The agency resolved the case by opting for "deferred action," meaning that Balderas was allowed to remain in the United States, apply for a work permit and continue his studies at Harvard, and then later apply to renew the "deferred action" upon its expiration. This outcome, however, generated its own controversy, as critics argued that the notoriety of the case enabled an Ivy League student to jump the queue ahead of people who have waited for years to move through the U.S. immigration system legally. Some also worried that the Dream Act would create an incentive for parents in other countries, particularly Mexico, to break U.S. immigration laws by calculating that the hazards of an illegal entry would reap dividends later when their children became U.S. citizens.

Had Balderas been deported back to Mexico, he would have faced difficult odds of returning to Harvard anytime soon. Normally, international students accepted at American colleges and universities apply for what the U.S. government classifies as an F-1 student visa to gain legal entry into the United States. This visa is not available to undocumented immigrant students living in the United States at the time they apply to universities, as the student visa requires a permanent residence overseas. When students who are undocumented immigrants, such as Eric Balderas, are sent back to their countries of birth, their history of illegal residency in the United States prevents them from obtaining the student visa for a period of at least ten years, and often immigrants seeking to return to the United States after being deported have to wait even longer.

Balderas had little to say publicly and told reporters that he contemplated suicide during his detention and that he had no memories of Ciudad Acuna, his hometown in Mexico. Once his case received deferred action, Balderas posted a statement to his supporters on Facebook:

> There are many other young, undocumented students that find themselves in my situation. All of these students are still struggling and, like all other Americans, we are also contributing members of society that have a lot to offer to this country. We must pass the DREAM Act because it's the only thing that will keep us here where we belong. This is only a small victory but the sense of urgency for passing the DREAM Act now should not be taken away.[59]

And yet, alongside the supporters who joined the Facebook page for Eric Balderas, many other Facebook groups and bloggers reacted with contempt and alarm as they followed the Balderas story and the sit-ins that supporters of the Dream Act held in congressional offices during the summer of 2010. Wrote one anonymous blogger:

> These are flagrant lawbreakers, in this country illegally, illegally using taxpayer funded services and facilities. And now they further break the

law through civil disobedience, openly proclaiming their illegal status in order to influence a law that will flip a switch and make it all go away for them? . . . Somebody help me understand how this is in the best interests of the country as a whole and more immediately our national security? Somebody help me understand how this doesn't make Arizona's case for them?[60]

Some of the blog's readers replied to the posting by speculating that the Dream Act fits into a global conspiracy against the American middle class in which cheaper labor from undocumented immigrant workers will continue to bid down wages in the United States and drive growing numbers of U.S. citizens from their jobs. As a reader identified as Donovan posted: "Illegal immigration isn't going away—it can't. Offset the high cost of currently politically useful (public-sector) unions with lower cost illegals . . . perfectly content with a standard of living below that of the native (relative term) population but for the illegals, a significant step up. U.S. pay will continue to go down to a closer parity globally; at which time maybe *some* manufacturing will return to the U.S." Another reader identified as Dr. Doom wrote: "I think the grand plan is to run the system into the entropy pit, eliminating the middle class, and making the poor all the moron [sic] poorer." From supporters of Arizona's new law to critics of birthright citizenship and opponents of the Dream Act, the rising tide of anti-immigration sentiment in the United States is bound up with public anxieties that globalization and its related dynamics are hollowing out the American dream and causing great economic dislocation and distress for vast numbers of the country's citizens.

This became all the more obvious in September and October 2011, as a new social movement emerged and targeted citizen outrage more directly toward the centers of economic and political power in the United States. Thousands descended on lower Manhattan to take part in "Occupy Wall Street" protests, and a wider "Occupy Together" movement quickly swelled to more than six hundred communities across the United States and nearly one hundred cities around the world. Adopting the slogan "We are the 99%," this leaderless but highly networked movement catapulted a long-simmering issue to the center of public debate: the sharply widening disparities during the past thirty years between the wealthiest 1 percent of the population and everyone else. The organizers of the global movement, similar to their counterparts who launched the Arab Spring, argued that their aim was "to express a feeling of mass injustice" in politics and economics. Echoing the rhetoric of the American Revolution, the group published a "Declaration of Occupation of New York City" and took to calling the private park they occupied in lower Manhattan by its original name, Liberty Park. As noted in the declaration:

> A democratic government derives its just power from the people, but corporations do not seek consent to extract wealth from the people and the Earth; and that no true democracy is attainable when the process is determined by economic power. We come to you at a time when corporations, which place profit over people, self-interest over justice, and oppression over equality, run our governments. We have peaceably assembled here, as is our right, to let these facts be known.[61]

CONCLUSION

Despite many signs that masses of Americans have been turning apprehensively inward, one should take care to avoid oversimplifying the story of immigration in the United States during the first decade of the twenty-first century. While the backlash against immigrants often dominates the headlines, the word on the street in many communities is notably more upbeat: never before have so many immigrants from so many places converged harmoniously upon a single country as much as in today's United States. Thriving immigrant communities continue to infuse new cosmopolitan vitality into the country's largest cities, especially in the global destination of New York City, where the urban villages along the "7" subway line in Queens have been transformed into districts far more vibrant, hospitable, and safe than a generation ago. Moreover, recent arrivals of immigrants have revitalized many smaller cities that had lost their populations once factories moved away decades earlier. The decaying mill city of Lewiston, Maine, for instance, is in the midst of revival thanks in part to a growing community of refugees from Somalia who have found the community affordable and child-friendly despite the cold winters. And today's immigrants to the United States, unlike their forebears a century ago, often stay closely involved in the communities they have left behind, thanks to digital communications technology, relatively affordable air travel, and the ease of wiring money almost instantly around the world.[62]

Taken together, the debates in the United States surrounding Arizona's new immigration law, the future of birthright citizenship, and the stalled Dream Act serve to illustrate the confluence of migration, political activity, and public space as three key elements in today's tricky relationship between globalization and citizenship. As immigrants flow into the United States from a wider range of sending countries than past generations, forceful political movements are pulling in opposite directions—some for inclusion, some for exclusion—and elected officials, as ever, respond as they gauge which direction the political winds are blowing within their constituencies. While recent patterns of global migration have turned the United States into a richer mosaic of cultural diversity, the American people, similar to their European counterparts examined in the previous chapter, remain divided as to how they want to approach immigration in the years to come, and dynamics of globalization trigger much of this uncertainty. This is why state governments are taking a higher profile and divergent pathways in U.S. immigration politics, with some states becoming more restrictive while others work to accommodate their growing immigrant populations. During the summer of 2011, the states of California and Illinois both decided not to wait for Washington and approved their own versions of the Dream Act.

Nevertheless, powerful imagery endures of the United States as a nation of immigrants—and a sanctuary for immigrants. President Obama followed a long rhetorical tradition in appealing to this quintessential element of the American experience when he gave a speech in May 2011 in the border city of El Paso, Texas. Two competing rallies just outside the event reinforced how divisive immigration has become in American politics: a group of advocates for immigrants called upon Obama to follow up his campaign promises to put through reforms such as the Dream Act, while another group chanted slogans such as "Border security first" and "Amnesty? Never!" Obama, for his part, tried to straddle the divide. He told the crowd that "being a nation of laws goes hand in hand with being a nation of immigrants" and relayed the story of José Hernández, the son of an undocumented farm worker, who dreamed of being an astronaut: "A few years later, he found himself more than 100 miles above the surface of the Earth, staring out of the window of the shuttle Discovery, and was remembering the boy in the California fields with that crazy dream that in America everything is possible. Think about that, El Paso. That's the American dream right there. That's what we're fighting for."[63]

CHAPTER 6

CONCLUSION:
RISING INDIVIDUALS,
RESILIENT STATES

As we have observed from the case studies in this book, the relationship between globalization and citizenship today comes down to a dual dynamic: even as campaigns for civil rights and democracy around the world are intensifying and speeding up in the digital media age, and public recognition of global interdependence continues to rise, the institution of national citizenship is hardening in many countries as governments tighten border controls and large segments of their populations turn inward against immigration and, in some cases, the broader idea of multiculturalism. In the first chapter, we outlined three definitional frames of citizenship: rights and duties, democratic empowerment and participation, and sentiments of allegiance, belonging, loyalty, and identity. It is helpful now to relate the issues and events discussed throughout this book to these definitional frames in order to gain further perspective on the relationship between globalization and citizenship in the present day.

We have seen how struggles for basic rights around the world remain paramount in pursuit of democratic citizenship, with demands from citizens and social movements for the rule of law and democratic political institutions continuing to gain in global resonance. We have seen how the new technology has motivated activists in established constitutional democracies, emerging democracies, and stalwart (or in some cases, tottering) dictatorships to push for access to the Internet as a basic right of the twenty-first century, with its full range of content and networking platforms seen as vital elements of a rapidly emerging global public space for dialogue and debate. And we have also seen how national judiciaries and formative international courts, at least within Europe, have become critically important vehicles for citizens and immigrants alike to assert their rights in confronting discrimination and social exclusion within their host countries, often tracing back, at least in part, to public anxiety over globalization. From the U.S. District Court ruling against portions of Arizona's controversial immigration law to a series of cases at the European Court of Human Rights and the European Court of Justice—aimed at lending cultural minorities and immigrants measures of legal recognition and protection that can trump hostile national circumstances—judicial institutions and individual plaintiffs, civic groups and legal advocates that bring forward key cases serve as essential vehicles in advancing and interpreting citizenship rights especially in the current global era.

Also highlighting how the full promise of citizenship remains incomplete around the world, many social and economic rights such as the right to education, the right to health care, the right to earn a decent living wage, and the right to fair and safe working conditions have been compromised as economic globalization continues apace. Indeed, growing public concern and righteous anger over these compromises have fueled the emerging Occupy Together movement, and the recent financial crisis has left these rights in greater jeopardy in many countries, especially in the United States, where many basic civil rights governing workplaces, such as the right to collective bargaining, have come under outright attack. For all the philosophical coherence and symbolic impact of the United Nations Universal Declaration of Human Rights, and the related international covenants on civil and political rights and social and economic rights, in practice human rights remain substantially contingent upon the extent that domestic political institutions choose to affirm and uphold these rights.

Even in those countries that have most recently embarked on democratic transitions, basic rights and the promises of democratic citizenship that require background social conditions of mutual respect and fair treatment have yet to be fulfilled, especially for women. The same night Egyptians triumphed in Hosni Mubarak's exit from the presidential palace, a reporter covering the story for an American television network suffered a brutal sexual assault in public while covering the celebrations on the streets of Cairo, with a crowd of men shouting, "Jew, Jew!" as they attacked her.[1] And Egypt's military authorities forced several female protesters from the January 25 uprising to submit to what they called "virginity tests" while they were detained; Amnesty International reported that the women were also beaten, tortured with electric shocks, and threatened with prostitution charges.[2]

While oppressive governments still trample on the inherent dignity of many people around the world, word of these sorts of crimes now spreads instantly. More civil society organizations fighting for change are forming and flourishing, especially across the Global South, and as a result, public tolerance of human rights abuses continues to fall sharply. Especially since national governments now compete openly with each other in the never-ending race for global credibility—with closely watched annual rankings released by think tanks and advocacy groups charting how countries measure up on indicators ranging from the standing of women to political corruption—missteps, backsliding, or acts of wrongdoing by any particular government, in the eyes of global monitors, ultimately will blemish its reputation and, in many cases, undermine its power.

This leads us to citizenship as democratic empowerment and participation, and when we examine the practices of citizenship in the most recent phases of globalization, we see a rising trend of what international relations scholar Joseph Nye has labeled "power diffusion," in which civil society actors networked across borders increasingly mobilize to challenge state power in highly visible ways.[3] While the observation that globalization increases transnational activism is now obvious, something new and exciting is afoot in the ways that everyday people around the world—and especially young adults living in dictatorships—are engaging communications technology and social media platforms to raise their voices and mobilize their emerging online communities with the goal of leveraging political and social change. Not only do the closely related dynamics of globalization and power diffusion lead to campaigns organized and sometimes carried out mainly in cyberspace, as in the case of Operation Avenge Assange, but they also create the conditions for small incidents to go viral and occasionally spark momentous historical events. The revolutions in Tunisia and Egypt trace back to citizen outrage over the deaths of two young men, both of them victims of police brutality. Both incidents occurred in provincial cities but quickly gained national and then global profiles, thanks initially to online communication among citizens that spearheaded political movements before catching the attention of Al Jazeera and other global news organizations.

However, the trend of "power diffusion" meets its match in a forceful counterdynamic: power consolidation by national governments. We have seen how national governments seeking to maintain their grips on power, both in absolute terms and relative to nonstate actors, resort to measures that sometimes violate norms of democracy and human rights. China's censorship practices, detentions of democracy activists, and disruptions of political gatherings fall into this category, and so does the harsh detention of U.S. Army officer Bradley Manning. Multinational corporations and financiers operate on both sides of the divide between power consolidation and power diffusion, depending on the circumstances. In some cases, they side at least tacitly in favor of power diffusion and against governments that overreach their hold on power; recall how Facebook staffers worked to outmaneuver the Tunisian government's "keystroke loggers" that were stealing user names and passwords and providing them to the dictatorship, and also how stock traders around the world swiftly pulled their money out of Egypt when Hosni Mubarak's besieged government pulled the plug on the Internet. In other cases, though, multinationals throw their weight behind power-consolidating states, just as high-tech companies such as Cisco and Yahoo! have been criticized for enabling China's Internet surveillance and censorship, while PayPal, MasterCard, and Visa cut off financial conduits to WikiLeaks following its release of U.S. diplomatic cables. The chairman of technology giant Google, Eric Schmidt, has openly raised concerns that the heavy reliance upon the Internet by democracy activists across North Africa and the Middle East could have the effect of prompting many governments to tighten Internet restrictions even further; it could also place Google employees at risk of occasional arrest and torture in countries that have classified much of the content obtained through its search engines as illegal.[4]

Finally, with respect to sentiments of citizen allegiances, belonging, identity, and loyalty, what is striking from the case studies in this book is the extent to which so many young, globally aware activists are inspired mainly by *national* dreams. From the undocumented immigrants in the United States campaigning for the Dream Act to the likes of Wael Ghonim, Liu Xiaobo, and millions more who are not household names, the roots of what could be framed as "assertive citizenship" seem driven substantially by deep national senses of belonging and liberating national visions for the future. National citizenship as a primary basis of political identity and loyalty remains highly resilient in the global era, and considerable segments of the public frame their national identities in singular and exclusionary terms. The growing political support across Europe for far-right parties and, on occasion, rabidly xenophobic political leaders, as well as the populist sentiments in the United States targeting immigration, remind us that narrow outlooks on nationalism and citizenship continue to run high in many political communities around the world. This is especially true in countries and regions plagued with economic instability and growing realizations that domestic political communities are no longer able to control their destinies. Recent government initiatives by the twenty-seven member states of the European Union to relaunch internal border controls, the campaigns across the United States to roll back citizenship rights guaranteed under the Fourteenth Amendment, and new laws on both continents cracking down on undocumented immigrants all stem from public fears associated with the risks, displacements, and uncertainties of globalization.

Still, today's interdependent and interconnected world has led growing segments of the population—especially younger generations in the world's more affluent, technologically sophisticated, and culturally diverse locales—to think of themselves as global citizens and to cast this citizenship as a complementary set of habits, practices, and dispositions alongside their more precisely defined national allegiances. The idea of "global citizenship" is now commonly invoked in public discourse and infused into the mission statements, programs, and policies of countless schools, colleges, and universities, as well as hundreds of businesses, civil society organizations, and governing institutions at all levels. The practices of global citizenship today have provided us with strong evidence countering the skeptics who argue that to be a citizen of the world is to be a citizen of an abstraction, and relatively few self-described global citizens take the approach of Julian Assange and his conscious decision to remain remote and detached from any local political community, out of a preference for maintaining "mental independence" as an outsider. Instead, people who try to live as global citizens commonly do so through ethical commitments, cross-cultural engagement, and participation in a wide variety of causes, often largely within their immediate local communities, in ways that render the concept rich, complex, and tangible—even if the latitude of the concept stretches beyond what many legal and political philosophers would consider sufficiently precise.[5] A more fundamental concern emerging about contemporary approaches to global citizenship is not that it is too remote or abstract but that the idea often seems too closely associated with the privileges, self-centeredness, and strategic impulses of those endowed with the luxury to contemplate it in the first place.

Even as so many people turn inward, and global citizenship, too, remains especially incomplete, we are reminded how fates across borders, shaping all life on the planet, have become truly interlinked—across not only space but also time. Each and every hour, global online media sources relay sobering reports of human suffering, humanitarian disasters, and environmental degradation that underscore how many people, and indeed the earth itself, remain in highly vulnerable, even perilous circumstances. The prolonged nuclear catastrophe that accompanied the massive March 2011 earthquake and tsunami in northeastern Japan reminded us how some expedient "solutions" to global problems, such as the depletion of energy resources, that might appear efficient to some analysts in the short term, actually impose huge costs and dangers. Aside from nuclear accidents that poison the air, water, and land and contaminate food supplies, leaving behind incalculable consequences for public health, the toxic nuclear waste being generated today in power plants around the world will remain for hundreds of thousands of years.

Just as the dimensions of citizenship have expanded throughout history, perhaps the moment has arrived for the idea of citizenship to become more expansive across time. At its core, what would a concept of "generational citizenship" look like? Thinking back to Henry Shue's definition of "moral rights" as the basis for rational and justified demands that essential goods be "socially guaranteed against standard threats,"[6] what basic rights would our descendants justifiably demand from us, especially in relation to sustainability in all its forms? What kinds of corresponding obligations should we then strive to fulfill today, across many overlapping political communities, for the good of future generations? Framing and advancing a model of generational citizenship offers one possible new endeavor to bring the concept of citizenship, at its heart, into a closer relationship with globalization—and the rising field of global studies—in the years to come.

Notes

CHAPTER 1: A DUAL DYNAMIC BETWEEN GLOBALIZATION AND CITIZENSHIP

1. John Locke, *Second Treatise on Government*, ed. C. B. MacPherson (Indianapolis: Hackett, 1980).

2. Henry Shue, *Basic Rights: Subsistence, Affluence and U.S. Foreign Policy*, 2nd ed. (Princeton: Princeton University Press, 1996), 13.

3. Seyla Benhabib, "Cosmopolitanism and Democracy: Affinities and Tensions," *The Hedgehog Review* 12, no. 3 (2009): 30.

4. Thomas Jefferson et al., "The Declaration of Independence," July 4, 1776, at http://www.archives.gov/exhibits/charters/declaration_transcript .html (accessed June 11, 2011).

5. See Judith Shklar, *American Citizenship: The Quest for Inclusion* (Cambridge: Harvard University Press, 1991).

6. See Peter Schuck, *Citizens, Strangers and In-Betweens: Essays on Immigration and Citizenship* (Boulder: Westview Press, 2000).

7. I am indebted to Stephen Collins for reminding me of this point. See Aristotle, *The Politics of Aristotle,* translated with an introduction by Ernest Barker (Oxford: Clarendon Press, 1961), 105–9.

8. Benedict Anderson, *Imagined Communities, Reflections on the Origin and Spread of Nationalism* (New York: Verso, 1991).

9. T. H. Marshall, *Class, Citizenship and Social Class* (Cambridge: Cambridge University Press, 1963), 26.

10. Adrian Oldfield, *Citizenship and Community: Civic Republicanism and the Modern World* (London: Routledge, 1990), 8.

11. Joshua Yates, "Mapping the Good World: The New Cosmopolitans and Our Changing World Picture," *The Hedgehog Review* 12, no. 3 (2009): 7–27.

12. Pico Iyer, "The Nowhere Man," *Prospect*, February 20, 1997, at http://www.prospectmagazine.co.uk/1997/02/thenowhereman (accessed on March 11, 2011).

13. David Held, Anthony McGrew, David Goldblatt, and Jonathan Perraton, *Global Transformations: Politics, Economics and Culture* (Cambridge: Polity Press, 1999), 16.

14. Ulrich Beck, *What Is Globalization?* (Cambridge: Polity Press, 2000), 11.

15. Anthony Giddens, *The Consequences of Modernity* (Cambridge: Polity Press, 1990), 21.

16. James N. Rosenau, *Distant Proximities: Dynamics beyond Globalization* (Princeton: Princeton University Press, 2003).

17. Jan Aart Scholte, *Globalization: A Critical Introduction*, 2nd ed. (London: Palgrave MacMillan, 2005), 16.

18. Roland Robertson and Habib Haque Khondker, "Discourses of Globalization: Preliminary Considerations," *International Sociology* 13 (March 1998): 25–40.

19. Malcolm Waters, *Globalization*, 2nd ed. (London: Routledge, 2001), 3.

20. Benjamin R. Barber, *Strong Democracy: Participatory Politics for a New Age* (Berkeley: University of California Press, 1984), 223.

21. Shklar, *American Citizenship*, 1.

22. Martha Nussbaum, "Patriotism and Cosmopolitanism," in *For Love of Country: Debating the Limits of Patriotism*, ed. Joshua Cohen (Boston: Beacon Press, 1996), 11–15.

23. Nussbaum, "Patriotism and Cosmopolitanism," 13–14.

24. Martha Nussbaum, "Toward a Globally Sensitive Patriotism," *Daedalus* 137, no. 3 (2008): 78–93.

25. Mitchell Cohen coined the phrase "rooted cosmopolitanism," framing it as "a dialectical concept . . . which accepts a multiplicity of roots and branches and that rests on the legitimacy of plural loyalties, of standing in

many circles, but with common ground." See Mitchell Cohen, "Rooted Cosmopolitanism," *Dissent* 39, no. 4 (1992): 483.

26. Kwame Anthony Appiah, *Cosmopolitanism: Ethics in a World of Strangers* (New York: Norton, 2006), xviii–xix.

27. Peter Singer, *One World: The Ethics of Globalization* (New Haven: Yale University Press, 2004), 175.

28. David Held, "The Transformation of Political Community: Rethinking Democracy in the Context of Globalization," in *Democracy's Edges*, eds. Ian Shapiro and Casiano Hacker-Cordón (Cambridge: Cambridge University Press), 97.

29. Held, "The Transformation of Political Community," 95.

30. Held, "The Transformation of Political Community," 99.

31. Robert A. Dahl, "A Democratic Dilemma: System Effectiveness versus Citizen Participation," *Political Science Quarterly* 109, no. 1 (1994): 23–34.

32. Will Kymlicka, "Citizenship in an Era of Globalization: Commentary on Held," in *Democracy's Edges*, eds. Ian Shapiro and Casiano Hacker-Cordón (Cambridge: Cambridge University Press), 124–25.

33. Alexander Wendt, "A Comment on Held's Cosmopolitanism," in *Democracy's Edges*, eds. Ian Shapiro and Casiano Hacker-Cordón (Cambridge: Cambridge University Press), 124–25.

34. Sidney Tarrow, *The New Transnational Activists* (Cambridge: Cambridge University Press, 2005), 56.

35. Alison Brysk and Gershon Shafir, eds., *People Out of Place: Globalization, Human Rights, and the Citizenship Gap* (London: Routledge, 2004).

36. Rogers Brubaker, *Citizenship and Nationhood in France and Germany* (Cambridge: Harvard University Press, 1992), 31.

37. These statistics are compiled by the International Organization for Migration, at http://www.iom.int/jahia/Jahia/pid/241 (accessed December 31, 2010).

38. Andrzej Kapiszewski, "Arab versus Asian Migrant Workers in the GCC Countries," *United Nations Expert Group Meeting on International Migration and Development in the Arab Region*, May 22, 2006, at http://www.un.org/esa/population/meetings/EGM_Ittmig_Arab/P02_Kapiszewski.pdf (accessed December 21, 2010).

39. Here we see a much more dramatic rise during the past ten years; the total amount of estimated remittances sent home by migrants in 2000 totaled US$132 billion. In 2009, an estimated $316 billion of the $414 billion in remittances was sent to developing countries. Statistics compiled by *International Organization for Migration*, at http://www.iom.int/jahia/Jahia/pid/241 (accessed December 31, 2010). Thanks to Charles Harns for pointing me to this data.

40. Lourdes Medrano, "Obama as Border Cop: He's Deported Record Numbers of Illegal Immigrants," *The Christian Science Monitor,* August 12, 2010, at http://www.csmonitor.com/USA/Justice/2010/0812/Obama-as-border-cop-He-s-deported-record-numbers-of-illegal-immigrants (accessed June 17, 2011).

41. Steven Vertovec, "Circular Migration: The Way Forward in Global Policy?" Working Paper of the International Migration Institute, University of Oxford, 2007, at http://www.imi.ox.ac.uk/pdfs/imi-working-papers/wp4-circular-migration-policy.pdf (accessed February 28, 2011). See also Frans Bieckmann and Roeland Muskens, "Creating a Virtuous Circle," *The Broker: Connecting Worlds of Knowledge,* March 22, 2007, at http://www.thebrokeronline.eu/en/Magazine/articles/Creating-a-virtuous-circle (accessed February 28, 2011).

42. In May 2009 the online *Urban Dictionary* added a definition of twitizen: "twitter user who not only uses twitter to keep in touch with people they know in 'real' life but often to keep in touch with people they know solely through twitter or cyber space." See "twitizen," *Urban Dictionary,* at http://www.urban-dictionary.com/define.php?term=twitizen (accessed February 1, 2011).

43. Margaret E. Keck and Kathryn Sikkink, *Activists beyond Borders: Advocacy Networks in International Politics* (Ithaca: Cornell University Press, 1998).

44. Maggie Hyde, "Fla. Church Plans to Burn Qurans on 9/Anniversary," *Religion News Service,* 21 July 11, 2010, at http://pewforum.org/Religion-News/Fla-church-plans-to-burn-Qurans-on-9-11-anniversary.aspx (accessed February 1, 2011).

45. Terry Jones, quoted in "Pastor Weighing Plans to Burn Qurans amid U.S. Warnings," *CNN,* September 7, 2010, at http://articles.cnn.com/2010-09-07/us/florida.quran.burning_1_petraeus-islamic-qurans?_s=PM:US (accessed February 1, 2011).

46. Barack Obama, "Exclusive: President Obama Says Terry Jones' Plan to Burn Korans Is 'A Destructive Act,'" *ABC News,* September 9, 2010, at http://abcnews.go.com/GMA/president-obama-terry-jones-koran-burning-plan-destructive/story?id=11589122 (accessed February 1, 2011).

47. Paul Adams, "Petraeus: Koran Burning Plan Will Endanger U.S. Troops," *BBC News,* September 7, 2010, at http://www.bbc.co.uk/news/world-south-asia-11209738 (accessed February 1, 2011).

48. Joshua Cohen, "Editor's Preface," in *For Love of Country: Debating the Limits of Patriotism,* ed. Joshua Cohen (Boston: Beacon Press, 1996), vii.

CHAPTER 2: GLOBAL MEDIA, MOBILIZATION, AND REVOLUTION

1. Václav Havel, quoted by Jim Clancy, "Vaclav Havel: Arab Protesters Have It Harder Than My Generation in '89," *CNN,* March 8, 2011, at http://

edition.cnn.com/2011/WORLD/europe/03/07/czech.havel.arab.unrest/index
.html (accessed March 23, 2011).

2. "Poll Results Prompt Iran Protests," *Al Jazeera English,* June 14, 2009, at
http://english.aljazeera.net/news/middleeast/2009/06/2009613172130303995
.html (accessed January 11, 2011).

3. Hamid Dabashi, quoted by Jon Leyne, "How Iran's Political Battle
Is Fought in Cyberspace," *BBC News,* February 11, 2010, at http://news.bbc
.co.uk/2/hi/middle_east/8505645.stm (accessed January 11, 2011).

4. Austin Heap, quoted by Leyne, "How Iran's Political Battle Is Fought
in Cyberspace."

5. Leyne, "How Iran's Political Battle Is Fought in Cyberspace."

6. Habib Bourguiba served as Tunisia's first president from 1957, after Tunisia gained independence from France, until 1987, when Ben Ali took power.

7. Robert Godec, quoted by Ian Black, "WikiLeaks Cables: Tunisia Blocks
Site Reporting 'Hatred' of First Lady," *Guardian,* December 7, 2010, at http://
www.guardian.co.uk/world/2010/dec/07/wikileaks-tunisia-first-lady (accessed
March 25, 2011).

8. Yasmine Ryan, "The Tragic Life of a Street Vendor," *Al Jazeera
English,* January 20, 2011, at http://english.aljazeera.net/indepth/featu
res/2011/01/201111684242518839.html (accessed March 25, 2011).

9. Rochdi Horchani, quoted by Yasmine Ryan, "How Tunisia's Revolution Began," *Al Jazeera English,* January 26, 2011, at http://english.aljazeera
.net/indepth/features/2011/01/2011126121815985483.html (accessed March
25, 2011).

10. Mona Eltahawy, "Tunisia's Jasmine Revolution," *Washington Post,*
January 15, 2011, at http://www.washingtonpost.com/wp-dyn/content
/article/2011/01/14/AR2011011405084.html (accessed March 25, 2011).

11. News organizations in France reported that Ben Ali and his wife took
1.5 tons of gold bars with them as they left the country, but Tunisia's central
bank insisted that the country's 6.8 tons of gold stocks remained unchanged.
"Tunisian Central Bank Denies Ben Ali Fled with Gold," *Radio France In-
ternationale,* January 22, 2011, at http://www.english.rfi.fr/africa/20110122
-tunisian-central-bank-denies-ben-ali-fled-gold (accessed March 25, 2011).

12. Moncef Marzouk, quoted by Alexandra Zavis, "Former Dissident
Sworn in as Tunisia's President," *Los Angeles Times,* December 13, 2011,
at http://latimesblogs.latimes.com/world_now/2011/12/tunisia-president
-moncef-marzouki.html (accessed December 30, 2011).

13. Najib Chebbi, quoted in "Tunisia Installs Moncef Marzouki as President," *Reuters,* December 13, 2011, at http://www.guardian.co.uk/world/2011/
dec/13/tunisia-moncef-marzouki-president (accessed December 30, 2011).

14. Joe Sullivan, quoted by Alexis Madrigal, "The Inside Story of How
Facebook Responded to Tunisian Hacks," *Atlantic,* January 24, 2011, at http://

www.theatlantic.com/technology/archive/2011/01/the-inside-story-of-how
-facebook-responded-to-tunisian-hacks/70044 (accessed February 2, 2011).

15. Madrigal, "The Inside Story of How Facebook Responded to Tunisian
Hacks."

16. Rim Abida, quoted by Madrigal, "The Inside Story of How Facebook
Responded to Tunisian Hacks."

17. Madrigal, "The Inside Story of How Facebook Responded to Tunisian
Hacks."

18. "Mid-East Bloggers Hail Change in Tunisia," *BBC News Africa,* January 15, 2011, at http://www.bbc.co.uk/news/world-africa-12200029 (accessed
February 2, 2011).

19. Bint Masreya, at http://www.bentmasreya.net (accessed February 2,
2011).

20. Gigi Ibrahim, quoted by Mona Eltahawy, "Tunisia's Jasmine Revolution."

21. Marwa Awad, "Autopsy Says Egypt Activist Choked, Protest Planned,"
Reuters, June 23, 2010, at http://af.reuters.com/article/egyptNews/idAFLDE65
M22620100623?pageNumber=2&v (accessed February 2, 2011).

22. As of February 2011, a copy of the video on YouTube had been viewed
15,559 times. See "ABO ESLAM & Mido Magdy," at http://www.youtube.com/
watch?v=elTj8mErGDI&feature=player_embedded#! (accessed February 2,
2011).

23. As of June 2011, a video of the 10-minute interview had been viewed
more than 331,000 times on YouTube. See http://www.youtube.com/watch?v
=JOFsuLBfnfo&feature=related (accessed June 26, 2011).

24. An English language version of the organization's website can be
found at http://www.arabist.net/blog/2010/6/14/the-murder-of-khaled-said
.html (accessed February 2, 2011).

25. "Activists Blame Police for Egyptian's Death," *Egyptian Gazette Online,*
June 12, 2010, at http://213.158.162.45/~egyptian/index.php?action=news&
id=8943&title=Activists%20blame%20police%20for%20Egyptian's%20death
(accessed February 2, 2010).

26. The website can be found at http://www.elshaheeed.co.uk. See "Mid-
East Bloggers Hail Change in Tunisia," *BBC News,* January 15, 2011, at http://
www.bbc.co.uk/news/world-africa-12200029 (accessed January 31, 2011).

27. Mona Eltahawy, "Facebook, YouTube and Twitter Are the New Tools
of Protest in the Arab World," *Washington Post,* August 7, 2010, at http://www
.washingtonpost.com/wp-dyn/content/article/2010/08/06/AR2010080605094
.html (accessed February 2, 2011).

28. Lobna Darwish, quoted by Maha Ben Abdeladhim and Sébastian
Seibt, "Thousands Call for Mubarak to Resign in Coordinated Protests across
Egypt," *France 24,* January 26, 2011, at http://www.france24.com/en/20110125

-tunisia-facebook-twitter-coordinate-protests-egypt-mubarak-resign-cairo (accessed January 28, 2011).

29. Maha Ben Abdeladhim and Sébastian Seibt, "Thousands Call for Mubarak to Resign."

30. Mohamed ElBaradei, at http://twitter.com/elbaradei, January 13, 2011 (accessed February 2, 2011).

31. Ayman Noor, at http://twitter.com/ayman_nour (accessed February 2, 2011).

32. Hamza Hendawi and Hadeel Ah-Shalchi, "Egyptian President Asks Cabinet to Resign," Associated Press, January 29, 2011, at http://news.yahoo.com/s/ap/20110128/ap_on_re_mi_ea/ml_egypt_protest (accessed January 29, 2011).

33. Alaa Al Aswany, "Police Alone Can't Keep Rulers in Power," *Guardian,* January 27, 2011, at http://www.guardian.co.uk/commentisfree/2011/jan/27/police-power-egypt-battle-protesters (accessed January 28, 2011).

34. Ahdaf Soueif, "It's Egypt's Young Who Are Leading the Protests," *Guardian,* January 27, 2011, at http://www.guardian.co.uk/commentisfree/2011/jan/27/ahdaf-soueif-cairo-protest (accessed January 28, 2011).

35. Abdel Halim Hafez, quoted by Anthony Shadid, "Obama Urges Faster Shift of Power in Egypt," *New York Times,* February 2, 2011, at http://www.nytimes.com/2011/02/02/world/middleeast/02egypt.html (accessed February 2, 2011).

36. Matt Bradley, "Mubarak's Trial to Start in August," *Wall Street Journal,* June 1, 2011, at http://online.wsj.com/article/SB10001424052702303657404576359283425162982.html (accessed June 22, 2011).

37. Michael R. Blood, "Cheney Calls Mubarak a Good Friend, US Ally," Associated Press, February 6, 2011, at http://news.yahoo.com/s/ap/20110206/ap_on_re_us/us_reagan_cheney (accessed February 6, 2011).

38. Craig Labovitz, quoted by Hazma Hendawi and Sarah El Deeb, "Egypt: Internet Down, Police Counterterror Unit Up," Associated Press, January 28, 2011, at http://news.yahoo.com/s/ap/20110128/ap_on_bi_ge/ml_egypt_protest (accessed January 29, 2011).

39. Jordan Robertson, "The Day Part of the Internet Died: Egypt Goes Dark," Associated Press, January 28, 2011, at http://news.yahoo.com/s/ap/20110128/ap_on_hi_te/us_egypt_protest_internet_outage (accessed January 29, 2011).

40. Ghonim's "Farmville" comment referred to the popular Internet simulation game and not the rural town in North Carolina. See Wael Ghonim, at http://twitter.com/Ghonim (accessed February 1, 2011).

41. Wael Ghonim, quoted by Ian Black, "Wael Ghonim Anointed Voice of the Revolution by Tahrir Square Faithful," *Guardian,* February 8,

2011, at http://www.guardian.co.uk/world/2011/feb/08/wael-ghonim-tahrir square?INTCMP=SRCH (accessed March 25, 2011).

42. Wael Ghonim, quoted in "Google Executive Is Released in Egypt," *CNN*, February 7, 2011, at http://articles.cnn.com/2011-02-07/world/egypt .google.executive_1_tweet-google-executive-cairo?_s=PM:WORLD (accessed March 26, 2011).

43. Reem El-Komi quoted by Ian Black, "Wael Ghonim Anointed Voice of the Revolution."

44. See http://twitter.com/mennagamal, as well as http://twitter.com/an gelsavant and http://twitter.com/Desert_Dals.

45. Wael Ghonim, quoted by Sam Gustin, "Wael Ghonim Leaving Google to Launch Tech NGO in Egypt," *Wired,* April 25, 2011, at http://www.wired .com/epicenter/2011/04/ghonim-leaves-google (accessed June 22, 2011).

46. Kristof had 987,791 Twitter followers as of February 2011—more followers, in fact, than the daily printed edition of the *Times,* which has been sharply declining in recent years and fell just below 900,000 during the latter half of 2010. See Jeremy W. Peters, "Newspaper Circulation Falls Broadly but at Slower Pace," *New York Times,* October 25, 2010, at http://media decoder.blogs.nytimes.com/2010/10/25/newspaper-circulation-falls-broadly -but-at-slower-pace (accessed February 1, 2011).

47. Nicholas Kristof, at http://twitter.com/nickkristof (accessed February 1, 2011).

48. Nicholas Kristof, "Exhilarated by the Hope in Cairo," *New York Times,* January 31, 2011, at http://www.nytimes.com/2011/02/01/opinion/01kristof .html (accessed February 1, 2011).

49. "Egypt Shuts Down Al Jazeera Bureau," *Al Jazeera English,* January 30, 2011, at http://english.aljazeera.net/news/middleeast/ 2011/01/201113085252994161.html (accessed February 1, 2011).

50. Marc Lynch, quoted by Robert Worth and David Kirkpatrick, "Seizing a Moment, Al Jazeera Galvanizes Arab Frustration," *New York Times,* January 27, 2011, at http://www.nytimes.com/2011/01/28/world/middleeast/28jazeera .html (accessed February 2, 2011).

51. Worth and Kirkpatrick, "Seizing a Moment, Al Jazeera Galvanizes Arab Frustration."

52. These cable systems were in Washington, D.C.; Toledo, Ohio; and Burlington, Vermont. See William Douglas, "As Arab World Roils, Al-Jazeera Finds Its 'CNN moment,'" *McClatchy Newspapers,* March 23, 2011, at http:// www.kansascity.com/2011/03/23/2746284/as-arab-world-roils-al-jazeera.html (accessed March 28, 2011).

53. Ben Hartman, "Analysis: Tahrir Square Had Twitter, Mubarak the Muscle," *Jerusalem Post,* February 4, 2011, at http://www.jpost.com/Middle East/Article.aspx?id=206715 (accessed February 5, 2011).

54. Nicholas Thompson, "Is Twitter Helping in Egypt?" *New Yorker*, January 27, 2011, at http://www.newyorker.com/online/blogs/newsdesk/2011/01/is-twitter-helping-in-egypt.html (accessed February 2, 2011).

55. Leila Marzouk, quoted by Reem Abdellatif, "Thousands Rally for Alleged Torture Victim Essam Atta," *Global Post*, October 29, 2011, at http://www.globalpost.com/dispatch/news/regions/middle-east/egypt/111029/thousands-rally-alleged-torture-victim-essam-atta (accessed October 30, 2011).

56. Ahmed Faouzi Khenissi, quoted by Scott Sayare, "Now Feeling Free, but Still without Work, Tunisians Look toward Europe," *New York Times*, March 23, 2011, http://www.nytimes.com/2011/03/24/world/africa/24tunisia.html (accessed March 28, 2011).

57. Julian Assange, quoted by Patrick Kingsley, "Julian Assange Tells Students That the Web Is the Greatest Spying Machine Ever," *Guardian*, March 15, 2011, at http://www.guardian.co.uk/media/2011/mar/15/web-spying-machine-julian-assange (accessed March 28, 2011).

58. Blocking the word "jasmine" proved to be a tricky business, however. As the *New York Times* reported, a popular Chinese folk song is named "Jasmine," and Chinese activists posted video clips of the country's president, Hu Jintao, singing the song, "forcing censors to have to decide if they should take down videos of senior leaders that could be explained as an expression of patriotism." See Ian Johnson, "Calls for a 'Jasmine Revolution' in China Persist," *New York Times*, February 23, 2011, at http://www.nytimes.com/2011/02/24/world/asia/24china.html (accessed March 28, 2011).

59. Eunice Yoon, "Getting Harassed by the Chinese Police," *CNN*, February 28, 2011, at http://business.blogs.cnn.com/2011/02/28/getting-harassed-by-the-chinese-police (accessed March 28, 2011).

60. Jonathan Watts, "Inner Mongolia Protests Prompt Crackdown," *Guardian*, May 30, 2011, at http://www.guardian.co.uk/world/2011/may/30/mongolia-protests-communist-party-crackdown (accessed June 22, 2011).

CHAPTER 3: A TALE OF TWO CITIZENS

1. Marina Kamenev, "Support for Assange from His Mother and (Most of) His Motherland," *Time*, December 14, 2010, at http://www.time.com/time/world/article/0,8599,2036881,00.html (accessed April 13, 2011).

2. Liu Xiaobo, quoted by Tania Branigan, "Liu Xiaobo—A Democratic Hero Forged in the Fire of Tiananmen Square," *Guardian*, December 9, 2010, at http://www.guardian.co.uk/world/2010/dec/09/liu-xiaobo-nobel-peace-prize-winner (accessed February 27, 2011).

3. China signed the International Covenant on Civil and Political Rights in October 1998 (not yet ratified) and the International Covenant on Economic, Social and Cultural Rights in October 1997 (ratified in March 2001).

4. Liu Xia, quoted by Michael Bristow, "Liu Xiaobo: 20 Years of Activism," *BBC News*, December 9, 2010, at http://www.bbc.co.uk/news/world-asia -pacific-11492131 (accessed April 25, 2011).

5. Liao Yiwu, quoted by Branigan, "Liu Xiaobo—A Democratic Hero."

6. Charter 08's call for privatization generated criticism among many socialist and social democratic critics of economic globalization who otherwise supported Charter 08 and condemned the arrest and imprisonment of Liu Xiaobo. As one writer argued: "With this call, Charter '08 has become a tool for privatization and as such in service of the new rich and party officials. In place of the Chinese Communist Party's (CCP) crony privatization the Charter '08 wants a 'fair and competitive' privatization. It is not clear how it will be done. It is really ironic that the authors of Charter '08 have drafted this document at a moment of the greatest global market failure since 1929." See Au Loong-yu, "A Critical Defense of Charter '08," ATC 143, November-December 2009, at http://www.solidarity-us.org/current/node/2442 (accessed June 26, 2011).

7. Jonathan Mirsky, "Words on Trial in Beijing," *New York Times*, December 18, 2009, at http://www.nytimes.com/2009/12/19/opinion/19iht -edmirsky.html (accessed April 26, 2011).

8. *The 1997 Criminal Code of the People's Republic of China*, translated with an introduction by Wei Luo (Buffalo, NY: William S. Hein & Co, 1998), 73.

9. Beichen, quoted by Jane Macartney, "International Outcry after Chinese Dissident Liu Xiaobo Sentenced to 11 Years," *Times of London*, December 26, 2009, at http://www.timesonline.co.uk/tol/news/world/asia/article 6967856.ece (accessed April 26, 2011).

10. Ai Weiwei, quoted by Jonathan Watts, "Chinese Human Rights Activist Liu Xiaobo Sentenced to 11 Years in Jail," *Guardian*, December 25, 2009, at http://www.guardian.co.uk/world/2009/dec/25/china-jails-liu-xiaobo (accessed April 26, 2011).

11. Macartney, "International Outcry."

12. Liu Xiaobo, "I Have No Enemies: My Final Statement," December 23, 2009, at http://www.hrichina.org/content/3208 (accessed February 27, 2011).

13. David Leigh and Luke Harding, *WikiLeaks: Inside Julian Assange's War on Secrecy* (New York: PublicAffairs, 2011), 13–14.

14. Nikki Barrowclough, "Keeper of Secrets," *The Age*, May 22, 2010, at http://www.theage.com.au/national/keeper-of-secrets-20100521-w230 .html#ixzz1LYOZOR8e (accessed April 15, 2011).

15. Julian Assange, quoted by John Goetz and Marcel Rosenbach, "WikiLeaks Founder Julian Assange on the 'War Logs': 'I Enjoy Crushing Bastards," *Der Spiegel*, July 26, 2010, at http://www.spiegel.de/international/ world/0,1518,708518,00.html (accessed April 14, 2011).

16. Julian Assange, "Why the World Needs WikiLeaks," *TED.com Talks*, at http://www.ted.com/talks/julian_assange_why_the_world_needs_WikiLeaks .html (accessed April 15, 2011).

17. Raffi Katchadourian, "No Secrets: Julian Assange's Mission for Total Transparency," *New Yorker*, June 7, 2010, at http://www.newyorker.com/ reporting/2010/06/07/100607fa_fact_khatchadourian#ixzz1L4T3WM92 (accessed April 14, 2011).

18. Katchadourian, "No Secrets."

19. Barrowclough, "Keeper of Secrets."

20. WikiLeaks, at http://twitter.com/#!/wikileaks (accessed June 19, 2011).

21. Esther Addley, "After WikiLeaks: 'A Priest of Free Speech' Who Wanted to Reveal Everything except His Own Story," *Guardian*, February 5, 2011, at http://www.guardian.co.uk/media/2011/feb/05/julian-assange-reveal -everything (accessed April 15, 2011).

22. Norm Cohen and Brian Stelter, "Iraq Video Brings Notice to a Web Site," *New York Times*, April 6, 2010, at http://www.nytimes.com/2010/04/07/ world/07WikiLeaks.html (accessed April 15, 2011).

23. Julian Assange, quoted by Barrowclough, "Keeper of Secrets."

24. Adam L. Penenberg, "WikiLeaks' Julian Assange: 'Anarchist,' 'Agitator,' 'Arrogant' and a Journalist." January 28, 2011, at http://www.washing tonpost.com/wp-dyn/content/article/2011/01/28/AR2011012803042.html (accessed April 16, 2011).

25. "WikiLeaks—Submissions," at http://www.WikiLeaks.ch/Submis sions.html (accessed April 16, 2011).

26. Charlie Savage, "U.S. Tries to Build Case for Conspiracy by WikiLeaks," *New York Times*, December 15, 2010, at http://www.nytimes.com/2010/12/16/ world/16wiki.html (accessed April 16, 2011).

27. Eric Schmitt and Helene Cooper, "Leaks Add to Pressure on White House over Strategy," *New York Times*, July 26, 2010, at http://www.nytimes .com/2010/07/27/world/asia/27WikiLeaks.html (accessed April 16, 2011).

28. While U.S. military documents estimated that nearly 110,000 people in Iraq, including at least 66,000 civilians, were killed since the start of the U.S.-led invasion in March 2003, other estimates have placed the total civilian death toll as high as 650,000. David Leigh, "Iraq War Logs Reveal 15,000 Previously Unlisted Civilian Deaths," *Guardian*, October 22, 2010, at http:// www.guardian.co.uk/world/2010/oct/22/true-civilian-body-count-iraq (accessed June 21, 2011).

29. Nick Davies, Jonathan Steele, and David Leigh, "Iraq War Logs: Secret Files Show How US Ignored Torture," *Guardian*, October 22, 2010, at http://www.guardian.co.uk/world/2010/oct/22/iraq-war-logs-military-leaks (accessed June 21, 2011).

30. See Daniel Domscheit-Berg, *Inside WikiLeaks: My Time with Julian Assange at the World's Most Dangerous Website* (New York: Random House, 2011).

31. Leigh and Harding, *WikiLeaks,* 72–83.

32. Online conversation between Bradley Manning and Adrian Lamo, quoted by Leigh and Harding, *WikiLeaks,* 77–79.

33. Adrian Lamo, quoted by Kevin Poulson and Kim Zetter, "U.S. Intelligence Analyst Arrested in WikiLeaks Video Probe," *Wired,* June 6, 2010, at http://www.wired.com/threatlevel/2010/06/leak (accessed April 19, 2011).

34. Leigh and Harding, *WikiLeaks,* 77.

35. Brian Todd, "Attorney for WikiLeaks Suspect Says He's Seen No Evidence on Documents," *CNN,* August 31, 2010, at http://articles.cnn.com/2010-08-31/us/wikileaks.suspect.attorney_1_bradley-manning-wikileaks-website-leaker?_s=PM:US (accessed April 19, 2011).

36. Glenn Greenwald, quoted by Ed Pilkington, "PJ Crowley Resigns over Bradley Manning Remarks," *Guardian,* March 13, 2011, at http://www.guardian.co.uk/world/2011/mar/13/pj-crowley-resigns-bradley-manning-remarks (accessed April 19, 2011).

37. Bruce Ackerman, "Bradley Manning's Inhumane Treatment," *Guardian,* April 11, 2011, at http://www.guardian.co.uk/commentisfree/cifamerica/2011/apr/11/bradley-manning-julian-assange (accessed June 20, 2011). The full list of signatures can be found at http://balkin.blogspot.com/2011/03/statement-on-private-mannings-detention.html.

38. Ellen Nakashima, "WikiLeaks Suspect's Treatment 'Stupid,' U.S. Official Says," *Washington Post,* March 12, 2011, at http://www.washingtonpost.com/wp-dyn/content/article/2011/03/11/AR2011031106542.html (accessed April 19, 2011).

39. Ed Pilkington, "Bradley Manning's Jail Conditions Improve Dramatically after Protest Campaign," *Guardian,* May 4, 2011, at http://www.guardian.co.uk/world/2011/may/04/bradley-manning-jail-conditions-improve (accessed June 20, 2011).

40. Scott Shane and John F. Burns, "U.S. Subpoenas Twitter over WikiLeaks Supporters," *New York Times,* January 8, 2011, at http://www.nytimes.com/2011/01/09/world/09wiki.html (accessed April 19, 2011).

41. Birgitta Jonsdottir, quoted by Shane and Burns, "U.S. Subpoenas Twitter."

42. Julian Assange, quoted in "WikiLeaks' Julian Assange Tells of 'Smear Campaign,'" *BBC News,* December 17, 2010, at http://www.bbc.co.uk/news/uk-12015140 (accessed April 18, 2011).

43. Numerous celebrities offered to contribute funds to raise the bail; among them, filmmaker Michael Moore, film director Ken Loach, socialite

Jemima Khan, investigative journalist and documentary maker John Pilger, novelist and historian Tariq Ali, and British caterer Sarah Saunders, who made the largest pledge on record of £150,000. Nick Collins, "WikiLeaks: Celebrities Offer to Pay Julian Assange's Bail," *Telegraph,* December 15, 2010, at http://www.telegraph.co.uk/news/worldnews/wikileaks/8202499/WikiLeaks -celebrities-offer-to-pay-Julian-Assanges-bail.html (accessed April 18, 2011).

44. Clifton Fernandes, quoted by Hamish McDonald, "Fey General Who Ignited a Cyber War," *Sydney Morning Herald,* December 11, 2010, at http:// www.smh.com.au/technology/technology-news/fey-general-who-ignited-a -cyber-war-20101210-18sxk.html (accessed April 19, 2011).

45. Julian Assange, "Julian Assange Answers Your Questions," *Guardian,* December 3, 2010, at http://www.guardian.co.uk/world/blog/2010/dec/03/ julian-assange-wikileaks (accessed April 18, 2011).

46. Kwame Anthony Appiah, "Why I Nominated Liu Xiaobo," *Foreign Policy,* October 8, 2010 (original letter dated January 29, 2010), at http:// www.foreignpolicy.com/articles/2010/10/08/why_i_nominated_liu_xiaobo (accessed February 27, 2011).

47. Jiang Yu, quoted by Jonathan Watts, "Chinese Human Rights Activist Liu Xiaobo Sentenced to 11 Years in Jail."

48. Ma Zhaoxu, quoted in "China's Nobel Anger as Liu Xiaobo Awarded Peace Prize," *BBC News,* October 8, 2010, at http://www.bbc.co.uk/news/ world-asia-pacific-11505164 (accessed February 27, 2011).

49. Geoff Dyer, "Beijing Denounces Nobel for Liu Xiaobo," *Financial Times,* October 8, 2010, at http://www.ft.com/cms/s/0/787aa112-d2b9-11df -9166-00144feabdc0.html#axzz1Nu7Vtxwr (accessed February 26, 2011).

50. Liu Xiaobo, quoted by Jonathan Mirsky, "Jailed for Words: Nobel Laureate Liu Xiaobo," *New York Review of Books,* October 11, 2010, at http://www .nybooks.com/blogs/nyrblog/2010/oct/11/jailed-for-words-nobel-laureate-liu -xiaobo (accessed June 20, 2011).

51. "Liu Xiaobo—Only Nobel Peace Laureate Still Detained," *Human Rights House,* November 21, 2010, at http://humanrightshouse.org/Articles/ 15463.html (accessed May 25, 2010).

52. Quoted by Debbi Wilgoren, Keith Richburg, and Chris Richards, "Liu Xiaobo, Jailed in China, Honored in Absentia by Nobel Committee," *Washington Post,* December 10, 2011, at http://www.washingtonpost.com/wp-dyn/ content/article/2010/12/10/AR2010121001670.html (accessed June 20, 2011).

53. Sakharov was not allowed to leave the Soviet Union; Suu Kyi was under house arrest in Burma; and Walesa feared he would not be allowed to reenter Poland if he left for Oslo.

54. John Lee, "China's National Insecurity," *Wall Street Journal,* December 20, 2010, at http://online.wsj.com/article/SB10001424052748703581204576032922836761948.html (accessed April 27, 2011).

55. Mark Mackinnon, "With China's Peace Prize, the Only Winner Is China," *Globe and Mail,* December 9, 2010, at http://www.theglobeandmail.com/news/world/asia-pacific/with-chinas-peace-prize-the-only-winner-is-china/article1830872 (accessed April 27, 2011).

56. Liu Xiaobo, quoted by Andrew Higgins, "How China Branded Nobel Winner Liu Xiaobo a Traitor," *Washington Post,* December 11, 2010 at http://www.washingtonpost.com/wp-dyn/content/article/2010/12/10/AR2010121006244.html (accessed April 27, 2011).

57. He Guanghua, quoted by Higgins, "How China Branded Nobel Winner Liu Xiaobo a Traitor."

58. Barry Sautman and Yan Hairong, "Do Supporters of Nobel Winner Liu Xiaobo Really Know What He Stands For?" *Guardian,* December 15, 2010, at http://www.guardian.co.uk/commentisfree/2010/dec/15/nobel-winner-liu-xiaobo-chinese-dissident (accessed April 28, 2011).

59. Liang died shortly after the Nobel committee announced its selection of Liu Xiaobo.

60. Xiao Feng, quoted by Andrew Jacobs, "Tirades against Nobel Aim at Audience in China," *New York Times,* December 10, 2010, at http://www.nytimes.com/2010/12/11/world/asia/11china.html (accessed April 27, 2011).

61. See "China's Nobel Attacks Aim for Domestic Ears; Beijing's Challenge: How to Smear Award without Raising Recipient's Profile," *International Herald Tribune,* December 13, 2010, 4.

62. Xiang Yu, quoted by Cara Anna, "Despite Censorship, the Internet-Savvy in China Learn Who Their Nobel Peace Prize Winner Is," Associated Press, December 8, 2010.

63. Václav Havel and Desmond Tutu, "China Must Release Liu Xiaobo—or Lose Its Credibility," *Observer,* December 5, 2010, at http://www.guardian.co.uk/commentisfree/2010/dec/05/liu-xiabao-nobel-havel-tutu (accessed February 26, 2011).

64. Geoff Dyer, "Beijing Denounces Nobel for Liu Xiaobo," *Financial Times,* October 8, 2010, at http://www.ft.com/cms/s/0/787aa112-d2b9-11df-9166-00144feabdc0.html#axzz1Nu7Vtxwr (accessed February 26, 2011).

65. Mrs. Clinton reportedly made this statement during a meeting in March 2009 with then Australian prime minister Kevin Rudd. See "US Embassy Cables: Hillary Clinton Ponders US Relationship with Its Chinese 'Banker,'" *Guardian,* December 4, 2010, at http://www.guardian.co.uk/world/us-embassy-cables-documents/199393 (accessed May 25, 2011).

66. Sarah Palin, quoted in "Hunt Wikileaks Chief Down like Osama bin Laden: Sarah Palin Demands Assange Is Treated like Al Qaeda Terrorist," *Daily*

Mail, December 1, 2010, at http://www.dailymail.co.uk/news/article-1334341/WikiLeaks-Sarah-Palin-demands-Julian-Assange-hunted-like-Al-Qaeda-terrorist.html#ixzz1NvubKCan (accessed February 28, 2011).

67. Stephanie Condon, "Congress Lashes Out at WikiLeaks," *CBS News,* November 29, 2010, at http://www.cbsnews.com/8301-503544-162-20023964–503544.html (accessed February 28, 2011).

68. Tom Flanagan, quoted in "WikiLeaks Founder Assange Should Be Assassinated," *Jerusalem Post,* December 1, 2010, at http://www.jpost.com/International/Article.aspx?id=197544 (accessed February 26, 2011).

69. Julian Assange, quoted by Lesley Ciarula Taylor, "WikiLeaks' Julian Assange Lashes Out at Former Stephen Harper Aide," *Toronto Star,* December 3, 2010, at http://www.thestar.com/news/world/article/901031--wikileaks-julian-assange-lashes-out-at-former-stephen-harper-aide (accessed February 26, 2011).

70. Assange, "Julian Assange Answers Your Questions."

71. Declan McCullagh, "MasterCard Pulls Plug on WikiLeaks Payments," *CNET News,* December 6, 2010, at http://news.cnet.com/8301-31921-3-20024776-281.html#ixzz1O5mHhddS (accessed May 25, 2011).

72. "WikiLeaks: Swiss Bank Shuts Julian Assange's Account," *BBC News,* December 6, 2010, at http://www.bbc.co.uk/news/uk-12569462 (accessed May 25, 2011).

73. Gregg Housh, quoted by Ravi Somaiya, "Hundreds of WikiLeaks Mirror Sites Appear," *New York Times,* December 5, 2011, at http://www.nytimes.com/2010/12/06/world/europe/06wiki.html (accessed May 25, 2011).

74. Gregg Keizer, "Pro-WikiLeaks Cyber Army Gains Strength; Thousands Join DDoS Attacks," *ComputerWorld,* December 9, 2010, at http://www.computerworld.com/s/article/9200659/Pro_WikiLeaks_cyber_army_gains_strength_thousands_join_DDoS_attacks (accessed June 20, 2011).

75. John Perry Barlow, quoted by Noam Cohen, "Web Attackers Find a Cause in WikiLeaks," *New York Times,* December 9, 2011, at http://www.nytimes.com/2010/12/10/world/10wiki.html (accessed February 27, 2011).

76. Noam Chomsky, quoted by McDonald, "Fey General Who Ignited a Cyber War."

77. Scott Burchill, quoted by McDonald, "Fey General Who Ignited a Cyber War."

78. A detailed account of the rape allegations can be found in Leigh and Harding, *WikiLeaks,* 145–63.

79. Israel Shamir and Paul Bennett, "Assange: The Amazing Adventures of Captain Neo in Blonde Land . . . ," *Counterpunch,* August 27–29, 2010, at http://www.counterpunch.org/shamir08272010.html (accessed April 15, 2011).

80. Johanne Hildebrandt, quoted by Esther Addley, "After WikiLeaks: 'A Priest of Free Speech' Who Wanted to Reveal Everything Except His Own Story."

81. David Brooks, "The Fragile Community," *New York Times,* November 29, 2010, at http://www.nytimes.com/2010/11/30/opinion/30brooks.html (accessed February 26, 2011).

82. Assange, "Julian Assange Answers Your Questions."

83. "WikiLeaks Shows 21st-Century Secrets Harder to Keep," Reuters, November 29, 2010, at http://www.reuters.com/article/2010/11/29/us-wikileaks-lessons-idUSTRE6AR38520101129 (accessed June 19, 2011).

84. Christopher Meyer, quoted in "WikiLeaks Shows 21st-Century Secrets Harder to Keep."

85. Michael Cox, quoted in "WikiLeaks Shows 21st-Century Secrets Harder to Keep."

86. Robert Wright, "Is Julian Assange Helping the Neocons?" *New York Times,* December 7, 2010 (accessed February 26, 2011).

87. Andrew Couts, "Faced with Anti-Government Protests, China May Raise Its 'Great Firewall' Even Higher," *Digital Trends,* February 22, 2011, at http://www.digitaltrends.com/computing/faced-with-anti-government-protest-china-may-raise-its-great-firewall-even-higher (accessed May 25, 2011).

88. Calum MacLeod, "Chinese Create Online Jokes to Vent Political Frustration," *USA Today,* December 29, 2010, at http://www.usatoday.com/tech/news/2010-12-29-chinainternet29_CV_N.htm (accessed June 19, 2011).

89. Murong Xuecun, quoted by Jeremy Page, "New Chinese Call for 'Jasmine' Protest Circulates Online," *Wall Street Journal,* February 24, 2011, at http://online.wsj.com/article/SB100014240527487045205045761622441105 69256.html (accessed February 27, 2011).

90. Matthew Lee, "U.S. to Boost Support for Cyber Dissidents," Associated Press, February 15, 2011, at http://abcnews.go.com/US/wireStory?id=12918050 (accessed June 7, 2011).

91. Hillary Rodham Clinton, quoted by Lee, "U.S. to Boost Support for Cyber Dissidents."

92. Hillary Rodham Clinton, quoted by Lee, "U.S. to Boost Support for Cyber Dissidents."

93. "In Conversation with Julian Assange Part II," *WikiLeaks,* June 15, 2011, at http://www.wikileaks.org/In-Conversation-with-Julian,107.html (accessed June 20, 2011).

CHAPTER 4: EUROPE'S INWARD TURN

1. Robert Schuman, "Declaration of May 9, 1950," at http://europa.eu/abc/symbols/9-may/decl_en.htm (accessed 2 December 20, 2010).

2. Keith B. Richburg, "A Generation on the Move in Europe," *Washington Post*, July 22, 2003, at http://www.washingtonpost.com/ac2/wp-dyn/A25821 -2003Jul21?language=printer (accessed December 20, 2010).

3. See Willem Maas, "Migrants, States, and EU Citizenship's Unfulfilled Promise," *Citizenship Studies* 12, no. 6 (2008): 583–96.

4. Citizens of Romania and Bulgaria, the two most recent entrants (joining the European Union in 2007), will have the right to live and work in any member state in 2014, when a seven-year waiting period will expire.

5. "EU Citizenship—Your Rights in the EU," European Commission, at http://ec.europa.eu/justice/policies/citizenship/policies_citizenship_intro_ en.htm (accessed January 11, 2011).

6. Suzanne Mulvehill, quoted by Andrew Abramson, "With U.S. in Slump, Dual Citizenship in E.U. Countries Attracts Americans," *Palm Beach Post*, June 8, 2008, at http://www.palmbeachpost.com/search/content/ local_news/epaper/2008/06/07/s1a_dual_citizenship_0608.html (accessed December 20, 2010).

7. Lauren Berg, quoted by Andrew Abramson, "With U.S. in Slump, Dual Citizenship in E.U. Countries Attracts Americans."

8. Eric Hammerle, quoted by Andrew Abramson, "With U.S. in Slump, Dual Citizenship in E.U. Countries Attracts Americans."

9. "Illiterate Turkish Man Denied German Citizenship," *Local*, February 26, 2009, at http://www.thelocal.de/society/20090226-17673.html (accessed December 21, 2010).

10. Ms. Velez told a journalist that the registry official advised her to choose a saint's name but that she wanted to keep her given name: "My name is part of my personality. If they force me to change it, I'll change it to a Basque name and see what they say then." Spain long prohibited names in the Basque minority language, but they have become common since the dictatorship of General Francisco Franco ended in 1975. See "No Darling, Spain Tells Aspiring Citizen," Reuters, January 19, 2007, at http://www.reuters.com/article/2007/01/19/ us-spain-names-odd-idUSL1930664920070119 (accessed February 19, 2011).

11. Samantha Crozier, quoted in "British Soldier's Wife Told to Leave Country," *Daily Telegraph*, March 17, 2008, at http://www.telegraph.co.uk/ news/1581931/British-soldiers-wife-told-to-leave-country.html (accessed February 19, 2011).

12. "Muslim Woman Denied French Citizenship for 'Radical' Practice," *France 24*, July 16, 2008, at http://www.france24.com/en/20080712-france -muslim-woman-immigration-denied-french-citizenship-radical-practice -islam-burqa (accessed December 21, 2010).

13. Emmanuelle Prada-Bordenave, quoted in "Muslim Woman Denied French Citizenship."

14. Nicolas Sarkozy, quoted in "French Cabinet Approves Veil Ban," *Al Jazeera English,* May 19, 2010, at http://english.aljazeera.net/news/europe/2010/05/201051911313208338.html (accessed December 21, 2010).

15. Nicolas Sarkozy, quoted in "Sarkozy Says Burqas Are 'Not Welcome' In France," Associated Press, June 22, 2009, at http://www.msnbc.msn.com/id/31487882/ns/world_news-europe (accessed December 21, 2010).

16. Faiza Silmi, quoted by Katrin Bennhold, "A Veil Closes France's Door to Citizenship," *New York Times,* July 19, 2009, at http://www.nytimes.com/2008/07/19/world/europe/19france.html (accessed December 21, 2010).

17. Raphael Liogier, quoted in "France Moves Closer to Banning Full Muslim Veil," Associated Press, January 15, 2010, at http://www.msnbc.msn.com/id/34874754/ns/world_news-europe (accessed December 21, 2010).

18. Daniele Lochak, quoted in "Muslim Woman Denied French Citizenship for 'Radical' Practice," *France 24,* July 16, 2008, at http://www.france24.com/en/20080712-france-muslim-woman-immigration-denied-french-citizenship-radical-practice-islam-burqa (accessed December 21, 2010).

19. Fadela Amara, quoted by Bennhold, "A Veil Closes France's Door to Citizenship."

20. Taj Hargey, quoted in "French Cabinet Approves Veil Ban," *Al Jazeera English,* May 19, 2010, at http://english.aljazeera.net/news/europe/2010/05/201051911313208338.html (accessed December 21, 2010).

21. Jean-François Copé, "Tearing Away the Veil," *New York Times,* May 4, 2010, at http://www.nytimes.com/2010/05/05/opinion/05cope.html (accessed December 21, 2010).

22. Copé, "Tearing Away the Veil."

23. Ronald P. Sokol, "Veiled Arguments," *International Herald Tribune,* July 14, 2010, at http://www.nytimes.com/2010/07/15/opinion/15iht-edsokol.html (accessed December 21, 2010).

24. Dominique Vanneste, quoted by Peter Allen, "Nothing Will Stop Us Coming to Britain," *Daily Express,* at http://www.express.co.uk/posts/view/131652/Nothing-will-stop-us-coming-to-Britain (accessed December 31, 2010).

25. Emma Jane Kirby, "Hope Dims in the Calais Jungle," *BBC News,* September 19, 2009, at http://news.bbc.co.uk/2/hi/programmes/from_our_own_correspondent/8262800.stm (accessed December 31, 2010).

26. Sandy Buchan, quoted by Martin Mazurkiewicz and Elena Becatoros, "French Police Bulldoze Migrant Camp," Associated Press, September 22, 2009, at http://www.huffingtonpost.com/2009/09/22/calais-french-police-bull_n_294480.html (accessed on December 31, 2010).

27. Eric Besson, quoted by Mazurkiewicz and Becatoros, "French Police Bulldoze Migrant Camp."

28. Georgia Trismpioti, quoted by Nicole Itano, "Greece Plans to Lock Up Illegal Migrants," *GlobalPost*, July 13, 2009, at http://www.globalpost.com/dis patch/europe/090710/greece-plans-lock-illegal-migrants (accessed December 30, 2010).

29. Lefteris Papadimas and Jan Strupczewski, "EU, IMF Agree $147 Billion Bailout for Greece," Reuters, May 2, 2010, at http://www.reuters.com/article/ idUSTRE6400PJ20100502 (accessed December 29, 2010).

30. Thomas Hammarberg, "Need to Halt Transfers of Asylum Seekers to Greece: Commissioner Hammarberg Intervenes in the Strasbourg Court," *Council of Europe*, September 1, 2010, at http://www.coe.int/t/commissioner/ news/2010/100901strasbourgcourt_EN.asp (accessed January 5, 2011).

31. "Afghan Wins Key Asylum Case at European Court," *BBC News*, January 21, 2011, at http://www.bbc.co.uk/news/world-europe-12255470 (accessed March 30, 2011).

32. Itano, "Greece Plans to Lock Up Illegal Migrants."

33. "Greece Plans Turkey Border Fence to Tackle Migration," *BBC News*, January 4, 2011, at http://www.bbc.co.uk/news/world-europe-12109595 (accessed January 5, 2011).

34. Margot Dickson, "Case Watch: A European Victory for Immigrants' Rights," *Open Society Foundations*, May 19, 2011, at http://blog.soros .org/2011/05/case-watch-a-european-victory-for-immigrants-rights (accessed June 24, 2011).

35. Paola la Rosa, quoted by Olly Lambert, "Italy's Lampedusa Left in Crisis after Arab Spring," *BBC News*, June 14, 2011, at http://www.bbc.co.uk/ news/world-europe-13747558 (accessed June 25, 2011).

36. Bernardino de Rubeis, quoted by Lambert, "Italy's Lampedusa Left in Crisis after Arab Spring."

37. Jorge Carazas, quoted by Elisabetta Povoledo, "Immigrants Rally for a Nationwide Strike in Italy," *New York Times*, March 1, 2010, at http://www .nytimes.com/2010/03/02/world/europe/02iht-italy.html (accessed January 6, 2011).

38. Or Northern League, which at times has advocated for the more prosperous northern regions of Italy to break away from the rest of the country.

39. Povoledo, "Immigrants Rally for a Nationwide Strike in Italy."

40. Elisabetta Povoledo, "Italy Struggles with Immigration and Aging," *New York Times*, June 22, 2008, at http://www.nytimes.com/2008/06/22/world/ europe/22iht-migrants.4.13893156.html (accessed January 6, 2011).

41. Maurizio Ambrosini, quoted by Povoledo, "Immigrants Rally for a Nationwide Strike in Italy."

42. Luigi Manconi, quoted by John Hooper, "Southern Italian Town World's 'Only White Town' after Ethnic Cleansing," *Guardian*, January 11,

2011, at http://www.guardian.co.uk/world/2010/jan/11/italy-rosarno-violence
-immigrants (accessed December 29, 2010).

43. Flavio Di Giacomo, quoted by Rachel Donaldo, "Race Riots Grip
Italian Town, and Mafia Is Suspected," New York Times, January 10, 2010,
at http://www.nytimes.com/2010/01/11/world/europe/11italy.html (accessed
December 29, 2010).

44. Roberto Saviano, quoted by Donaldo, "Race Riots Grip Italian Town."

45. Silvio Berlusconi, quoted by Nick Squires, "Italy Does Not Want to
Become Multiethnic, Says Silvio Berlusconi," Daily Telegraph, May 11, 2009,
at http://www.telegraph.co.uk/news/worldnews/europe/italy/5305030/Italy
-does-not-want-to-become-multi-ethnic-says-Silvio-Berlusconi.html (accessed
December 29, 2010).

46. Giovanna Melandri, quoted by Squires, "Italy Does Not Want to Become Multiethnic."

47. Dario Franceschini, quoted by Deepa Babington, "Berlusconi's Anti-
immigration Comments Spur Outcry," Reuters, May 10, 2009, at http://
uk.reuters.com/article/idUKTRE5491CC20090510 (accessed December 29,
2010).

48. Angela Merkel, quoted by Kate Connolly, "Angela Merkel Declares
Death of German Multiculturalism," Guardian, October 17, 2010, at http://
www.guardian.co.uk/world/2010/oct/17/angela-merkel-germany-multicultur
alism-failures (accessed December 29, 2010).

49. Robert Marquand, "Why 13 Percent of Germans Would Welcome a
'Führer,'" Guardian, October 15, 2009, at http://www.csmonitor.com/World/
Europe/2010/1015/Why-13-percent-of-Germans-would-welcome-a-Fuehrer
(accessed December 29, 2010).

50. Miriam Franchina, quoted in "Italian Far-Right on Facebook: 'Kill
Them All in Zingonia,'" European Union Times, October 30, 2009, at http://
www.eutimes.net/2009/10/italian-far-right-on-facebook-kill-them-all-in-zin
gonia (accessed on December 29, 2010).

51. "Italian Far-Right on Facebook: 'Kill Them All in Zingonia.'"

52. David Lev, "Swiss Debate Grows over Mosque Minaret Ban," Arutz
Sheva, September 31, 2009, at http://www.israelnationalnews.com/News/
News.aspx/133400 (accessed December 5, 2010).

53. David Diaz-Jogeix, quoted by Nick Cumming-Bruce and Steven Er-
langer, "Swiss Ban Building of Minarets on Mosques," New York Times, November 29, 2009, at http://www.nytimes.com/2009/11/30/world/europe/30swiss
.html (accessed December 5, 2010).

54. Ulrich Schüler, quoted by Lev, "Swiss Debate Grows over Mosque
Minaret Ban."

55. Swiss Council of Religions, quoted by Lev, "Swiss Debate Grows over
Mosque Minaret Ban."

56. Mutalip Karaademi, "Muslim Leader in Langenthal Defends Building of Minarets," Swissinfo.ch, October 6, 2009, at http://www.swissinfo.ch/eng/multimedia/video/Muslim_response.html?cid=1012770 (accessed December 5, 2010).

57. Peter Stamm, "Switzerland's Invisible Minarets," *New York Times*, December 4, 2009, at http://www.nytimes.com/2009/12/05/opinion/05stamm.html (accessed December 5, 2010).

58. Nick Cumming-Bruce, "Swiss Ban on Minaret Building Meets Widespread Criticism," *New York Times*, November 30, 2009, at http://www.nytimes.com/2009/12/01/world/europe/01iht-swiss.html (accessed December 5, 2010).

59. Eveline Widmer-Schlumpf, quoted in Cumming-Bruce, "Swiss Ban on Minaret Building Meets Widespread Criticism."

60. Abdel Majri, quoted in Cumming-Bruce, "Swiss Ban on Minaret Building Meets Widespread Criticism."

61. Stress, quoted by Michael Kimmelman, "In Quiet Switzerland, Outspoken Rapper Takes on the Far Right," *New York Times*, May 27, 2009, at http://www.nytimes.com/2009/05/28/arts/music/28abroad.html (accessed December 5, 2010).

62. Unidentified woman, quoted by Andrew Bomford, "Desperate Lives of Calais Migrants," *BBC News*, March 13, 2009, at http://news.bbc.co.uk/2/hi/europe/7941060.stm (accessed on December 31, 2010).

CHAPTER 5: IMMIGRATION POLITICS AND THE CONTESTED AMERICAN DREAM

1. For the immigration statistics throughout this section, see Raymond L. Cohn, "Immigration to the United States," *Economic History Association*, February 1, 2010, at http://eh.net/encyclopedia/article/cohn.immigration.us (accessed January 20, 2011).

2. Adam Liptak, "Power to Build Border Fence Is above U.S. Law," *New York Times*, April 8, 2008, at http://www.nytimes.com/2008/04/08/us/08bar.htm (accessed January 20, 2011).

3. Spencer S. Hsu, "Work to Cease on 'Virtual Fence' Along U.S.-Mexico Border," *Washington Post*, March 16, 2010, at http://www.washingtonpost.com/wp-dyn/content/article/2010/03/16/AR2010031603573.html (accessed January 20, 2011).

4. Trent Franks, quoted by Warren Richey, "Legal Challenges to Arizona Immigration Law Multiply," *Christian Science Monitor*, April 29, 2010, at http://www.csmonitor.com/USA/Justice/2010/0429/Legal-challenges-to-Arizona-immigration-law-multiply (accessed January 20, 2011).

5. Barack Obama, "Remarks by the President at Naturalization Ceremony for Active-Duty Service Members," White House, Office of the Press Secretary, April 23, 2010, at http://m.whitehouse.gov/the-press-office/remarks-president -naturalization-ceremony-active-duty-service-members (accessed January 20, 2011).

6. Jan Brewer, quoted by Douglas Stanglin, "Arizona Governor Blames Obama Administration for Failing on Immigration," *USA Today*, April 23, 2010, at http://content.usatoday.com/communities/ondeadline/post/2010/04/obama-arizonas-immigration-law-could-undermine-basic-notions-of-fair ness/1 (accessed January 20, 2011).

7. Jan Brewer, "Statement by Governor Jan Brewer," State of Arizona: Office of the Governor, April 23, 2010, at http://www.azgovernor.gov/dms/upload/PR_042310_StatementByGovernorOnSB1070.pdf (accessed January 20, 2011).

8. Brewer, "Statement by Governor Jan Brewer."

9. The campaign adviser, Charles Coughlin, stated that Corrections Corporation of America had "neither directly, nor indirectly attempted to influence immigration policy, including SB 1070, and absolutely did not engage anyone in the Governor's Office on [the] signature of that bill." See Morgan Loew, "Brewer Linked to Private Prisons Housing Illegal Immigrants," KPHO-TV, Phoenix, August 31, 2010, at http://www.kpho.com/iteam/24834877/detail.html (accessed on January 20, 2011).

10. Morgan Loew, "Feds: Drug Cartels Getting Guns from Arizona," KPHO-TV, November 19, 2010, at http://www.kpho.com/iteam/25858698/detail.html (accessed January 20, 2011).

11. Richey, "Legal Challenges to Arizona Immigration Law Multiply."

12. Richey, "Legal Challenges to Arizona Immigration Law Multiply."

13. Some Arizona churches with substantial immigrant populations reported that attendance at weekly services dropped as much as 30 percent after the law was signed in April 2010.

14. Roger Mahony, "Arizona's Dreadful Immigrant Law," *Cardinal Roger Mahony Blogs L.A.*, April 18, 2010, at http://cardinalrogermahonyblogsla .blogspot.com/2010/04/arizonas-new-anti-immigrant-law.html (accessed January 21, 2011).

15. Mahony, "Arizona's Dreadful Immigrant Law."

16. Sara Miller Llana, "Mexico Issues Travel Warning over Arizona Immigration Law," *Christian Science Monitor*, at http://www.csmonitor.com/World/Americas/2010/0427/Mexico-issues-travel-warning-over-Arizona-immigra tion-law (accessed January 21, 2011).

17. Melissa Vertíz, quoted by Chris Hawley, "Activists Blast Mexico's Immigration Law," *USA Today*, May 25, 2010, at http://www.usatoday.com/news/world/2010-05-25-mexico-migrants_N.htm (accessed January 21, 2010).

18. "Who Is Boycotting Arizona?" *Arizona Republic*, August 27, 2010, at http://www.azcentral.com/business/articles/2010/05/13/20100513immigrat ion-boycotts-list.html (accessed January 20, 2011).

19. "Boycott Arizona!" at http://www.thepetitionsite.com/1/boycott-ari zona (accessed January 2, 2012).

20. Jeffrey M. Jones, "More Americans Favor Than Oppose Arizona Immi-gration Law," *Gallup*, April 29, 2010, at http://www.gallup.com/poll/127598/ americans-favor-oppose-arizona-immigration-law.aspx (accessed January 21, 2011).

21. Cited in Michael Truelsen, "70 percent of Arizona Voters Like Tough Immigration Law," *Tucson Sentinel*, April 21, 2010, at http://www.tucsonsen-tinel.com/local/report/042110_immigration_poll (accessed January 20, 2010).

22. "Firm Support for Arizona Immigration Law in U.S," *Angus Reid Global Monitor*, June 4, 2010, at http://www.angus-reid.com/polls/39032/firm_ support_for_arizona_immigration_law_in_us (accessed January 21, 2011).

23. Ben Johnson, quoted by Daniel B. Wood, "Opinion Polls Show Broad Support for Tough Arizona Immigration Law," *Christian Science Monitor*, April 30, 2010, at http://www.csmonitor.com/USA/Society/2010/0430/Opin ion-polls-show-broad-support-for-tough-Arizona-immigration-law (accessed January 20, 2011).

24. Barbara O'Connor, quoted by Wood, "Opinion Polls Show Broad Sup-port for Tough Arizona Immigration Law."

25. Linda Greenhouse, "Breathing While Undocumented," *New York Times*, April 26, 2010, at http://opinionator.blogs.nytimes.com/2010/04/26/ breathing-while-undocumented (accessed January 20, 2010).

26. "MALDEF Condemns AZ Governor Brewer for Signing Unconstitu-tional Anti-immigrant Bill," Mexican American Legal Defense and Educational Fund, April 23, 2010, at http://maldef.org/news/releases/maldef_condemns_ az_governor_042310 (accessed January 20, 2011).

27. Julia Preston, "Justice Dept. Sues Arizona over Its Immigration Law," *New York Times*, July 6, 2010, at http://www.nytimes.com/2010/07/07/ us/07immig.html (accessed January 21, 2011).

28. Eric Holder, quoted by Preston, "Justice Dept. Sues Arizona over Its Immigration Law."

29. Preston, "Justice Dept. Sues Arizona over Its Immigration Law."

30. Charles E. Schumer and Lindsey O. Graham, "The Right Way to Mend Immigration," *Washington Post*, March 19, 2010, at http://www.washing tonpost.com/wp-dyn/content/article/2010/03/17/AR2010031703115.html (ac-cessed January 21, 2011).

31. Gabriel Arana, "The Ridiculous Schumer-Graham Plan for Im-migration 'Reform,'" *TAPPED: The Group Blog of The American Prospect*, March 19, 2010, at http://www.prospect.org/csnc/blogs/tapped_archive

?month=03&year=2010&base_name=the_ridiculous_schumergraham_p (accessed January 21, 2011).

32. Susan Bolton, quoted by Randal C. Archibold, "Judge Blocks Arizona's Immigration Law," *New York Times*, July 28, 2010, at http://www.nytimes .com/2010/07/29/us/29arizona.html (accessed January 21, 2011).

33. Judge Bolton, who was appointed to the federal court by former U.S. president Bill Clinton, upheld some less controversial portions of the law, including provisions (not challenged by the U.S. Justice Department) that made it illegal to transport undocumented immigrants and banned city governments in Arizona from refusing to cooperate with U.S. government immigration officials.

34. Peter Spiro, "What's Next for Arizona: A Natural Death Would Be Better," *New York Times*, July 30, 2010 at http://www.nytimes.com/roomforde bate/2010/07/28/whats-next-on-arizonas-immigration-law/judicial-victory -may-not-help-immigrants (accessed January 20, 2011).

35. Daryl Metcalfe, quoted by Julia Preston, "State Lawmakers Outline Plans to End Birthright Citizenship, Drawing Outcry," *New York Times*, January 5, 2011, at http://www.nytimes.com/2011/01/06/us/06immig.html (accessed January 21, 2011).

36. "Amendment XIV," *Constitution of the United States*, National Archives and Records Administration, at http://www.archives.gov/exhibits/charters/ constitution_transcript.html (accessed January 21, 2011).

37. John Kavanagh, quoted by Marc Lacey, "Birthright Citizenship Looms as Next Immigration Battle," *New York Times*, January 4, 2011, at http://www .nytimes.com/2011/01/05/us/politics/05babies.html (accessed on January 20, 2011).

38. Gabriel Chin, quoted by Lacey, "Birthright Citizenship Looms as Next Immigration Battle."

39. Peter H. Schuck, "Birthright of a Nation," *New York Times*, August 13, 2010, at http://www.nytimes.com/2010/08/14/opinion/14schuck.html (accessed January 22, 2010).

40. Duncan Hunter, quoted in "U.S. Rep: Deport Illegal Immigrants' U.S.-Born Kids," Associated Press, April 30, 2010, at http://abcnews.go.com/US/ wireStory?id=10515582 (accessed January 21, 2011).

41. Gretchen Adamek, "Birthright Citizenship," *New York Times*, January 11, 2011, at http://www.nytimes.com/2011/01/12/opinion/l12immig.html (accessed January 22, 2011).

42. Deedee Garcia Blase, quoted by Julia Preston, "State Lawmakers Outline Plans to End Birthright Citizenship, Drawing Outcry," *New York Times*, January 5, 2011, at http://www.nytimes.com/2011/01/06/us/06immig.html (accessed January 21, 2011).

43. Devin Dwyer, "A New Baby Boom? Foreign 'Birth Tourists' Seek U.S. Citizenship for Children," *ABC News*, April 14, 2010, at http://abcnews .go.com/Politics/birth-tourism-industry-markets-us-citizenship-abroad/ story?id=10359956 (accessed January 24, 2011).

44. Barbara Demick, "The Baby Registry of Choice," *Los Angeles Times*, May 25, 2002, A1.

45. Chang Kyu Kim, quoted by Demick, "The Baby Registry of Choice."

46. Mark Krikorian, quoted by Dwyer, "A New Baby Boom?"

47. Ali Noorani, quoted by Dwyer, "A New Baby Boom?"

48. Selin Burcuoğlu, quoted by Işıl Eğrikavuk, "Birth Tourism in US on the Rise for Turkish Parents," *Hürriyet Daily News & Economic Review*, at http://www.hurriyetdailynews.com/n.php?n=birth-tourism-to-the-usa-ex plodes-2010-03-12 (accessed January 24, 2011).

49. The legislation also required eligible candidates for U.S. legal status to have lived in the United States for at least five years and to have either graduated from high school or have gained a high-school equivalency degree.

50. Barack Obama, "Statement by the President on the Senate Vote on the DREAM Act," The White House, Office of the Press Secretary, December 18, 2010, at http://www.whitehouse.gov/the-press-office/2010/12/18/statement -president-senate-vote-dream-act (accessed January 22, 2011).

51. Julia Preston, "Immigration Vote Leaves Obama's Policy in Disarray," *New York Times*, December 18, 2010, at http://www.nytimes.com/2010/12/19/ us/politics/19dream.html (accessed January 23, 2011). See also Daniel Kanstroom, *Deportation Nation: Outsiders in American History* (Cambridge: Harvard University Press, 2007).

52. Charles H. Kuck, "Obama Is to Blame for the Failure of Immigration Reform," *Immigration, Education and Globalization*, December 29, 2010, at http://usmexico.blogspot.com (accessed January 23, 2011).

53. Eliot Engel, quoted by Julie Hirschfeld Davis, "Bill to Help Some Illegal Immigrants May Be Doomed," Associated Press, December 8, 2010, at http:// www.boston.com/news/nation/washington/articles/2010/12/08/democrats_ face_long_odds_on_immigration_measure (accessed December 10, 2010).

54. Dana Rohrabacher, quoted by Davis, "Bill to Help Some Illegal Immigrants May Be Doomed."

55. Benita Veliz, "Students Stage DREAM Act Hunger Strike," *San Antonio Express-News*, November 10, 2010, at http://www.mysanantonio.com/ news/education/article/Students-stage-DREAM-Act-hunger-strike-807147 .php#ixzz1CKxoCfP0 (accessed January 23, 2011).

56. "Supporters of DREAM Act Begin Hunger Strike outside Senator Charles Schumer's Office," *Latin America News Dispatch*, June 2, 2010, at http://latindispatch.com/2010/06/02/supporters-of-dream-act-begin-hunger -strike-outside-senator-charles-schumers-office (accessed June 26, 2011).

57. Alina Cortes, quoted by David Herszenhorn, "Senate Blocks Bill for Young Illegal Immigrants," *New York Times*, December 18, 2010, at http://www.nytimes.com/2010/12/19/us/politics/19immig.html (accessed January 22, 2011).

58. "Promising Harvard Sophomore, Eric Balderas, Faces Deportation," *AllVoices: Local to Global News*, June 17, 2010, at http://www.allvoices.com/contributed-news/6099451-promising-harvard-sophomore-eric-balderas-faces-deportation (accessed January 23, 2011).

59. Eric Balderas, posting on "Keep Eric Home" at http://www.facebook.com/group.php?gid=118015094907966 (accessed January 24, 2011).

60. "I Don't Even Know Where to Begin," *Charlie Foxtrot Nation*, August 1, 2011, at http://charliefoxtrotnation.wordpress.com/2010/08/01/i-dont-even-know-where-to-begin (accessed January 24, 2011).

61. "Declaration of the Occupation of New York City," September 29, 2011, at http://www.nycga.net/resources/declaration (accessed October 30, 2011).

62. See Peggy Levitt, *Transnational Villagers* (Berkeley: University of California Press, 2001).

63. Barack Obama, quoted by Ed Vulliamy, "El Paso: The City Hears the First Battle Cries in America's Explosive Immigration Debate," *Guardian*, May 15, 2011, at http://www.guardian.co.uk/world/2011/may/15/el-paso-barack-obama-immigration (accessed June 27, 2011).

CHAPTER 6: CONCLUSION

1. For CBS correspondent Lara Logan's own description of what happened to her in Cairo on the night of February 11, 2011, see "Lara Logan Breaks Silence on Cairo Assault," *CBS News*, April 28, 2011, at http://www.cbsnews.com/stories/2011/04/28/60minutes/main20058368.shtml (accessed June 27, 2011).

2. "Egypt 'Virginity Tests' decried," *BBC News*, June 1, 2011, at http://www.bbc.co.uk/news/world-middle-east-13620712 (accessed June 27, 2011).

3. Joseph S. Nye, *The Future of Power* (New York: PublicAffairs, 2011).

4. "Google Chairman Warns of Censorship after Arab Spring," *BBC News*, June 27, 2011, at http://www.bbc.co.uk/news/world-us-canada-13935470 (accessed June 28, 2011).

5. Hans Schattle, *The Practices of Global Citizenship* (Lanham, MD: Rowman & Littlefield, 2008).

6. Henry Shue, *Basic Rights: Subsistence, Affluence and U.S. Foreign Policy*, 2nd ed. (Princeton: Princeton University Press, 1996), 13.

Acknowledgments

The issues and struggles presented in this book are truly signs of our times, and I am first indebted to the activists whose campaigns are chronicled here as well as the journalists who bring their stories to the world, often under difficult circumstances. Manfred Steger invited me to contribute to the Globalization series well before events would render this book all the more timely. I am most grateful to Manfred, Terrell Carver, and Susan McEachern for their trust, patience, and helpful comments on the manuscript. My colleagues at Yonsei University gave me the latitude to expedite this book and several other projects, and my research assistant, Boram Kim, compiled valuable source material for chapter 3. I wrote the book at the same time as I hosted a daily news and interview program on TBS-eFM, the English-language radio station in Seoul, and I thank the production team for bringing to my attention many developments that would find their way into the narrative.

Janice Braunstein and Cheryl Brubaker meticulously helped me refine the manuscript; as ever, any shortcomings in this book are entirely my own. I am also deeply grateful to many friends, family members, colleagues, and mentors, past and present, for their support and insights. Especially I wish to thank Yunkyung Choi and our children, Louise Marie and Benjamin Noam, as well as my parents, Arthur and Sheila Schattle, for their everlasting love and encouragement.

Seoul, Korea
January 2012

INDEX

reported admission of forwarding confidential U.S. government files to WikiLeaks, 73–74; reported correspondence with Julian Assange, 72; support from constitutional law scholars, 75

Mao Zedong, 62

market globalism, 105, 135

Marmara, 157

Marshall, Thomas H., 10

Marzouk, Leila, 55

Marzouki, Moncef, 36

Masriyah, Bint, 40

MasterCard, 91, 93, 170

Ma Zhaoxu, 81

McClelland, Robert, 78

Mediterranean Sea, 12, 117, 119, 121–22

Melandri, Giovanna, 125

Melbourne, 66–67

Merkel, Angela, 3, 126

Merzaban, Daliah, 49

Metcalfe, Daryl, 150

Mexican American Legal Defense and Educational Fund, 147–48

Mexico, 138, 142, 144, 146, 162–63

Meyer, Christopher, 96

Milan, 124, 126–27

military service, 8, 12, 72, 108, 116, 141, 154–58

mirror sites, 92

mobile phones, 30–31, 33–37, 46, 48, 51, 53, 66, 115, 146

Moore, Michael, 186n43

Morocco, 109, 127

mosques, 24, 127–132

Mott, Lucretia, 9

Mousavi, Mir-Hossein, 30–31, 33, 35–37

Mubarak, Gamal, 44

Mubarak, Hosni, 27, 42–50, 52, 54–57, 169–70

multiculturalism: advocacy of, 6, 16, 21–22, 68, 111, 125–26, 130, 132, 165; criticism of, 3, 26, 103–104, 111, 125–26, 134, 167; political motivations for denouncing, 5, 19, 110–11, 134

multiethnic societies, 125

Mulvehill, Suzanne, 106

Murong, Xuecun, 97

Muslim Brotherhood (Egypt), 45–46, 52

Muslim Educational Centre (U.K.), 111

National Alliance of Black Educators, 144

National Center for Health Statistics, 153

national citizenship, 5, 7, 9, 21, 25, 103, 105, 118, 150, 154, 167, 171

National Coalition of Latino Clergy and Christian Leaders, 142

National Council of Churches, 143

National Endowment for Democracy (U.S.), 84, 87

National Human Rights Commission (Mexico), 144

National Immigration Forum, 156

nationalism, 3, 10, 13–15, 25, 134, 171

National Urban League, 145

Native Americans, 123, 138

natural disasters, 20, 51, 172

naturalization, 136–37, 141, 150–51

neoliberalism, 135

Netherlands, 76, 107–8

netizens, 22, 24, 81, 92

news media, 2, 20; changing practices of journalists, 51–52;